Microsoft Works Suite 2001
fast&easy®

Patrice-Anne Rutledge
and Diane Koers

A DIVISION OF PRIMA PUBLISHING

To my family, with love for your thanks and support—Patrice

To Vern—Diane

© 2000 by Prima Publishing. All rights reserved. No part of this book may be reproduced or transmitted in any form or by any means, electronic or mechanical, including photocopying, recording, or by any information storage or retrieval system without written permission from Prima Publishing, except for the inclusion of brief quotations in a review.

 A Division of Prima Publishing

Prima Publishing and colophon are registered trademarks of Prima Communications, Inc. PRIMA TECH is a trademark of Prima Communications, Inc., Roseville, California 95661.

Microsoft, Windows, Works, and Internet Explorer are trademarks or registered trademarks of Microsoft Corporation. Mac and Macintosh are trademarks or registered trademarks of Apple Computer, Inc. Netscape is a registered trademark of Netscape Communications Corporation.

Important: Prima Publishing cannot provide software support. Please contact the appropriate software manufacturer's technical support line or Web site for assistance.

Prima Publishing and the authors have attempted throughout this book to distinguish proprietary trademarks from descriptive terms by following the capitalization style used by the manufacturers.

Information contained in this book has been obtained by Prima Publishing from sources believed to be reliable. However, because of the possibility of human or mechanical error by our sources, Prima Publishing, or others, the Publisher does not guarantee the accuracy, adequacy, or completeness of any information and is not responsible for any errors or omissions or the results obtained from the use of such information. Readers should be particularly aware of the fact that the Internet is an ever-changing entity. Some facts might have changed since this book went to press.

ISBN: 0-7615-3371-0

Library of Congress Catalog Card Number: 00-10961

Printed in the United States of America

00 01 02 03 04 DD 10 9 8 7 6 5 4 3 2 1

Publisher:
Stacy L. Hiquet

Marketing Manager:
Judi Taylor

Associate Marketing Manager:
Heather Buzzingham

Managing Editor:
Sandy Doell

Senior Acquisitions Editor:
Deborah Abshier

Project Editor:
Melody Layne

Copy Editor:
Kate Shoup Welsh

Technical Reviewer:
Dennis Teague

Proofreader:
Jan Zunkel

Interior Layout:
Danielle Foster

Cover Design:
Prima Design Team

Indexer:
Sharon Shock

Acknowledgments

I'd like to thank all the people at Pima Publishing who contributed to the creation of this book. To Debbie Abshier who suggested that I take on this project; to Melody Layne for her organizational and editorial contributions; and to Kate Shoup Welsh and Dennis Teague for their attention to detail. Also a special thanks to Diane Koers for her many contributions to this book, including writing parts VI and VII.

About the Authors

Patrice-Anne Rutledge is a best-selling computer book author who has written or contributed to over 20 books on topics such as Access, PowerPoint, Publisher, FrontPage, and Quicken. She wrote the highly-acclaimed *Access 2000 Fast & Easy* and *Access 97 Fast & Easy*, as well as *The Essential Publisher 97 Book*, all published by Prima Tech. She has also contributed to numerous international magazines and newspapers on topics such as technology, business, and travel and created the columns *Global Business Today* and *eCommunicate*. As both an independent consultant and member of the management team for leading technology firms, Patrice has been involved in many aspects of computing, including software development, localization, marketing, and technical communications. Patrice holds a degree in French Linguistics from the University of California and initially became fascinated with computers while pursuing a career as a technical translator. She resides in the San Francisco bay area where she enjoys good music and films, ethnic restaurants, and escaping to exotic destinations when she's not writing or working with computers.

Diane Koers owns and operates All Business Service, a software training and consulting business formed in 1988 that services the central Indiana area. Her area of expertise has long been in the word-processing, spreadsheets, and graphics areas of computing, as well as providing training and support for Peachtree Accounting Software. Diane's authoring experience includes twelve other Prima Tech *Fast & Easy* books (including *Windows Millennium Edition Fast & Easy*, *WordPerfect 9 Fast & Easy*, *Works 95 Fast & Easy*, *Works 2000 Fast & Easy*, *Office 2000 Fast & Easy* and *Lotus SmartSuite Millennium Edition Fast & Easy*) and she has co-authored Prima's *Essential Windows 98* and IDG's *Peachtree for Dummies*. She has also developed and written software-training manuals for her clients. Active in her church and civic activities, Diane enjoys spending her free time traveling and playing with her grandsons and her three Yorkshire Terriers.

Contents

Introduction

This new *Fast & Easy* book from Prima Publishing will help you use the many and varied features of Microsoft's popular Works Suite product. Works Suite is designed to answer most personal and professional computing needs with a program that has a user-friendly integrated design and a feature-rich environment.

Prima's *Fast & Easy* books teach by the step-by-step approach, using clear language and offering illustrations of exactly what is onscreen. *Microsoft Works Suite 2001 Fast & Easy* provides the tools to successfully learn Microsoft Works Suite 2001—including Word 2000, Money 2001 Standard, PictureIt! Publishing 2001, Encarta Encyclopedia Standard 2001, Streets & Trips 2001 as well as the Works spreadsheet, database manager, personal calendar system, and electronic address book. With the addition of Internet Explorer and Outlook Express, you'll also be able to surf the Web and send and receive e-mail.

Who Should Read This Book?

The easy-to-follow, highly visual nature of this book makes it the perfect learning tool for a beginning computer user. It is also ideal for those who are new to this version of Microsoft Works Suite, or those who feel comfortable with computers and software but have never used these types of programs before.

By using *Microsoft Works Suite 2001 Fast & Easy*, any level of user can look up steps for a task quickly without having to plow through pages of descriptions.

How This Book Is Organized

This book uses steps and keeps explanations to a minimum to help you learn faster. Included in the book are a few elements that provide some additional comments to help you master the program, without encumbering your progress through the steps:

- **Tips** offer shortcuts when performing an action, or a hint about a feature that might make your work in Microsoft Works quicker and easier.

- **Notes** give you a bit of background or additional information about a feature, or advice about how to use the feature in your day-to-day activities.

- **Cautions** warn you about common user mistakes and help you avoid pitfalls.

In addition, four helpful appendixes show you how to install Microsoft Works Suite, use the time-saving Microsoft Task Wizards, access the Web with Internet Explorer, enjoy e-mail capabilities with Outlook Express, and use the FoneSync software package included with Works to share phone and address information with your cellular phone.

Read and enjoy this *Fast & Easy* book. It certainly is the fastest and easiest way to learn Microsoft Works Suite 2001.

PART I

Discovering Microsoft Works Suite

1

Getting Started

Congratulations! You are ready to begin working with Microsoft Works Suite, an excellent integrated software application designed for homes, home offices, or other small businesses. In this chapter, you'll learn how to:

- Start the Works Suite program
- Use the Task Launcher
- Preview the various Works Suite components
- Exit Microsoft Works Suite

Starting Works Suite

When Microsoft Works Suite installs, the setup program creates several methods for you to begin using the software. If you have not yet installed Microsoft Works Suite, see Appendix A, "Installing Works Suite."

Using the Shortcut Icon

The fastest method to launch the Works Suite program is to use the shortcut placed on your Windows desktop.

1. Double-click on the **Microsoft Works Suite icon**. The Microsoft Works Task Launcher program will appear.

NOTE

You might be prompted to register your software. Follow the onscreen instructions to register.

Using the Start Menu

If your desktop doesn't have a shortcut icon, you can access Works Suite by using the Start button.

1. Click on **Start**. The Start menu will appear.

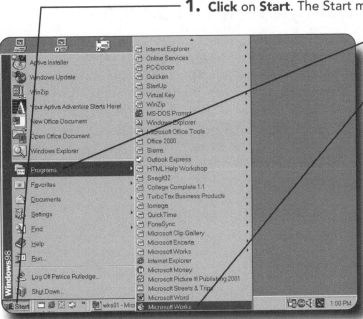

2. Click on **Programs**. The Programs menu will appear.

3. Click on **Microsoft Works**. The Works program will launch, and the Task Launcher will appear.

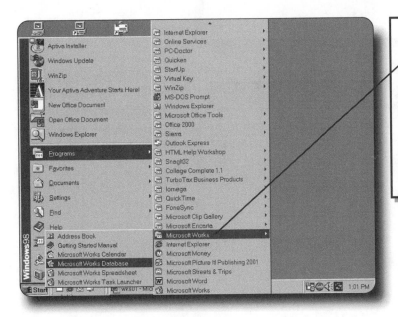

TIP

You can also click on the Microsoft Works folder and choose a Works component. This method bypasses the Task Launcher discussed in the next section.

Using the Task Launcher

From the Task Launcher, you can access various components, create new documents, open existing documents, or use one of the Task Wizards.

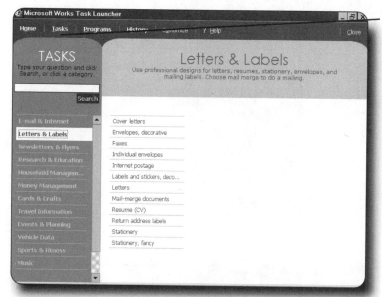

1a. **Click** on **Tasks**. A list of available Task Wizards, categorized by project type, will appear. Task Wizards are discussed in Appendix B, "Using Task Wizards."

OR

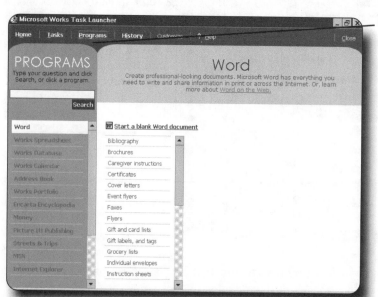

1b. **Click** on **Programs**. A listing of the Works Suite components will appear.

OR

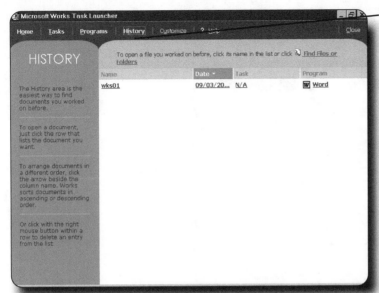

1c. **Click** on **History**. A list of previous Works Suite documents you've created and saved will appear here. For example, if you create and save a Word document, you can then view it in the History list.

From these menus, you can select the task, program, or document you want and then get started with Works Suite.

> **NOTE**
>
> If you have Microsoft Works 6.0 rather than Works Suite 2001, you'll note that the 6.0 product doesn't include Money, PictureIt! Publishing, Encarta, or Streets & Trips. It also substitutes its own word processing module for Microsoft Word.

Understanding the Components of Works Suite

Microsoft Works Suite is considered an *integrated* application. This means that all the components work as one single program.

Working with Works

Works is the foundation of Microsoft Works Suite and includes several modules.

Seeing Spreadsheets

You use spreadsheets to perform calculations and analyze financial or numerical information. Save time by letting the spreadsheet do the calculating for you.

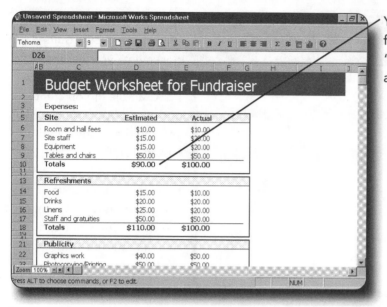

You'll learn how to create formulas in Chapter 12, "Working with Functions and Formulas."

Discovering Databases

Track names, addresses, and other data by designing a Works database.

You'll learn how to add records to a database in Chapter 17, "Working with Data."

Viewing the Calendar

Schedule events and meetings with the Microsoft Works Calendar.

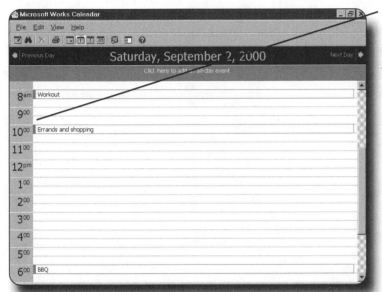

Chapter 30, "Managing Your Schedule with the Calendar," shows you how to keep your calendar up-to-date.

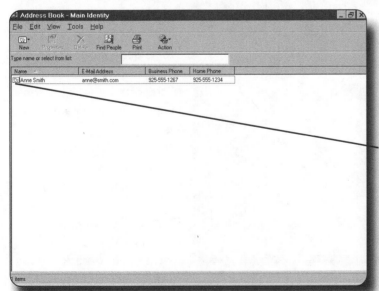

Scanning the Address Book

Use the Address Book to keep track of your family and friends.

Chapter 29, "Tracking People with the Address Book," shows you how to manage telephone numbers, e-mail addresses, birthdays, and much more.

Working with Word

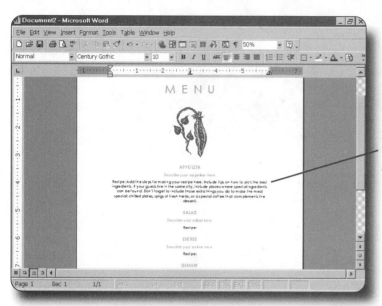

Create memos, letters, proposals, and other text-based documents using Microsoft Word, the word processing component of Works Suite.

You'll learn how to format text in Chapter 4, "Formatting a Document."

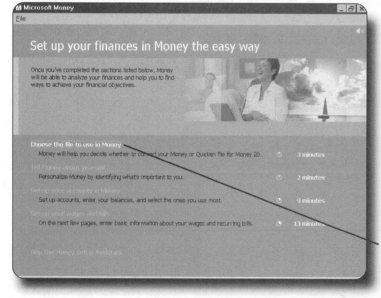

Managing Your Money

Works Suite includes the standard version of Microsoft Money, a personal financial management system that helps you track your income and expenses, create a budget, and make sound financial decisions.

Chapter 22, "Categorizing Your Financial Activities," teaches you to track various kinds of income and expenses.

Getting Creative with PictureIt! Publishing

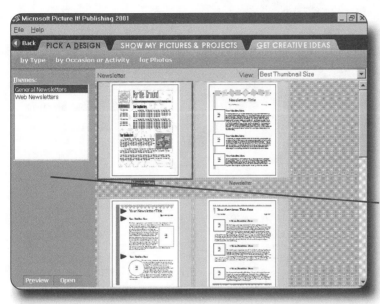

With PictureIt! Publishing, you can create newsletters, brochures, or colorful invitations; edit photos and pictures; and catalog images. It's a desktop publishing and photo editing application all in one.

See how you can scan and enhance photos in Chapter 27, "Working with Pictures and Photos."

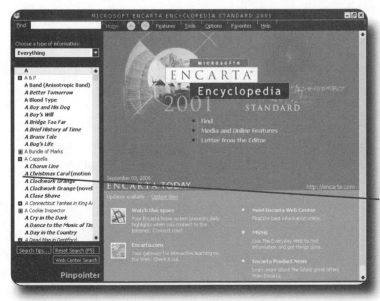

Expanding Your Knowledge with Encarta

Encarta is a multimedia encyclopedia with more than 36,000 current articles on a variety of topics.

You'll learn how to do in-depth research for a school report in Appendix C, "Researching with Works Suite."

Find Your Way with Streets & Trips

Never get lost again, thanks to door-to-door directions from Streets & Trips.

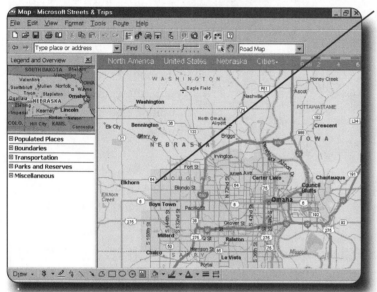

Find out how to get directions anywhere in the U.S. and Canada in Appendix C, "Researching with Works Suite."

Exiting Works Suite

When you are finished working with Works Suite, exit the program. This procedure protects your data and avoids possible program damage. It also frees up valuable computer memory that can be used for other programs.

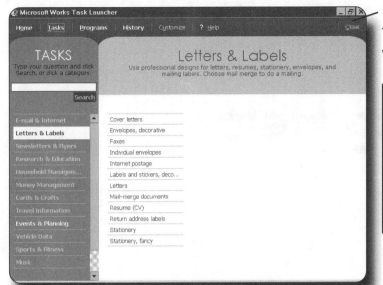

1. **Click** on **Close**.
The Works Suite program
will close.

TIP

It's recommended that
you save your
documents in and exit
other Works
components before
exiting Works Suite.

NOTE

If any documents are open that haven't been saved,
Works Suite asks whether you want to save changes to
those files. Click on Yes if you want to save your
document or click on No if you want to discard the
document. If you click on Yes, Works Suite prompts
you for a name for the file.

2

Getting Help

Although you'll find many answers to your questions in this book, there might be times when you'll need additional information. Microsoft supplies several types of assistance. In this chapter, you'll learn how to:

- Access the Help window
- Use the Help Contents and Index
- Install the Works Suite online manual
- Get help from the Web

Accessing Help

Help with Microsoft Works Suite is available in several ways. One method, using the Help window, shows you that help is only a mouse click away.

When you begin any of the Works core components (spreadsheet, database, calendar, address book, and so on), the Help window displays a menu of choices applicable to that type of document.

CAUTION

If you're using one of the other Works Suite components—such as Word, Money, or PictureIt! Publishing—you might have to access Help functionality from the Help menu of that program. Note that you'll access the Help functionality for that specific program, not for Works Suite itself, and it might differ slightly from the Works Help window you view in this chapter.

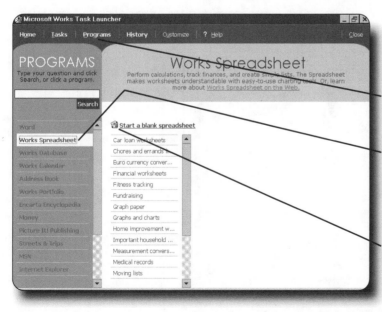

1. Start Microsoft **Works Suite**. The Works Task Launcher will appear.

2. Click on **Programs**. The Programs screen will appear.

3. Click on a Works **application**. A list of possible document types will appear.

4. Click on the **Start hyperlink** for that program, such as **Start a blank spreadsheet.** A blank document will appear.

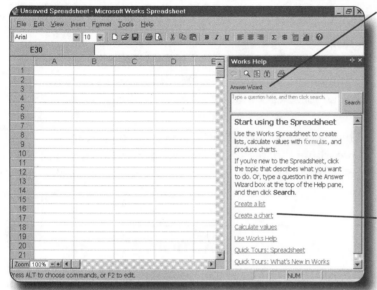

The Help window appears to the right of the document window.

TIP

If the Help window doesn't open automatically, press F1.

5. Click on a **topic**. The Help window will redisplay with information for the selected task.

NOTE

Some features might have multiple help topic levels.

TIP

Click on the Print button to print a copy of the help information.

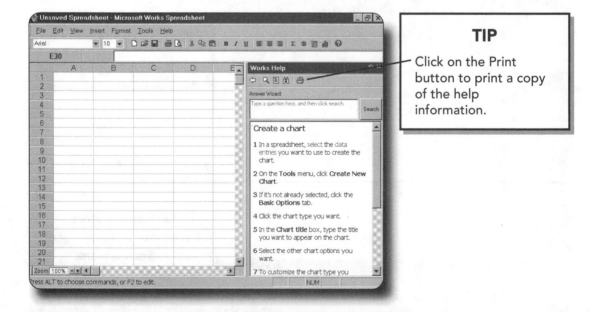

Asking the Answer Wizard

The Ask the Answer Wizard help function is another way to get help with Works core components. This feature enables you to research a Works feature by typing a question in your own words.

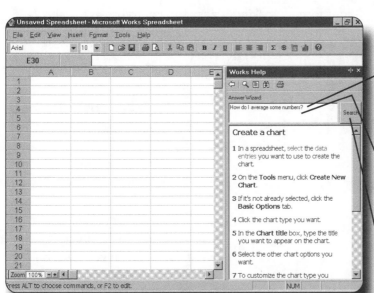

1. Click in the **Search text box**. The blinking insertion point will appear.

2. Type your **question**. The text will appear in the Search text box.

3. Click on **Search**. A list of possible topic matches will appear in the bottom of the Help window.

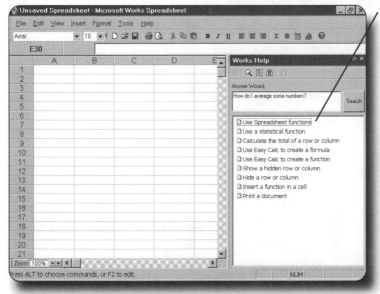

4. Click on the **topic** that most closely matches your request. Information on the feature will appear.

Looking Through the Help Contents

The Help Contents feature presents help information in a folder format, making it easy for you to browse available topics. This feature functions with core Works components.

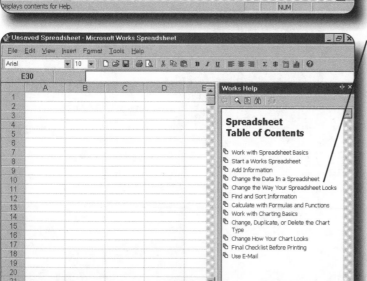

1. Click on **Help**. The Help menu will appear.

2. Click on **Contents**. The Help window will display a Table of Contents relevant to the Works component you are currently using. For example, if you have a spreadsheet open, the Spreadsheet Table of Contents will appear.

3. Click on a **general topic**. A list of subtopics will appear.

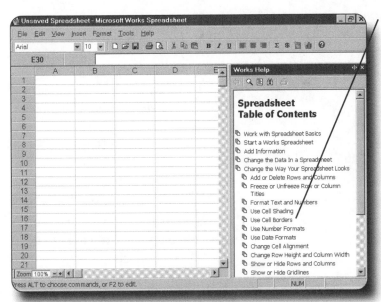

4. Click on the **subtopic** you want to view. The information on that topic will appear in the Help window.

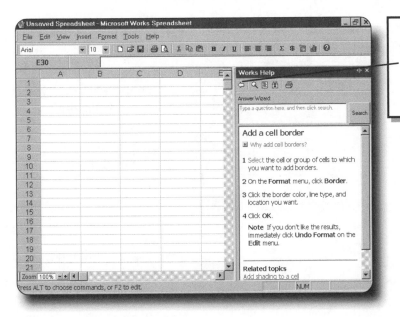

TIP

Click on the Back button to return to the previous Help screen.

Using the Help Index

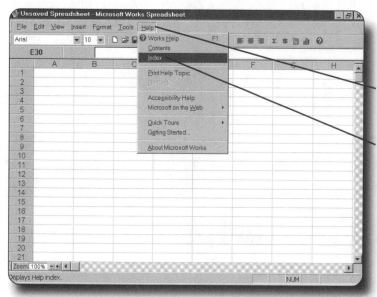

Works' help features for its core components also include an extensive index of topics.

1. **Click** on **Help**. The Help menu will appear.

2. **Click** on **Index**. A list of words relevant to the Works component you are using will appear.

The topics are listed alphabetically with some topics displaying a list of subtopics.

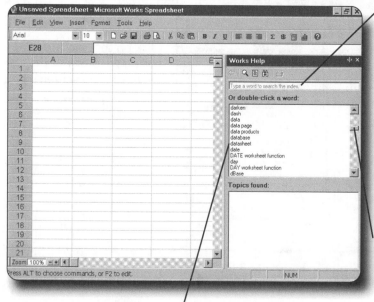

3a. **Type** the **word** that describes your topic (or the first characters of that word). If the word you typed is in the list, it will display; otherwise, the list will display the word that is closest alphabetically to the word you typed.

OR

3b. **Scroll** through the **list of topics** until you find the word that describes your topic.

4. **Double-click** on the desired **word**. The information will appear in the Help window.

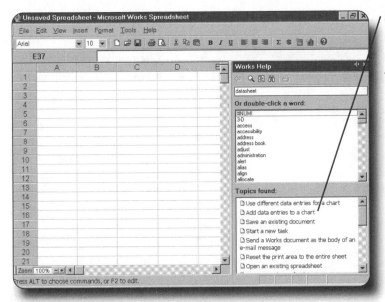

5. Click on the **topic** that most closely matches your request. Information on the feature will appear.

Managing the Help Window

If the Help window is in your way and you don't need it at the moment, close it.

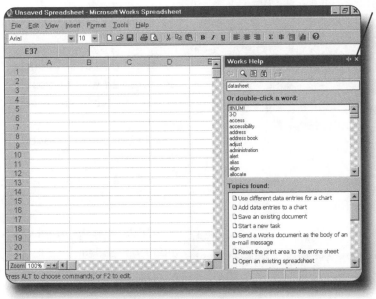

1. Click on the Help window **Close button**. The Help window will close.

You can reopen the Help window whenever you need it.

2. **Click** on **Help**. The Help menu will appear.

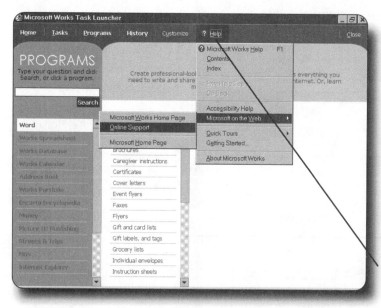

3. **Click** on **Works Help**. The Help window will reappear.

TIP

Press F1 to quickly reopen the Works Help window.

NOTE

For the remainder of this book, the Help window will not display.

Finding Help on the Web

Many sources of assistance are supplied with Microsoft Works. You've already seen several good resources. Another one is the World Wide Web. Microsoft includes technical support on its Web site.

1. **Click** on **Help**. The Help menu will appear.

2. Click on **Microsoft on the Web**. A submenu will appear.

3. Click on **Online Support**. If you are not connected to the Internet, you will be prompted to do so.

Internet Explorer 5.5 will launch, and the Microsoft Product Support Services page for Works will appear.

NOTE

Because Web pages change frequently, your screen might appear slightly different from the one shown in the figure.

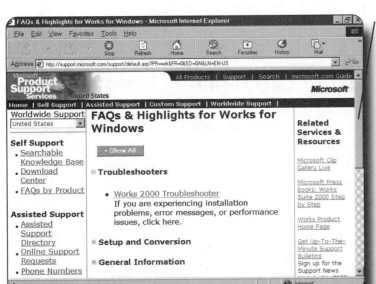

4. Scroll down the Web page. More options will appear.

From the Microsoft Product Support Services page, you can obtain technical support, view Frequently Asked Questions, download free templates and Task Wizards, or even communicate with other Microsoft Works users.

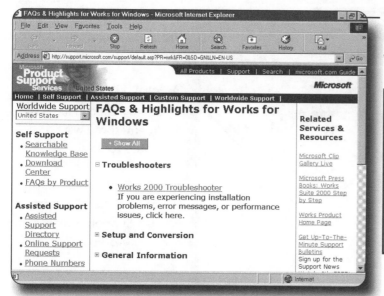

5. Click on the **Close button**. The Web browser will close.

NOTE

You might be prompted to close your Internet connection. You can either stay online or disconnect if you're finished accessing the Web.

TIP

If you're interested in receiving regular tips on using the many features of Works Suite, be sure to go to the MSN Works Web site at http://works.msn.com/ and sign up for the Microsoft Works E-News e-mail newsletter.

Using the Online Users Manual

You probably didn't receive any printed books with your Microsoft Works Suite program. Most manufacturers now include documentation on the CD that comes with the software.

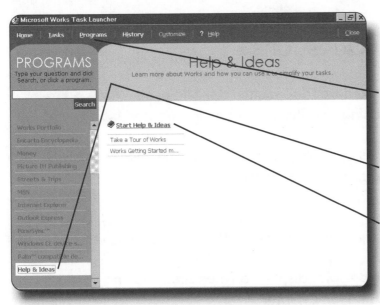

1. Start the Microsoft **Works Suite program.** The Task Launcher will appear.

2. Click on **Programs**. The Programs submenu will appear.

3. Click on **Help & Ideas**. A list of tasks will appear.

4. Click on **Start Help & Ideas.** An Internet Explorer window will open, displaying the user manual.

5. Click on **the Help topic** you want to view in the left pane of the window.

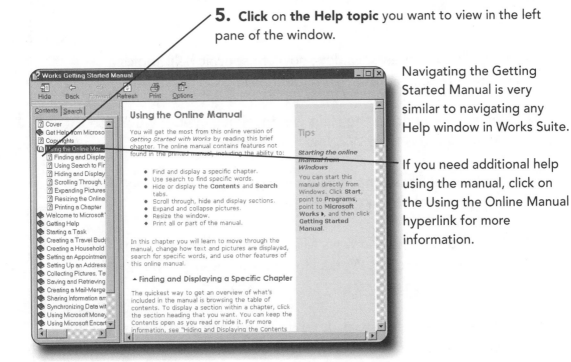

Navigating the Getting Started Manual is very similar to navigating any Help window in Works Suite.

If you need additional help using the manual, click on the Using the Online Manual hyperlink for more information.

Part 1 Review Questions

1. What is the fastest method to launch the Microsoft Works Suite program? *See "Using the Shortcut Icon" in Chapter 1*

2. What are the types of tasks you can do with the Task Launcher? *See "Discovering the Task Launcher" in Chapter 1*

3. What are the major components included with Works Suite? *See "Understanding the Components of Works Suite" in Chapter 1*

4. Where are the help topics displayed when first opening Works? *See "Accessing Help" in Chapter 2*

5. What is the Answer Wizard? *See "Asking the Answer Wizard" in Chapter 2*

6. In the Help Contents window, how are specific help topics indicated? *See "Looking Through the Help Contents" in Chapter 2*

7. What can you do to the Help window if it's in your way? *See "Managing the Help Window" in Chapter 2*

8. Want to get free e-mail tips on using Works Suite? *See "Finding Help on the Web" in Chapter 2*

9. What are some of the ways Microsoft can assist you when you access the Microsoft Works Home Page? *See "Finding Help on the Web" in Chapter 2*

10. Instead of printed books, how do many manufacturers provide documentation? *See "Using the Online Users Manual" in Chapter 2*

PART II

Creating Documents with Word

3

Getting Started with Word

When you need to create a letter, memo, or proposal, use Microsoft Word, the powerful word processing application that's part of Works Suite. Word processing is great for everything text-based—from the simplest letter to a professional-looking newsletter. In this chapter, you'll learn how to:

- Create a document
- Insert the current date
- Move around in a document
- Select and delete text
- Undo your mistakes
- Save a document

Opening a Blank Word Document

Use the Works Task Launcher to create a new Word document.

1. Start the **Microsoft Works Suite program**. The Task Launcher will appear.

2. Click on **Programs**. A listing of the Works Suite components will appear.

3. Click on **Word**. A listing of Word tasks will appear.

4. Click on **Start a blank Word document**. A blank Word document will appear.

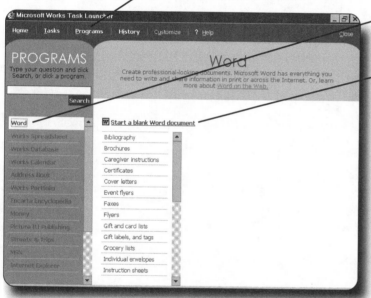

Exploring Word

If you've ever used word processing software before, the Microsoft Word screen should look relatively familiar. Like other Works Suite programs, you use a combination of menus and toolbars for navigation purposes. Word also offers its own online help window.

Working with Menus

You'll use Word menus to perform an action.

1. **Click** on **a menu category** on the menu bar. A list of related commands will appear.

2. **Click** on a **command**. The requested action will occur.

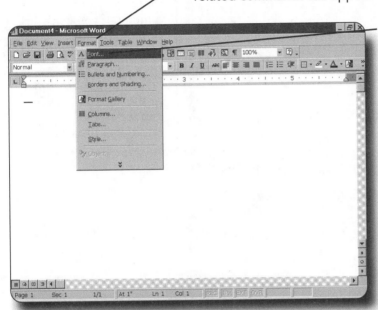

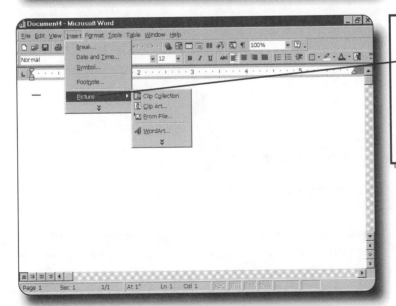

NOTE

An arrow displays to the right of some menu commands. Click on the command to view a submenu of additional choices.

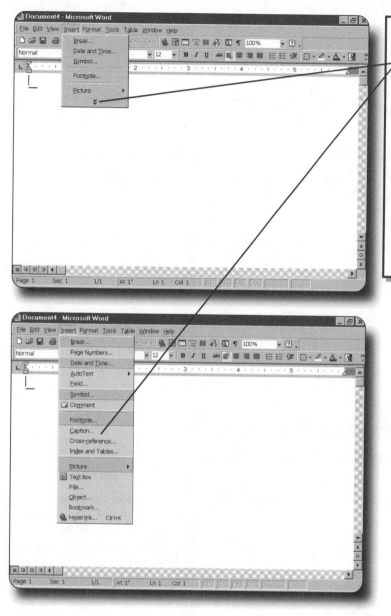

CAUTION

Microsoft Word automatically displays only the most common menu commands the first time you click on a menu. If you can't find the menu command you want, click on the double arrows at the bottom of the list; the list will expand to display additional choices.

Working with Toolbars

Toolbars are another way to perform an action in Word. The Standard and Formatting toolbars automatically display whenever you open Word.

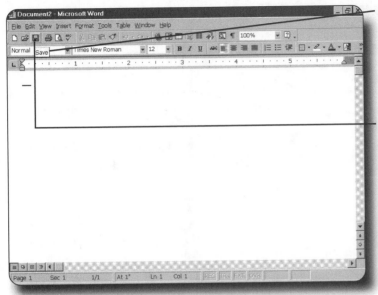

1. **Hover** over a **toolbar button**. Text explaining what this button does will appear. This is called a ScreenTip.

2. **Click** on a **toolbar button**. The corresponding action will occur.

Getting Help with Word

Microsoft Word includes its own help functionality that differs slightly from the Works Help window.

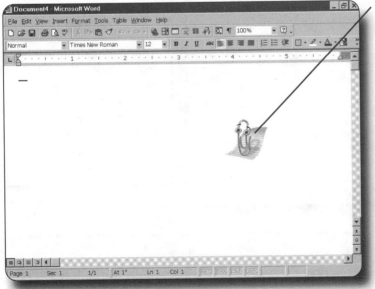

1a. **Click** on the **Office Assistant** if it displays on your screen. The assistant balloon will appear.

OR

1b. **Press F1** if the Office Assistant doesn't display on your screen. The assistant balloon will appear.

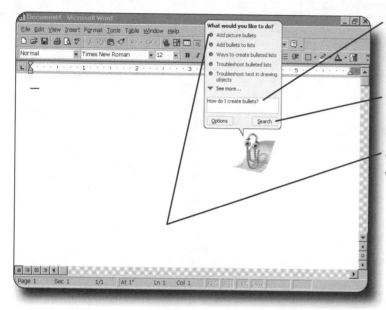

2. Enter your **question** or **keyword** in the balloon text box.

3. Click on **Search**. A list of help topics will appear.

4. Click on **the topic you want to view**.

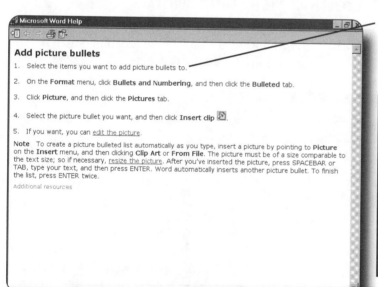

The Microsoft Word Help window will appear with related help information.

NOTE

The Microsoft Word Help window is similar to the Works Help window. Chapter 2, "Getting Help," covers more ways to get help with Works Suite programs.

TIP

To hide the Office Assistant, open the Help menu and click on Hide the Office Assistant.

Entering Text in a Document

When entering text in a Word document, press the Enter key only when you get to the end of a paragraph or when you want an extra blank line between paragraphs. If the word you are typing doesn't fit entirely at the end of the current line, Word puts it on the next line automatically. This is called *word wrap*.

You will find it to your benefit to "Type first. Edit later." That is, type the text into your document, and then go back and make any changes.

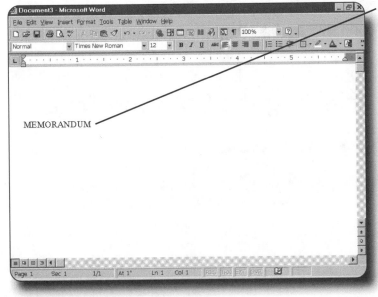

1. **Type** some **text**. The text you type will appear at the location of the insertion point.

If you make any mistakes while typing, you can press the Backspace key to erase any letter to the left of the blinking insertion point. You'll learn how to make other corrections later.

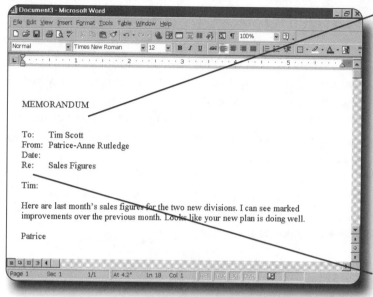

2. Press the **Enter key twice** when you have completed a paragraph. The insertion point will move down two lines.

NOTE

A paragraph consists of a single line of text, such as "Dear Sir," or multiple lines of text.

3. Continue typing until your document is complete.

Inserting the Date and Time

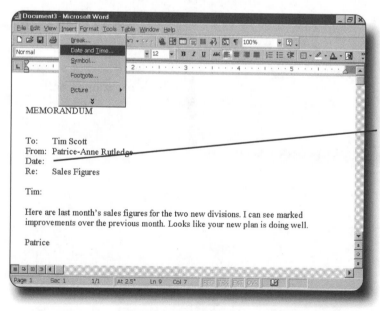

Instead of fishing around your desk looking for your calendar, let Word put today's date in your document.

1. Click the **mouse pointer** where you want to insert the date. The insertion point will blink.

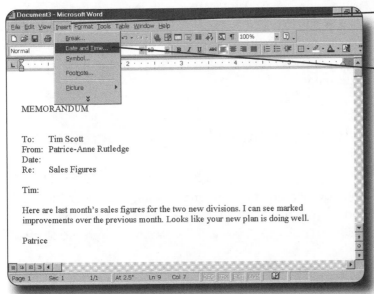

2. Click on **Insert**. The Insert menu will appear.

3. Click on **Date and Time**. The Date and Time dialog box will open.

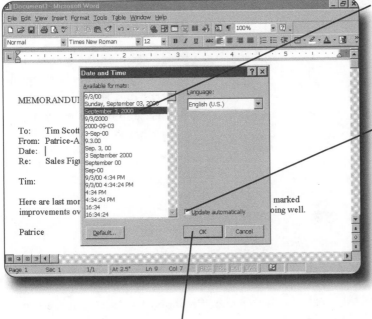

4. Click on a **date format**. The selected date format will be highlighted.

NOTE

If the Update automatically check box is checked, the date will change in the document every time the document is opened to reflect the current date. This is called a *dynamic* date. If you don't want the date to change (a *static* date), don't check this check box.

5. Click on **OK**. The date will be inserted into your document at the location of the insertion point.

Moving Around in a Document

Word provides several quick ways to move around a document.

Moving Around Using the Scroll Bar

When you move through a document using the scroll bar, the insertion point doesn't move—only the screen display moves. You must click in the document to move the insertion point to a new location when using the scroll bar.

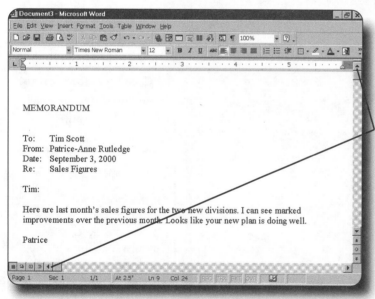

1. **Click** on the **arrow** at either end of the vertical scroll bar. The document onscreen will be moved up or down in the window.

2. **Click** on the **arrow** at either end of the horizontal scroll bar. The document onscreen will be moved left or right in the window.

Using the Go To Feature

To quickly move to a specific page of a document, you can use the Word Go To Feature.

1. **Click** on **Edit**. The Edit menu will appear.

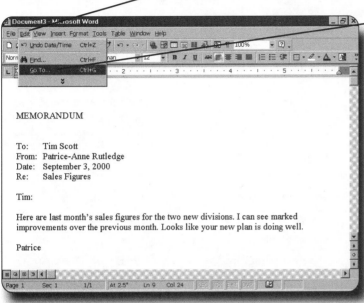

2. **Click** on **Go To**. The Find and Replace dialog box will open with the Go To tab displayed.

3. **Type** the desired **page number** in the Enter page number text box.

4. **Click** on **Go To**. The specified page will display.

5. **Click** on **Close**. The Find and Replace dialog box will close.

TIP

Pressing Ctrl+G is a shortcut for opening the Find and Replace dialog box with the Go To tab displayed.

Moving Around Using the Keyboard

You might prefer to use your keyboard to move around in your document. This minitable presents useful keyboard commands.

To Move	Do This
Right one word	Press Ctrl+Right Arrow
Left one word	Press Ctrl+Left Arrow
To the beginning of a line	Press Home
To the end of a line	Press End
To the beginning of the paragraph	Press Ctrl+Up Arrow
To the next paragraph	Press Ctrl+Down Arrow
Down one screen	Press Page Down
Up one screen	Press Page Up
To the beginning of the document	Press Ctrl+Home
To the end of the document	Press Ctrl+End
To a specified page number	Press Ctrl+G

Inserting Text

When Word is installed, it initially defaults to *insert* mode. When you want to add new text to a document, any existing text will move to the right to make room for the new text.

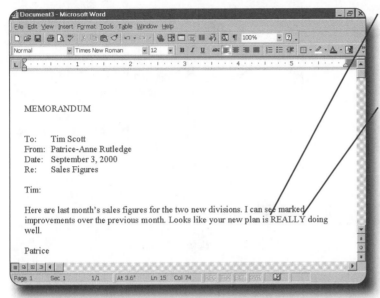

1. Click the **mouse** where you want to add text. The blinking insertion point will appear.

2. Type the **new text**. The new text will be inserted into the document.

NOTE

In this figure, the added word is in uppercase letters so that you can easily see the effect of inserting text.

Selecting Text

To move, copy, delete, or change the formatting of text, you first need to select it. When text is selected, it appears onscreen as light type on a dark background—just the reverse of unselected text. You can only select a sequential block of text at a time—not bits of text in different places.

1. To select a word, **double-click** on it. The word will be highlighted.

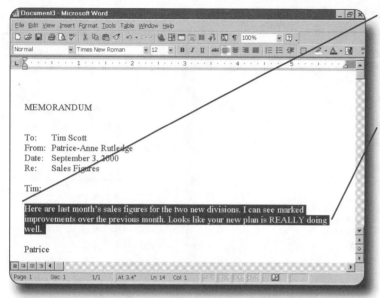

2. To select a paragraph, **position** the **mouse pointer** to the left side of a paragraph. The mouse pointer will point to the right.

3. **Double-click** the **mouse**. The entire paragraph will be highlighted.

4. **Click** on **Edit**. The Edit menu will appear.

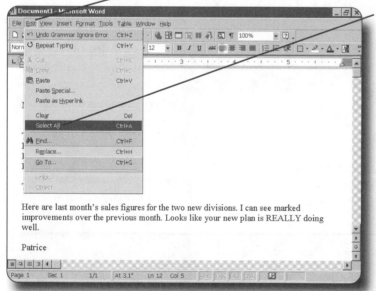

5. **Click** on **Select All**. The entire document will be highlighted.

TIP

Alternatively, you can select a block of text by clicking at the beginning of the text, pressing and holding down the mouse button, and then dragging across the text. Release the mouse button. The text will be highlighted.

Deselect text by clicking anywhere else in the document.

Deleting Text

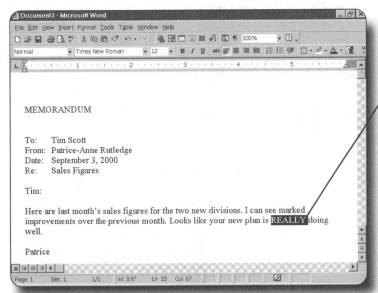

You can delete unwanted text one character, word, paragraph, or page—or any combination—at a time.

1. Select the **text** you want to delete. The text will be highlighted.

2. Press the **Delete key** on your keyboard. The text will be deleted.

As soon as the deleted text disappears, any text below or to the right of the deleted text moves up to fill in the space.

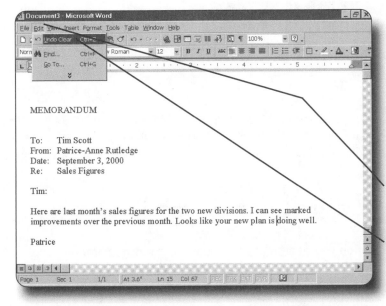

Undoing Mistakes

Microsoft Word has a wonderful feature called *undo*. This feature reverses the last step you performed.

1. Click on **Edit**. The Edit menu will appear.

2. Click on **Undo**. The last action you performed will be reversed.

NOTE

The Edit menu lists Undo with the feature last used. For example, if you last deleted text, it will read Undo Delete. If the last function was to underline text, the Undo will read Undo Underline.

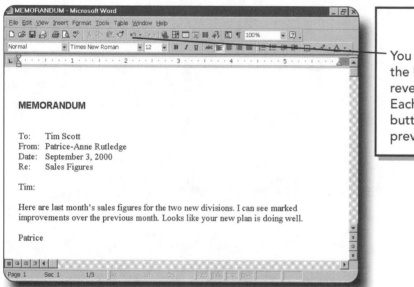

TIP

You can also click on the Undo button to reverse the last action. Each click of the Undo button reverses one previous step.

Saving a Document

For any number of reasons, your computer could fail you at any time. Saving your work not only preserves changes you make in the process of creating a document, but also files it electronically so that you can later find it and use it again.

Saving a Document the First Time

When you first create a document, it has no name. If you want to use that document later, you must name it so that Word can find it.

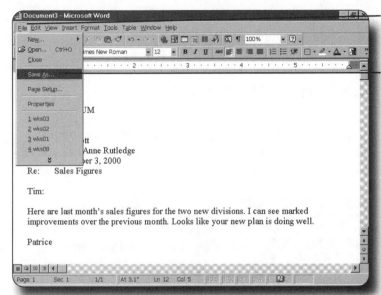

1. **Click** on **File**. The File menu will appear.

2. **Click** on **Save As**. The Save As dialog box will open.

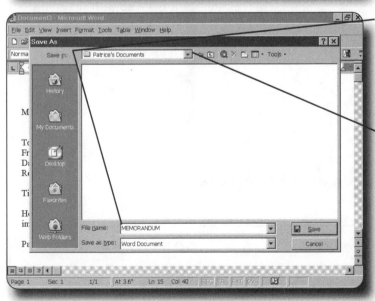

3. **Type** a **name** for your file in the File name text box. The file name will display.

NOTE

The Save in drop-down list shows folder options where you can save the document. The default folder that appears is usually My Documents, but this could vary depending on your version of Windows. If you don't want to save the document in this folder, or if you want to save it on another disk, click on the drop-down arrow to browse and locate another folder or disk.

4. Click on **Save**. Your document will be saved, and the name you specified will appear in the title bar.

Resaving a Document

As you continue to work on your document, you should resave it every ten minutes or so to help ensure that you do not lose any changes.

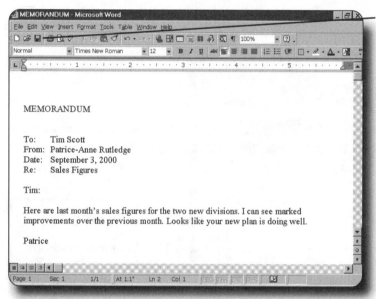

1. Click on the **Save** button. The document will be resaved with any changes. No dialog box will open because the document is resaved with the same name and in the same folder as previously specified.

TIP

If you want to save the document with a different name or in a different folder, click on File and then choose Save As. The Save As dialog box prompts you for the new name, or you can choose a different folder. When you undertake this action, the original document remains in place, and a copy of the document is saved according to your specifications.

4

Formatting a Document

Appearance is everything, so Word offers several ways to improve the appearance of your document through formatting. Formatting enables you to change the look of your document by changing the look of the text. In this chapter, you'll learn how to:

 Work with text properties

 Set paragraph alignment and indentation

 Set and delete tabs

 Work with bullets and numbering

Working with Text Attributes

You can change the appearance of text in a variety of ways. For example, you can make the text bold, underlined, or italic, as well as change the font typeface and size.

Making Text Bold

Applying the bold attribute to text makes the text characters thicker and darker.

1. **Select** the **text** to be bolded. It will be highlighted.

2. **Click** on the **Bold button**. The selected text will be in bold.

MEMORANDUM - Microsoft Word

File Edit View Insert Format Tools Table Window Help

Normal   Times New Roman   12

MEMORANDUM

To: Tim Scott
From: Patrice-Anne Rutledge
Date: September 3, 2000
Re: Sales Figures

Tim:

Here are last month's sales figures for the two new divisions. I can see marked improvements over the previous month. Looks like your new plan is doing well.

Patrice

Page 1   Sec 1   1/1   At 1.5"   Ln 4   Col 1

TIP

Repeat steps 1 and 2 to deselect the bold option.

Underlining Text

Using the underline attribute can call special attention to parts of your document.

1. **Select** the **text** you want to underline. The text will be highlighted.

2. **Click** on the **Underline button**. The selected text will be underlined.

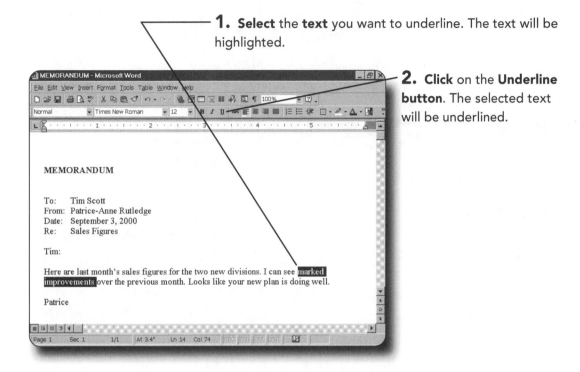

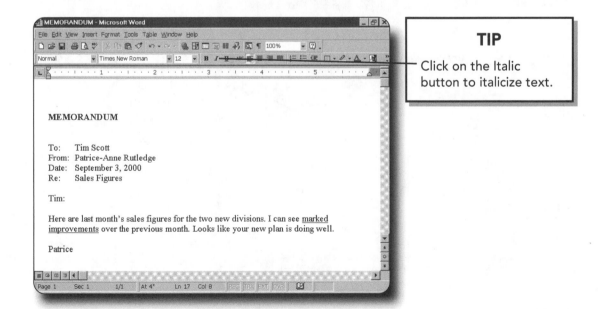

TIP

Click on the Italic button to italicize text.

Changing the Font Typeface

Changing the font typeface is another way to make text stand out from the rest of your document. The font selections available to you vary depending on which fonts are installed on your computer.

1. **Select** the **text** you want to change. The text will be highlighted.

2. **Click** on the **Font Name drop-down arrow**. A list of available fonts will appear.

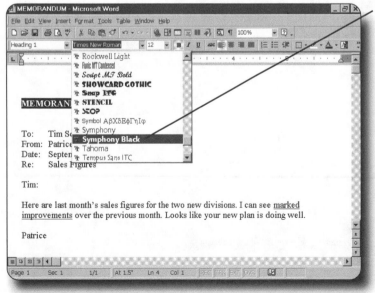

3. **Click** on a **font name** from the list. The font typeface change will be immediately applied to the selected text.

Selecting a Font Size

You might want to make portions of your text larger or smaller than the rest of the text in your document.

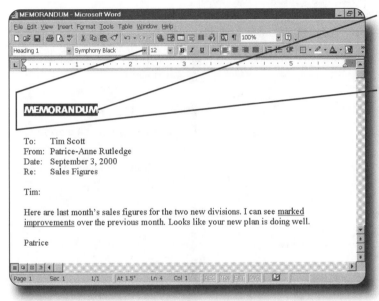

1. **Select** the **text** you want to change. The text will be highlighted.

2. **Click** on the **Font Size drop-down arrow.** A list of font sizes will appear.

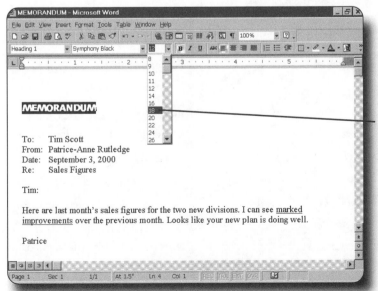

The larger the number, the larger the font size will be. For example, a 72-point font is one inch tall on the printed page.

3. **Click** on a **font size**. The font size change will be applied to the selected text.

Setting Other Text Attributes

Word has a dialog box that enables you to select text attributes in a single step, such as font, font size, underlining, italics, and so on.

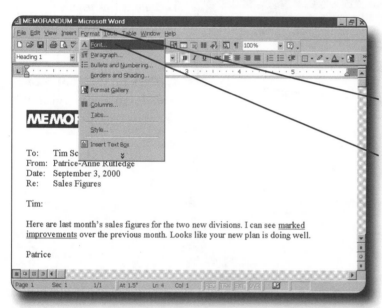

1. Select the **text** to be modified. The text will be highlighted.

2. Click on **Format**. The Format menu will appear.

3. Click on **Font**. The Font dialog box will open.

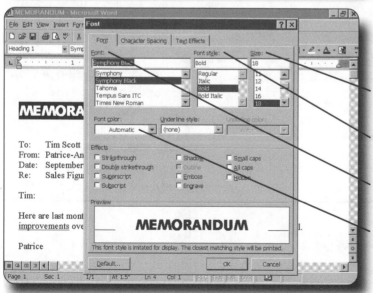

4. Click on any combination of the following **options**:

- **Size.** Click on a size in the displayed list.

- **Font style.** Click on a style in the displayed list.

- **Font.** Click on a name in the displayed list.

- **Font Color.** Click on the drop-down arrow and choose from the available colors.

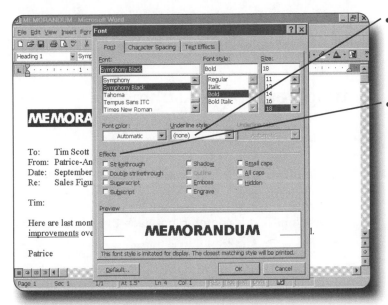

- **Underline Style.** Click on the drop-down arrow and choose from the available underline methods.

- **Effects.** Click on any desired choices.

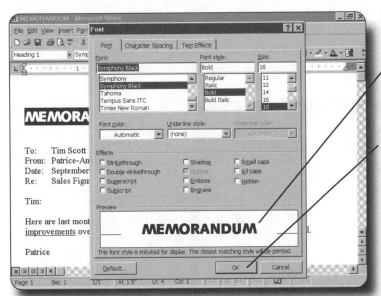

TIP

A preview of your selections appears in the Sample box.

5. Click on **OK**. The dialog box will close, and the selected options will be applied to the highlighted text.

Setting Paragraph Options

You might want to align certain paragraphs in your documents so that they are, for example, centered on a page. Headings and titles are examples of text that are usually centered. You also might need to indent paragraphs so that they stand out from other text.

Setting Paragraph Alignment

Four types of alignment are available:

- **Left align**. Text is even with the left margin but jagged on the right margin.

- **Center align**. Text is centered between the left and right margins.

- **Right align**. Text is even with the right margin but jagged on the left margin.

- **Justified**. Text is spaced evenly between the left and right margins.

1. **Click** the **mouse pointer** within the paragraph you want to align. The insertion point will blink at the selected location.

The four alignment choices are available as selections on the toolbar: Align Left, Center, Align Right, or Justify.

2a. **Click** on an **alignment button** to align the selected paragraph.

OR

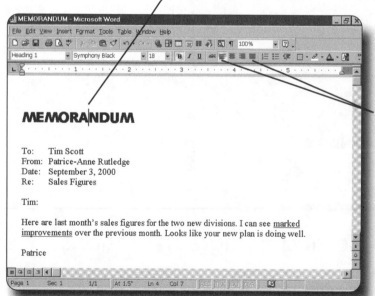

2b. **Click** on **Format**. The Format menu will appear.

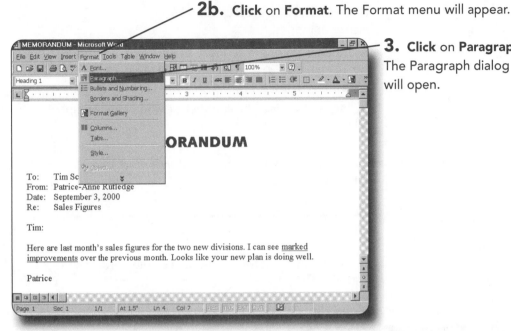

3. **Click** on **Paragraph**. The Paragraph dialog box will open.

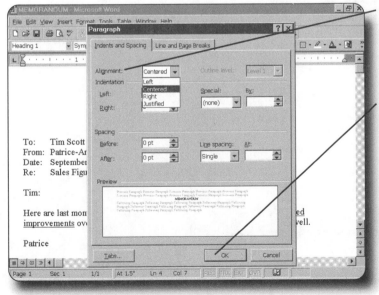

4. **Click** on the **drop-down arrow** and choose from the available alignments. The option will be selected.

5. **Click** on **OK**. The Paragraph dialog box will close.

TIP

Shortcut keys to align text include Ctrl+L to left align, Ctrl+E to center, Ctrl+R to right align, and Ctrl+J to justify.

Indenting Paragraphs

Sometimes you want to inset an entire paragraph from the left or right margins to emphasize it. This is known as *indenting*. Unlike a tab, which indents only the first line, all lines of the paragraph are inset when a paragraph is indented.

1. Select the **paragraphs** to be indented. The paragraphs will be highlighted.

TIP

Optionally, click the mouse in a single paragraph to be modified.

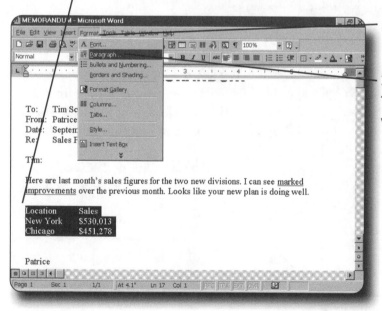

2. Click on **Format**. The Format menu will appear.

3. Click on **Paragraph**. The Paragraph dialog box will open.

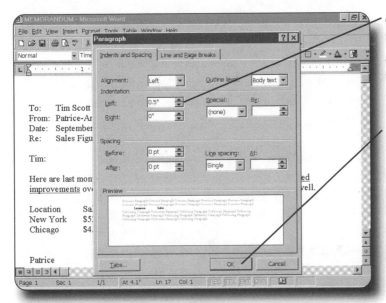

4. Click the **Left Indentation up/down arrows**. The indentation will increase .10 inch for each click.

5. Click on **OK**. The Paragraph dialog box will close.

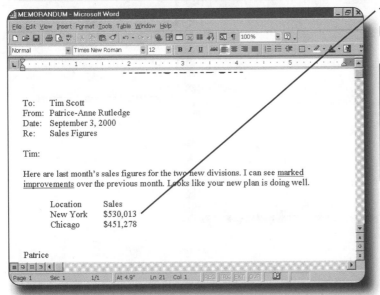

The selected paragraphs will be indented.

TIP

Alternatively, press the Tab key after selecting the text to automatically indent ½ inch.

Working with Tabs

Often you need to create columns of text in your document. Don't use your space bar to line up these columns—it's better accomplished by using tabs.

Displaying the Ruler

Setting and deleting custom tabs is easiest by using the ruler. If the ruler isn't already displayed, you'll need to turn it on. The display of the ruler can be turned on or off as needed.

1. **Click** on **View**. The View menu will appear.

2. If there is no check mark already next to it, **click** on **Ruler**. The ruler bar will display.

The ruler bar displays in inches.

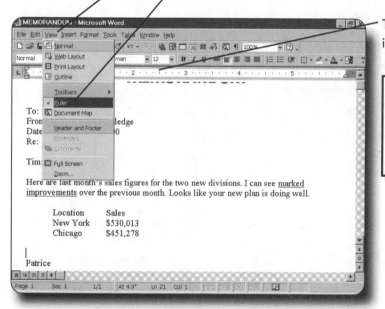

TIP

To turn off the display of the ruler, repeat steps 1 and 2.

Using the Default Tabs

By default, tabs are set at every ½ inch.

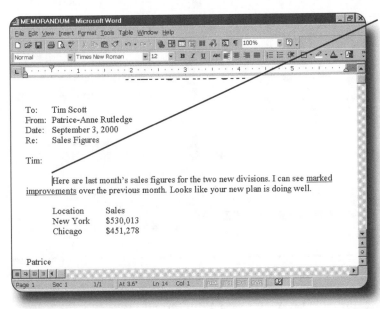

1. **Click** the **mouse pointer** at the beginning of a paragraph. The blinking insertion point will appear at the beginning of the paragraph.

2. **Press** the **Tab key**. The first line of the paragraph moves to the right ½ inch.

TIP

Press the Tab key again to indent the first line an additional ½ inch.

Setting Tabs

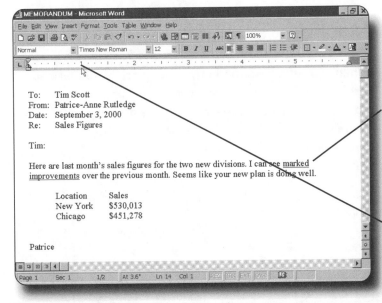

Use the ruler to create your own tab settings.

1. **Click** the **mouse pointer** in the paragraph to be modified. The blinking insertion point will appear in the paragraph.

2. **Position** the **mouse pointer** on the ruler. The mouse pointer will become a white arrow.

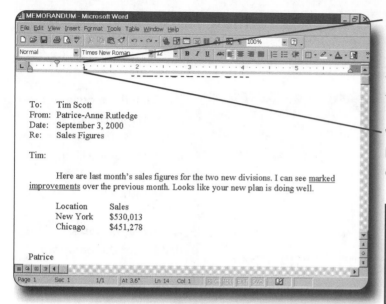

3. Click the **point of the arrow** on the ruler where you want to create a new tab. The tab will be set at that point.

Word indicates custom tabs by a small L-shaped character on the ruler.

NOTE

Custom tabs override the default tabs to the left of the custom tab.

TIP

Move a tab by clicking and dragging the tab marker to a new location on the ruler.

Modifying Tab Styles

When you set a custom tab by clicking on the ruler, Word inserts a left-aligned tab. You can modify any tab to be a right, centered, or decimal tab (for use with numbers containing decimals). You can even specify that a tab have dot leaders.

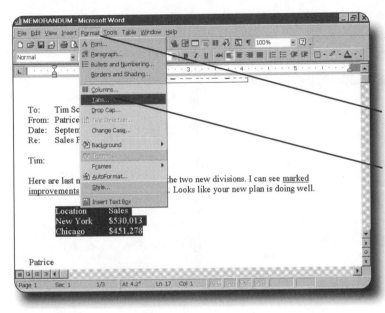

1. Select the **paragraphs** to be modified. The paragraphs will be highlighted.

2. Click on **Format**. The Format menu will appear.

3. Click on **Tabs**. The Tabs dialog box will open.

A list of custom tabs for the selected paragraphs displays.

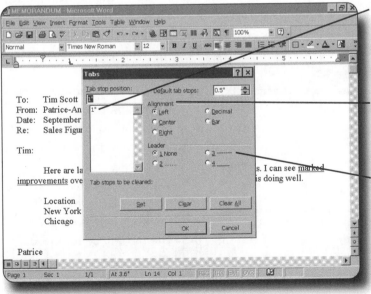

4. Click on the **tab stop position** you want to modify. The tab stop position will be highlighted.

5. Click on an **alignment**. The alignment option will be selected.

6. Optionally, **click** on a **leader** for the tab. The leader option will be selected.

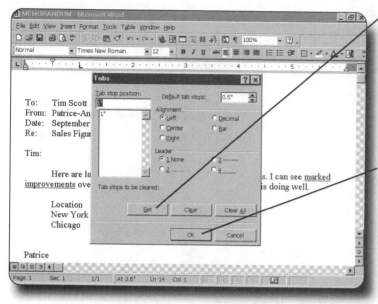

7. Click on **Set**. The changes will be recorded to the tab.

8. Repeat steps 4–7 for each tab that you want to modify.

9. Click on **OK**. The Tabs dialog box will close.

The tab changes will be applied to the selected paragraphs.

Deleting Tabs

Delete any tabs that were set in error or that you no longer want in the paragraph. Make sure your insertion point is in the paragraph that contains the tab you want to delete.

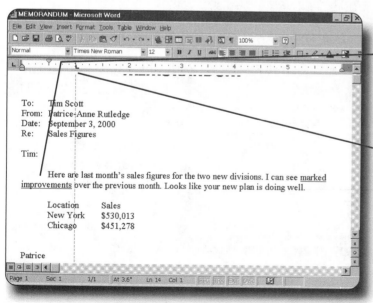

1. Click the **mouse** in the paragraph to be modified. The blinking insertion point will appear in the paragraph.

2. Drag the **unwanted tab** off the ruler anywhere into the body of the document. The tab will be removed.

Working with Bullets

Word makes it easy to create a bulleted paragraph.

Adding a Bullet

Often, indenting a paragraph or group of paragraphs is not enough to draw attention to it; you might want to add a symbol in front of it to emphasize it. This type of symbol is known as a *bullet*.

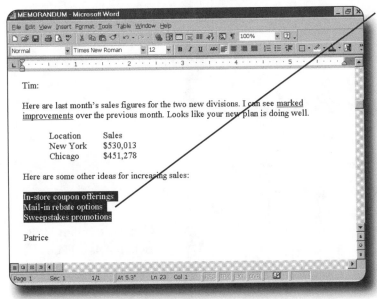

1. Select the **paragraphs** to bullet. The paragraphs will be highlighted.

2. Click on the **Bullets button**. The paragraph will be immediately bulleted and indented.

TIP

Repeat steps 1 and 2 to remove a bullet from a paragraph.

Changing a Bullet Style

Choose from a collection of bullet styles ranging from small, black, filled circles to check marks to funny little icons.

1. Select the **paragraphs** you want to modify. The paragraphs will be highlighted.

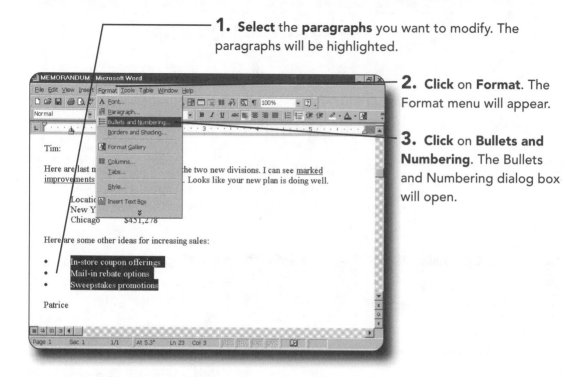

2. Click on **Format**. The Format menu will appear.

3. Click on **Bullets and Numbering**. The Bullets and Numbering dialog box will open.

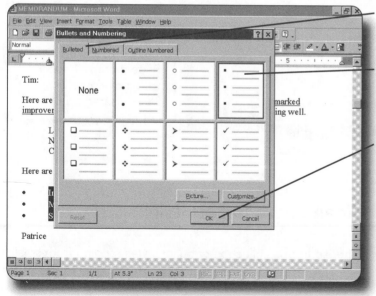

4. Click on the **Bulleted tab**.

5. Click on a **bullet style**. The bullet style will be highlighted.

6. Click on **OK**. The Bullets and Numbering dialog box will close, and the bulleted paragraphs will reflect the newly selected bullet style.

Creating a Numbered List

Creating a numbered list is preferable to just typing numbers; that way, when an item from the list is deleted or moved, all the remaining items are automatically renumbered.

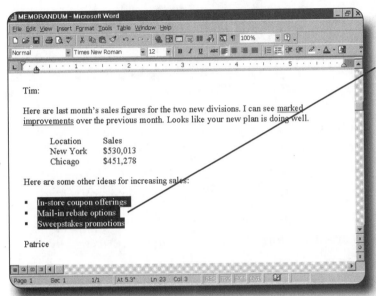

1. **Select** the **text** to be numbered. The paragraphs will be highlighted.

2. **Click** on the **Numbering button**.

The paragraphs will be immediately numbered.

TIP

Click on Bullets and Numbering from the Format menu to open the Bullets and Numbering dialog box. From there, you can select a different style for your numbered list from the Numbered or Outline Numbered tabs.

5

Working with Tables

Tables can greatly enhance both the look and readability of any Word document that contains detailed information. Using Word's table features makes it easy to create columns and rows and to enter columnar text. In this chapter, you'll learn how to:

- Create a table
- Modify a table's size
- Format a table

Creating a Table

Creating a table in Word is fast and easy.

1. Click the **mouse** where you want the table to appear. The blinking insertion point will appear.

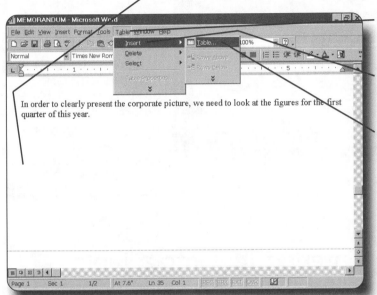

2. Click on **Table**. The Table menu will appear.

3. Click on **Insert**. The Insert submenu will appear.

4. Click on **Table**. The Insert Table dialog box will open.

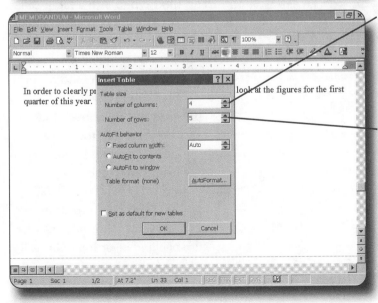

5. Click on the **up and down arrows** in the Number of columns field to indicate the number of columns for the table.

6. Click on the **up and down arrows** in the Number of rows field to indicate the number of rows for the table.

You can modify the number of rows and columns later.

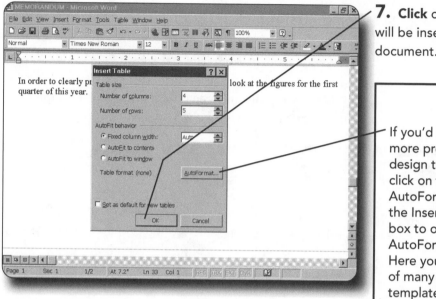

7. Click on **OK**. The table will be inserted into your document.

TIP

If you'd like to apply a more professional design to your table, click on the AutoFormat button in the Insert Table dialog box to open the Table AutoFormat dialog box. Here you can apply one of many format templates to the table you're creating.

Entering Text into a Table

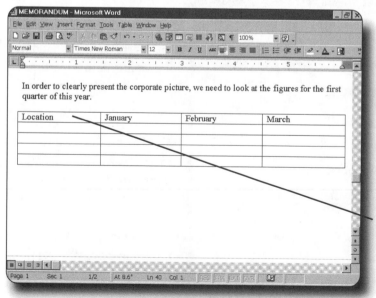

Text typed into a table cell is restricted by the boundaries of each table cell. Press the Tab key to move from one cell to the next, and press Shift+Tab to move the insertion point back to the previous cell. You can also use your arrow keys to move from cell to cell.

1. Click on the **cell** where you want to enter data. The blinking insertion point will appear in the cell.

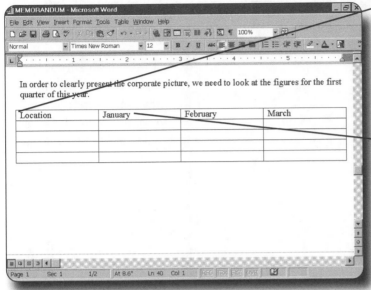

2. **Type** some **text**. The text will appear in the cell.

3. **Press** the **Tab** key. The insertion point will move to the next cell.

4. **Type** some **text**. The text will appear in the next cell.

5. **Repeat steps 1–4** to enter your data.

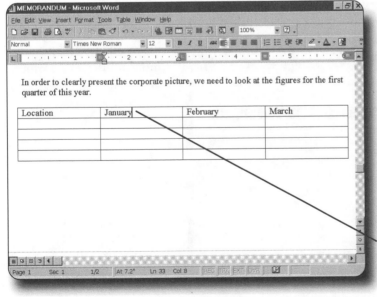

Selecting Table Cells

To modify a table, you'll need to select the cells you want to change. Pay close attention to the mouse pointer when attempting to select cells. The mouse pointer must be in the shape of a white arrow.

• To select a single cell, click on that cell.

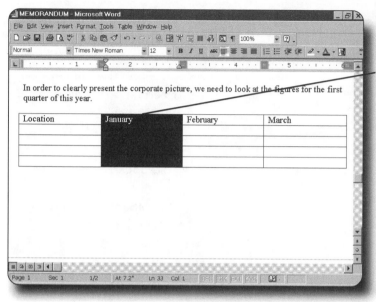

When selected, cells appear onscreen as all black.

- To select an entire column, position the mouse at the top of a column where the mouse turns into a black arrow pointing downward and then click.

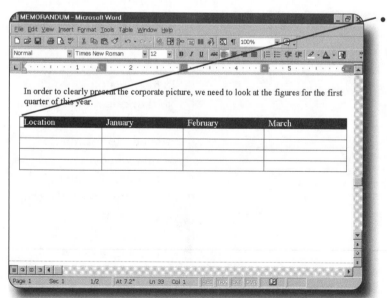

- To select an entire row, position the mouse to the left of the row where the mouse turns into a white arrow and then click.

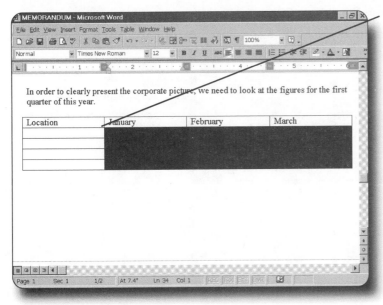

- To select a block of cells, click on the beginning cell, hold down the mouse button, and drag across the additional cells. Then release the mouse button.

Modifying Your Table

After you start working with a table, you might find that you need to add rows and columns, or you might want to make a column narrower or wider based on the text in that column.

Adding Rows at the End

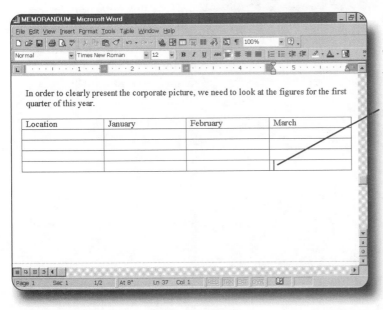

If you need additional rows at the end of your table, Word can quickly add them for you.

1. Click in the last **cell** of the table. The blinking insertion point will appear.

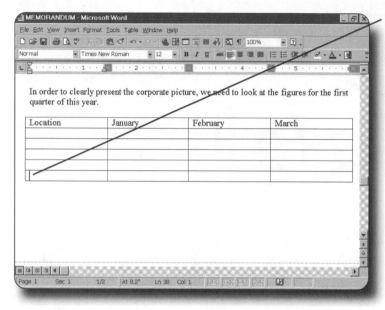

2. Press the **Tab key**. An additional row will be added to the table.

3. Repeat steps 1 and **2** for as many additional rows as needed.

Adding Rows in the Middle

When you add rows in the middle of a table, all existing rows below the new row are moved down.

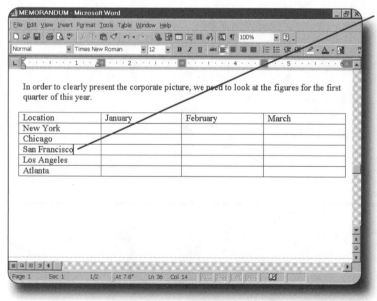

1. Click anywhere in the **row** above or below which you want the new row to appear. The blinking insertion point will appear, and a cell in that row will be selected.

2. **Click** on **Table**. The Table menu will appear.

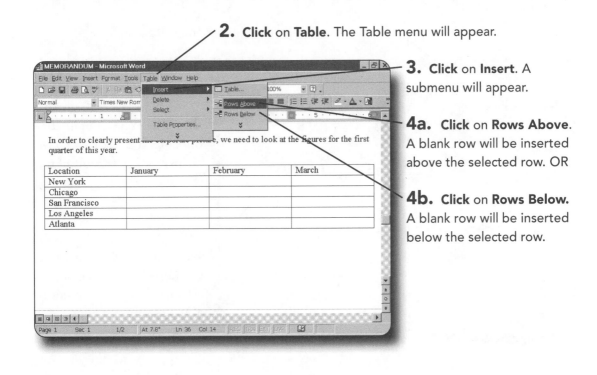

3. **Click** on **Insert**. A submenu will appear.

4a. **Click** on **Rows Above**. A blank row will be inserted above the selected row. OR

4b. **Click** on **Rows Below**. A blank row will be inserted below the selected row.

Inserting Columns

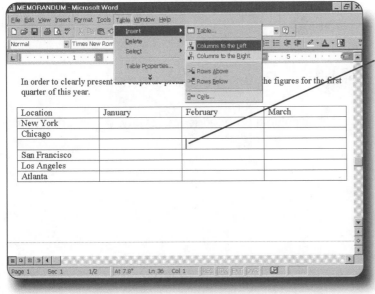

You can also insert new columns into your table.

1. **Click** anywhere in the **column** to the left or right of which you want the new column to appear. The blinking insertion point will appear.

2. Click on **Table**. The Table menu will appear.

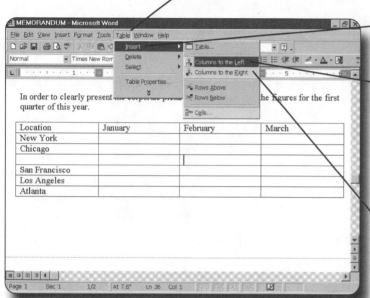

3. Click on **Insert**. A submenu will appear.

4a. Click on **Columns to the Left.** A blank column will be inserted to the left of the selected column.

OR

4b. Click on **Columns to the Right.** A blank column will be inserted to the right of the selected column.

TIP

If your table is now too wide for the page, see the section below on "Changing Column Width."

Deleting Rows or Columns

If a row or column is no longer necessary, you can delete it.

1. Select the **columns** or **rows** you want to delete. The entire column or row will be highlighted.

2. Click on **Table**. The Table menu will appear.

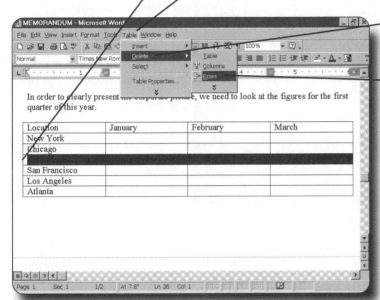

3. Click on **Delete**. A submenu will appear.

4. Click on either **Columns** or **Rows**, depending on what you want to delete. The selected rows or columns will be deleted.

NOTE

The Table menu choices will change depending on whether you've selected a column or a row in the table.

Changing Column Width

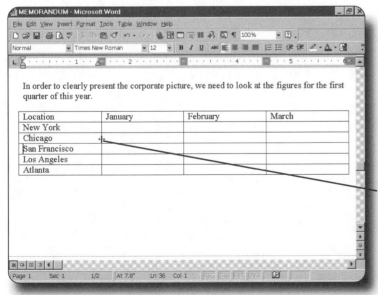

By default, all columns are equally spaced, and a table spans the entire width of the document from margin to margin.

1. Position the **pointer** over the right border of a column. The pointer will change to a black double-headed arrow.

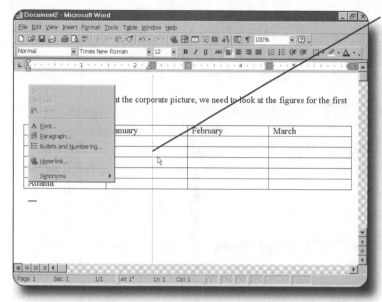

2. **Press and hold the mouse button** and **drag** the **border** until the column is the desired size. A dotted line will indicate the new column size.

3. **Release** the **mouse button**. The column will be resized.

6

Working with Page Layout

Word offers flexible page layout options that enable you to modify and format your documents in an endless variety of ways. For example, you might need to adjust the size of the text area of a document, or you might want to use headers and footers to repeat key information on each page of a document such as a company's name or the page number. These types of page layout features give your document a professional look. In this chapter, you'll learn how to:

- Set margins
- Change page size
- Change page orientation
- Add a header or footer

Setting Margins

The size of the text area is determined by the page margins. You can set left, right, top, and bottom margins.

By setting the margins, you control the amount of text area available. The default margin setting is 1 inch for the top and bottom margins and 1.25 inch for the left and right margins.

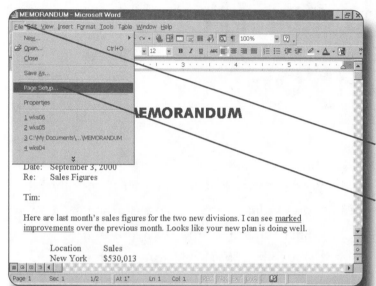

1. Click on **File**. The File menu will appear.

2. Click on **Page Setup**. The Page Setup dialog box will open.

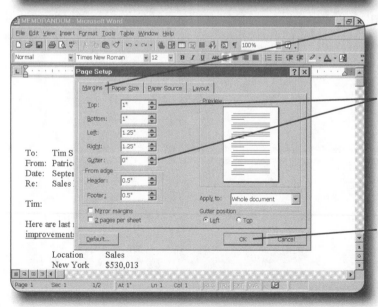

3. Click on the **Margins tab,** if necessary. The tab will come to the front.

4. Click on the **up and down arrows** for each margin in the Top, Bottom, Left, and Right margin spin boxes. The value in these boxes is measured in inches.

5. Click on **OK**. The Page Setup dialog box will close and the specified margin settings will be applied to the document.

Changing Page Size

Word lets you select from several page size options, which are based on the page size settings of your printer. Letter size (8½ by 11 inches) is the standard format, but you can also choose international, legal, notepaper, and envelope size settings.

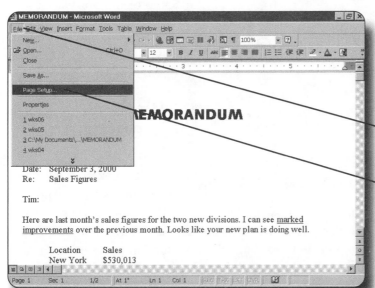

1. Click on **File**. The File menu will appear.

2. Click on **Page Setup**. The Page Setup dialog box will open.

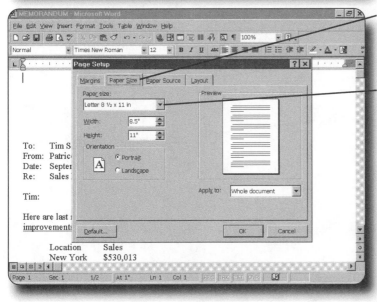

3. Click on the **Paper Size tab.** The tab will come to the front.

4. Click on the **Paper Size drop-down arrow.** The list of available page size options will appear.

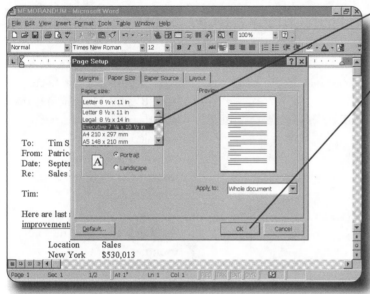

5. Click on a **page size**. The page size will be selected.

6. Click on **OK**. The Page Setup dialog box will close.

Changing Page Orientation

Word lets you print a document using either a portrait or landscape orientation. Portrait orientation prints the document in a vertical layout, along the short edge of the page whereas landscape orientation prints horizontally across the long edge of the page. Another way to look at it is that portrait positions the 8 ½-inch side of an 8 ½ by 11-inch page at the top and landscape positions the 11-inch side at the top.

1. Click on **File**. The File menu will appear.

2. Click on **Page Setup**. The Page Setup dialog box will open.

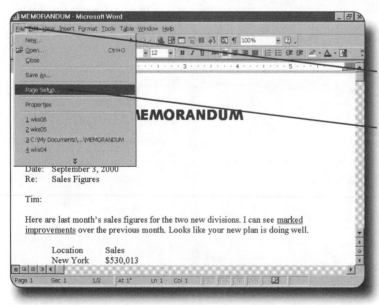

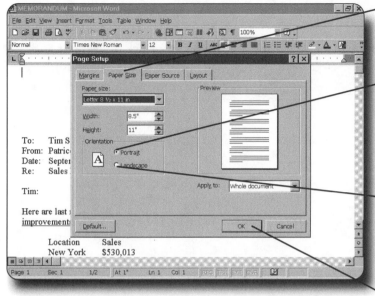

3. Click on the **Paper Size tab.** The tab will come to the front.

4a. Click on the **Portrait button**. The document's orientation will be portrait.

OR

4b. Click on the **Landscape button**. The document's orientation will be landscape.

5. Click on **OK**. The Page Setup dialog box will close.

Adding a Header or Footer

Two areas in a document are reserved for repeating text. When this text is at the top of a page, it is called a *header*. When this text is at the bottom of a page, it is called a *footer*. The header or footer area displays as a box with an outline at the top or bottom of the document.

Creating a Header or Footer

Examples of text you may want to place in a header or footer are the date the document was created, the document name, your company's name, or the current page number. The header and footer area are automatically created when you create a new document.

1. Click on **View**. The View menu will appear.

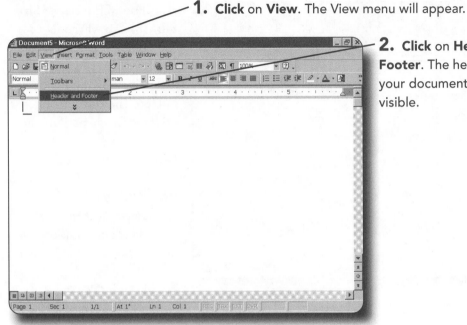

2. Click on **Header and Footer**. The header area of your document will become visible.

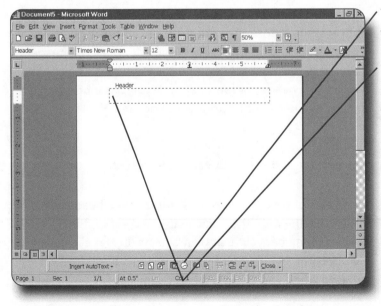

The Header and Footer toolbar will display.

The insertion point will be located in the header area of the document.

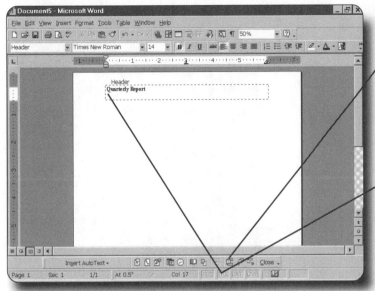

TIP

Click on the Switch Between Header and Footer button on the toolbar to move the insertion point to the document footer.

3. Type the header or footer **text**. The text will be added to the header or footer.

TIP

Format header or footer text using the same methods used to format the document body text. Formatting text was discussed in Chapter 4, "Formatting a Document."

Inserting a Page Number in a Header or Footer

When creating a header or footer, don't simply type a number for the page number because Word requires a special field to increment them.

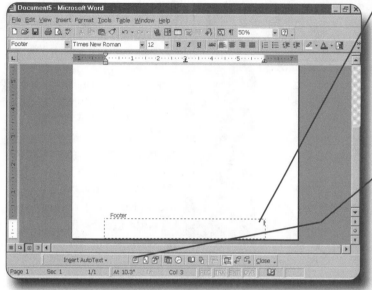

1. **Position** the **insertion point** at the location in the header or footer where you want the page number to be printed. The insertion point will be located in the header or footer area of the document.

2. **Click** on the **Insert Page Number button**. The number will be inserted into the header or footer. This number is, however, a programming code for the current page number. Word will change the numbers as you move along in the document.

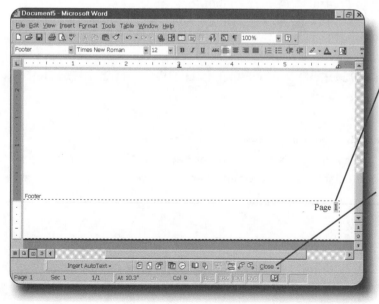

TIP

If you want the page number to be preceded by text, such as the word "Page," type the text in front of the page numbering field.

3. **Click** on the **Close** button. The document will return to the main editing screen.

7

Creating Reports

Reports are second only to letters in popularity and use. Whether you are a student, consultant, or other professional, you will have many uses for reports. Students often must do reports as part of their class work; professionals create reports for a variety of reasons ranging from cost and project justifications to recommendations and strategic directions. In this chapter, you'll learn how to:

- Add report page breaks
- Add report borders
- Add report footnotes

Inserting Page Breaks

When a page is full of text, Word automatically begins a new page. Sometimes, however, you want a new page to begin at a specific location. This is called a *page break*.

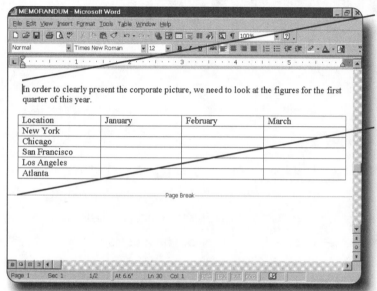

1. Click the **mouse** at the position where you want the new page to begin. The blinking insertion point will appear at that position.

Existing page breaks appear as a black line across the screen with the label "Page Break" in the center.

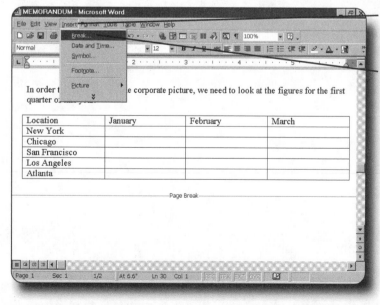

2. Click on **Insert**. The Insert menu will appear.

3. Click on **Break**. The Break dialog box will open.

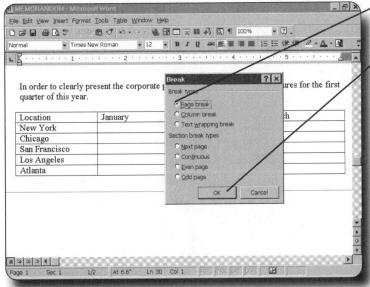

4. Click on the **Page Break** option.

5. Click on **OK**. The Break dialog box will close.

The insertion point will appear at the beginning of a new page.

Adding Borders

Decorate your document with a border. Word offers a variety of borders that you can use around a selected paragraph or the current page.

Applying a Paragraph Border

Add prominence to part of a page by placing a border around it.

1a. **Click** the **mouse pointer** in the paragraph around which you want to place a border. The blinking insertion point will appear.

OR

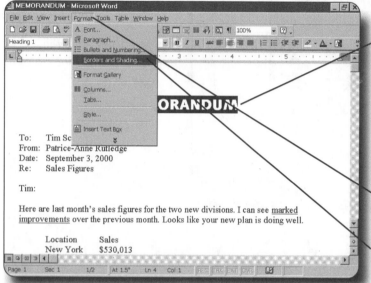

1b. **Highlight** (by clicking and dragging the mouse) one or more **paragraphs** around which you want to place a border. The paragraphs will be highlighted.

2. **Click** on **Format**. The Format menu will appear.

3. **Click** on **Borders and Shading**. The Borders and Shading dialog box will open.

4. **Click** on the **Borders tab**.

5. **Click** on a **Setting** option to determine the type of border you want— a box, a shadow, or a 3-D border, for example.

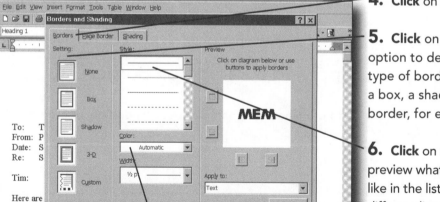

6. **Click** on a **Style**. You can preview what each style looks like in the list. There are many different line styles to choose from: single lines, double lines, thick or thin lines, and dashed or dotted lines.

7. **Click** on a **color** from the Color drop-down list. The color will apply to your border.

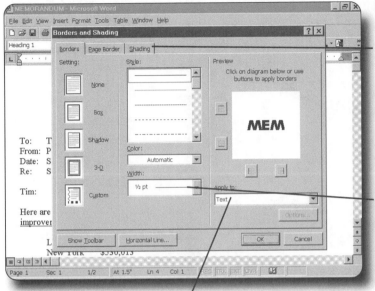

TIP

Optionally, apply a shading pattern by choosing from among the options in the Shading tab of the Borders and Shading dialog box.

8. Click on a **line width** from the Width drop-down list. The line width will apply to your border.

9. Click on either **Text or Paragraph** from the Apply to drop-down list. The border will apply to either the selected text or the entire paragraph depending upon your choice.

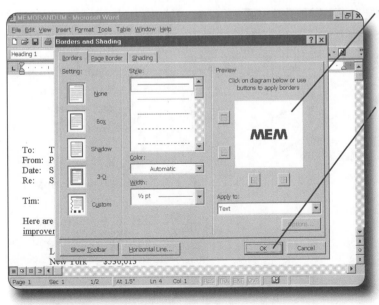

You can preview and modify your choices in the Preview box before accepting the border settings.

10. Click on **OK**. The Borders and Shading dialog box will close.

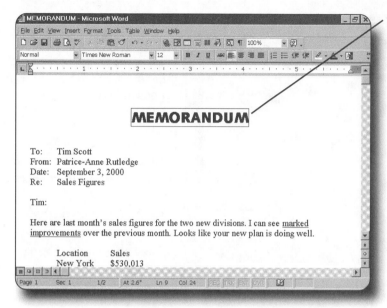

The paragraph border will be applied to the current or selected paragraphs.

Bordering Pages

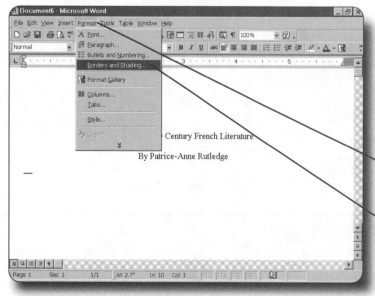

Works includes more than 150 pieces of decorative artwork that can be applied around each page of your document. Choose from simple lines, stars, hearts, leaves, and more.

1. **Click** on **Format**. The Format menu will appear.

2. **Click** on **Borders and Shading**. The Borders and Shading dialog box will open.

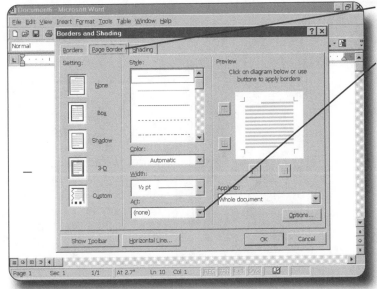

3. **Click** on the **Page Border tab**.

4. **Click** on the **Art drop-down arrow**. A selection of available styles will appear.

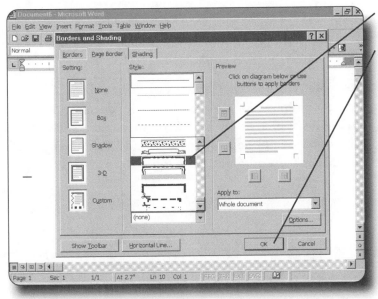

5. **Click** on an **art style**.

6. **Click** on **OK**. The Borders and Shading dialog box will close.

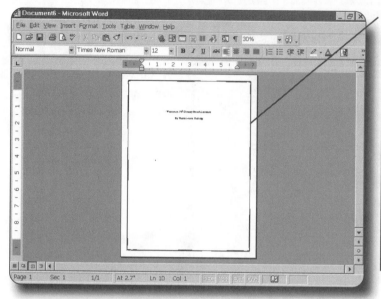

Each page of the entire document will have a decorative border.

TIP

If you'd rather apply a plain border to your page, follow the same steps as you did on the Borders tab for bordering a paragraph after highlighting the entire page.

Adding Footnotes and Endnotes

Footnotes and endnotes comment on and provide reference information for the text in your document. Footnotes appear at the bottom of the current page, whereas endnotes appear on a separate page at the end of the document. Footnotes and endnotes are automatically numbered for you.

1. **Click** the **mouse pointer** where you want to insert the footnote or endnote reference mark (usually, a superscripted number). The blinking insertion point will appear.

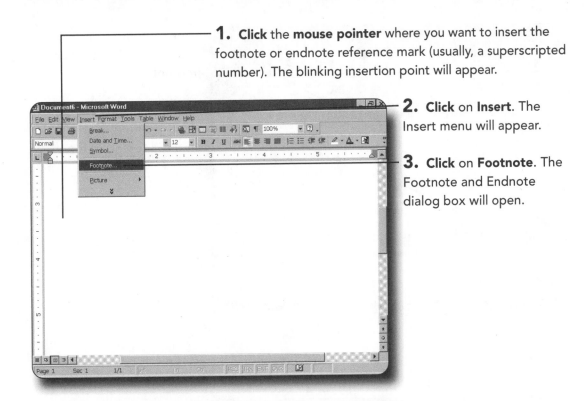

2. **Click** on **Insert**. The Insert menu will appear.

3. **Click** on **Footnote**. The Footnote and Endnote dialog box will open.

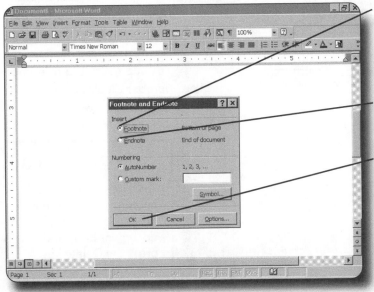

4a. **Click** on **Footnote**. The option will be selected.

OR

4b. **Click** on **Endnote**. The option will be selected.

5. **Click** on **OK**. The footnote or endnote reference will be added to the document, and the insertion point will be placed in the footnote or endnote area of the document.

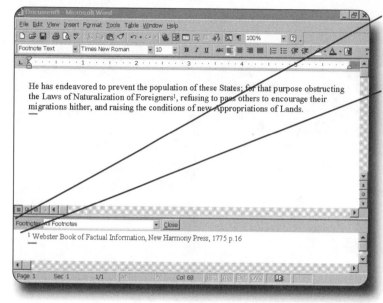

Word automatically includes a separator line for your footnotes.

6. Type the **text** of the note. The text will be entered for this note.

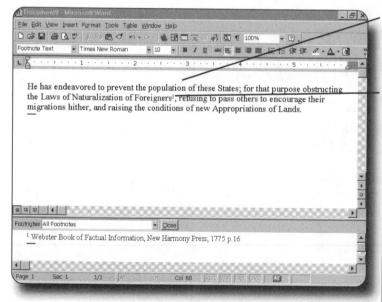

7. Click in the **document body.** You will return to the main text of the document.

The superscripted reference number displays in the document body.

TIP

To delete a footnote or endnote, highlight the reference number in the document body and press the Delete key. The corresponding footnote or endnote text will also be deleted.

8

Improving Your Writing

One goal of Microsoft Word is to make document creation as easy as possible. To reach this goal, several features have been included to improve your writing. For example, Word's spelling and grammar checker can catch many mistakes for you, and if you can't think of the exact word you want to use, the Thesaurus feature can help you out. You can use these and other features, such as Find and Replace, to improve your writing style. In this chapter, you'll learn how to:

- Use the Find and Replace features
- Check your spelling and grammar
- Use the Thesaurus feature

Using Find to Locate Text

Do you have a long document that you created, but you can't remember where you used a particular word or phrase? Use the Find feature to search for words or phrases in a document.

1. **Click** the **mouse** at the location to begin the search—usually the beginning of the document. The insertion point will appear at that location.

2. **Click** on **Edit**. The Edit menu will appear.

3. **Click** on **Find**. The Find and Replace dialog box will open with the Find tab selected.

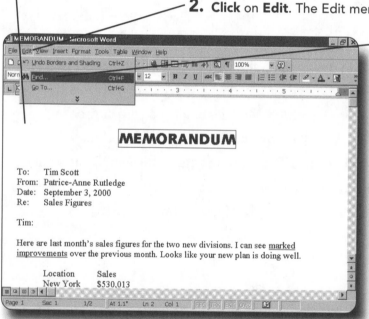

TIP

Another way to access the Find feature is to press Ctrl+F.

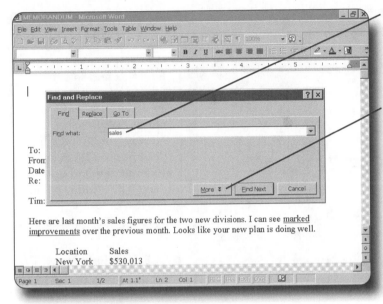

4. Type the **word or phrase** you want to locate. The text will appear in the Find what text box.

5. Optionally, **click** on **More** to expand the dialog box for additional options.

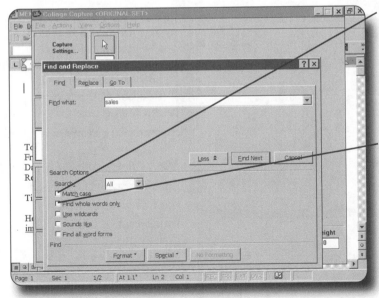

6. Click on the **Match case check box** if you want Word to search only for text that exactly matches the case of what you entered in the Find what text box.

7. Click on the **Find whole words only check box** if you want Word to search only for whole words that match what you entered in the Find what text box.

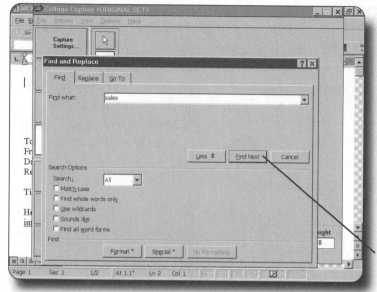

NOTE

If you type "and" in the Find box and select Find whole words only, Word will not find the words "Anderson," "candy," or "band." If you choose Match case, Word would find only "and." It would not find "AND" or "And."

8. Click on **Find Next**. The first occurrence of the found text will be highlighted.

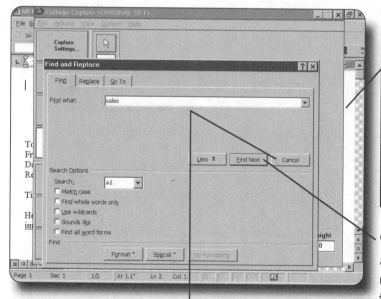

NOTE

Occasionally, the found text is hidden under the dialog box. You might have to move the Find and Replace dialog box by clicking and dragging on the title bar at the top of the dialog box.

9a. Click on **Find Next** again. Word will locate the next occurrence of the found text.

OR

9b. Click on **Cancel**. The Find and Replace dialog box will close, and the found text will remain highlighted.

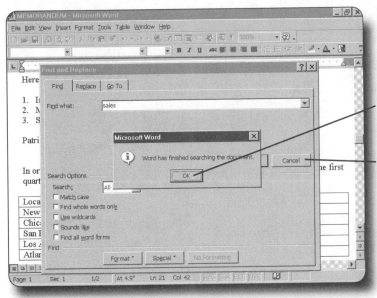

When the entire document has been searched, Word will advise you with a message box.

10. Click on **OK**. The message box will close.

11. Click on **Cancel**. The Find and Replace dialog box will close, and the last found text will remain highlighted.

Replacing Text

Use the Replace feature to exchange a word or phrase for something else. You can replace some or all occurrences of the word or phrase with other text.

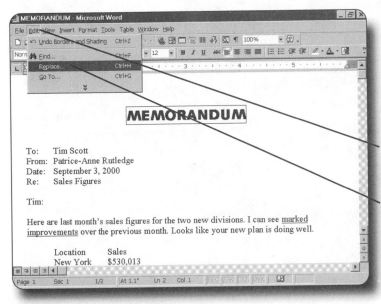

1. Click the **mouse** at the beginning of the document or where you want to begin the search. The insertion point will appear at that location.

2. Click on **Edit**. The Edit menu will appear.

3. Click on **Replace**. The Find and Replace dialog box will open with the Replace tab selected.

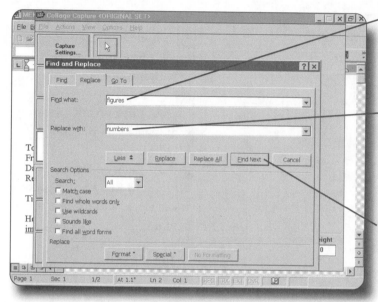

4. Type the **text** that you want to find in the Find what text box. The text will appear in the box.

5. Type the **text** in the Replace with text box that will replace the text entered in step 4. The text will appear in the box.

6. Click on **Find Next**. The first instance of the text will be highlighted.

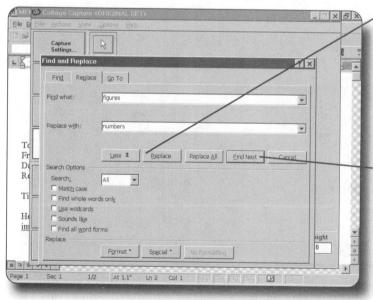

7a. Click on **Replace**. The replacement text will be placed in the document, and Word will search for the next occurrence of the text.

OR

7b. Click on **Find Next**. Word will leave the found text alone and go to the next occurrence.

8. Continue clicking on Find Next to view each instance of the text you want to find.

NOTE

If the Replace with text box is left blank and you click on Replace, Word deletes the search word or phrase.

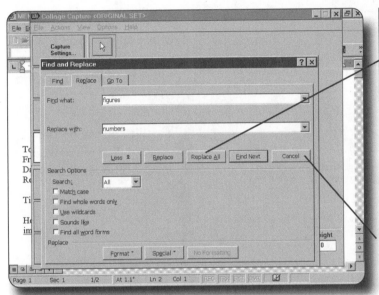

TIP

Click on Replace All to replace all occurrences of the search text at the same time. A message box advises you of the number of replacements. Click on OK to close the message box.

9. Click on **Cancel**. The Find and Replace dialog box will close.

Correcting Spelling and Grammatical Errors

Word has built-in dictionaries and grammatical rule sets that it uses to check your document. Word can identify possible problems as you type, and it also can run a special spelling and grammar check, which provides you with more information about the problems and tools for fixing them. These features aren't infallible; if you type "air" instead of "err," Word probably won't be able to tell that you're wrong. However, combined with a good proofreading, these tools can be very helpful.

Checking Spelling As You Go

By default, Word identifies problems right in your document as you type. Spelling errors have a red wavy line underneath them.

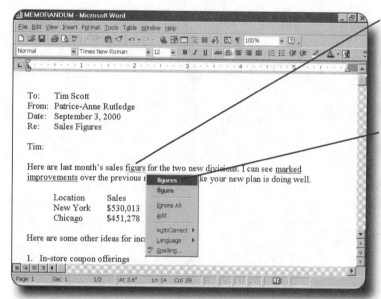

1. **Right-click** on a **word** of whose spelling you are unsure. The shortcut menu will appear with suggested corrections.

2. **Click** on the **correct spelling**. The misspelled word will be replaced with your selection.

Running a Spelling and Grammar Check

Word also enables you to check your grammar—another way to improve your writing. You can run a spelling and grammar check at the same time.

1. Click on **Tools**. The Tools menu will appear.

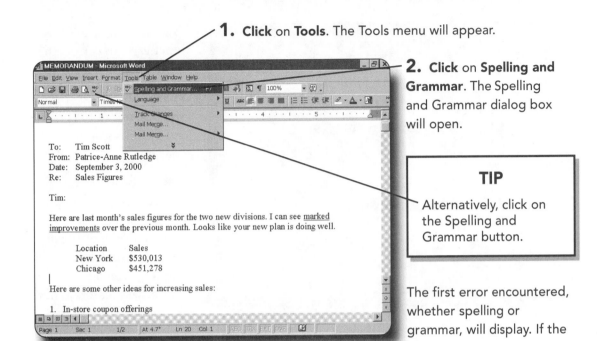

2. Click on **Spelling and Grammar**. The Spelling and Grammar dialog box will open.

TIP

Alternatively, click on the Spelling and Grammar button.

The first error encountered, whether spelling or grammar, will display. If the error is in spelling, it is identified in the Not in Dictionary text box. The Suggestions text box contains possible correct spellings for the word. In this example, the correct spelling is already highlighted.

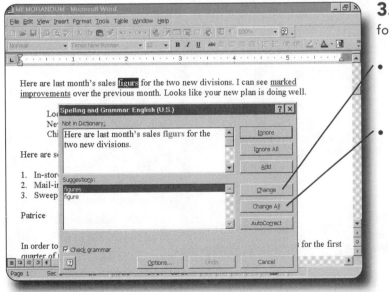

3. Click on **one** of the following options:

- **Change.** Choose this to change just this instance of the spelling mistake.

- **Change All.** Choose this if you think the mistake appears more than once within the document.

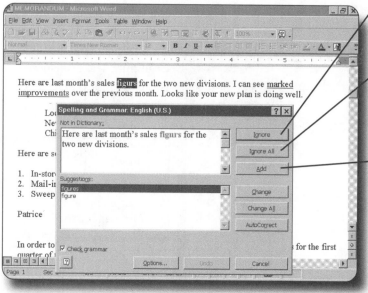

- **Ignore.** Choose this if you don't want to correct this instance of the spelling.

- **Ignore All.** Choose this if you don't want to correct any instances of the spelling.

- **Add.** Choose this to add a word, such as a proper name or legal term, to Word's built-in dictionary so that it won't be flagged as an error in the future. This feature is not available for all words.

After you choose one of these actions, the check will proceed to the next possible error.

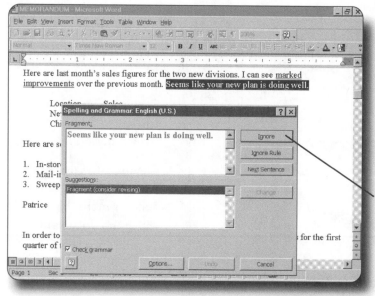

If Word finds a grammatical error, it will display it in the top text box, with a suggested revision or explanation of the error in the Suggestions text box.

4. Click on **one** of the following:

- **Ignore.** Choose this if you don't want to change this instance of the grammatical problem or if you want to modify it at a later time.

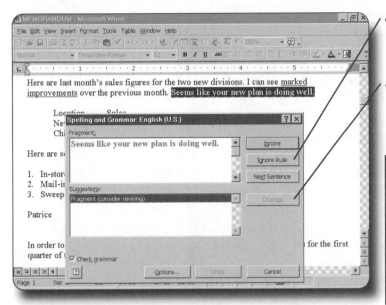

- **Ignore Rule.** Choose this to ignore all instances of the grammatical problem.

- **Change.** Choose this to make the suggested change.

NOTE

Sometimes, Word can't give a grammatical suggestion. In those cases, you'll need to correct the error yourself.

CAUTION

Do *not* rely on Word's Spell Check and Grammar features to catch all your errors. They are far from perfect and can miss many items. They can also flag errors when your text is really okay and can suggest wrong things to do to fix both real problems and false error reports. You alone know what you want your document to say. Proofread it yourself!

When all mistakes have been identified, Word will notify you that the spelling and grammar check is complete.

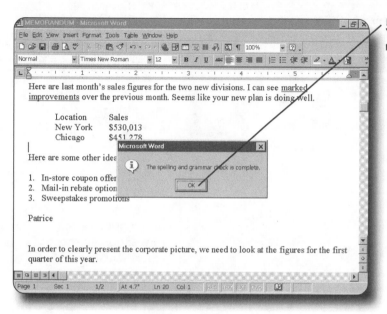

5. **Click** on **OK**. The message box will close.

Using the Thesaurus

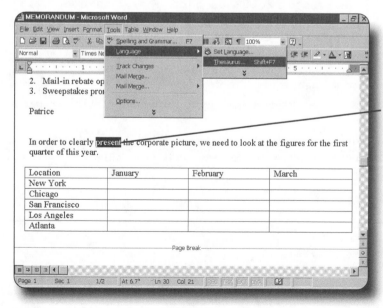

The Word Thesaurus gives you an easy way to find just the right words to use in your document.

1. **Highlight or click** on the **word** you want to replace. The blinking insertion point will appear in the word.

2. Click on **Tools**. The Tools menu will appear.

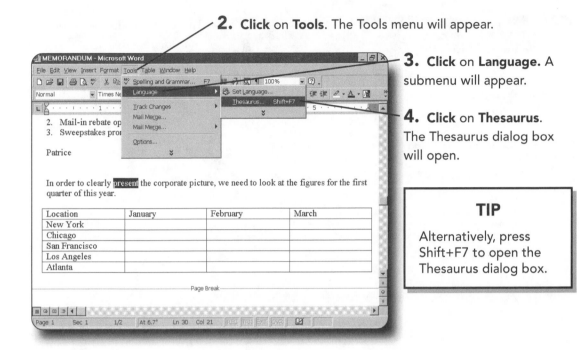

3. Click on **Language**. A submenu will appear.

4. Click on **Thesaurus**. The Thesaurus dialog box will open.

TIP

Alternatively, press Shift+F7 to open the Thesaurus dialog box.

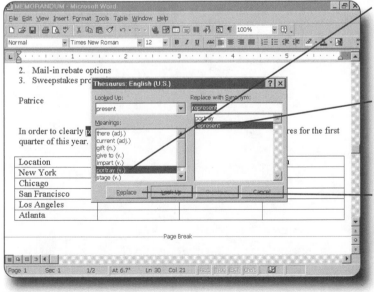

5. Click on a **meaning** in the Meanings list. Potential synonyms for that meaning will appear.

6. Click on a **word** from the Replace with Synonym list. The word will be highlighted.

7. Click on **Replace**. The Thesaurus dialog box will close.

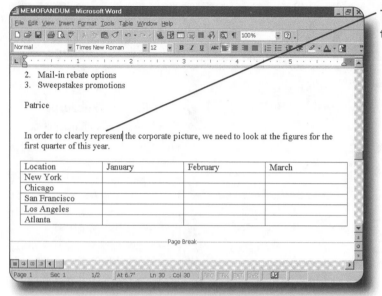

The word will be replaced in the document.

9

Completing Your Document

Your work on your Word document is coming to an end. The final steps include printing the document and then closing it. In this chapter, you'll learn how to:

- Print a document
- Create an envelope
- Open and close a document

Printing a Document

Word is a what-you-see-is-what-you-get (WYSIWYG) program, which means that text and other elements, such as graphics, appear onscreen the same way they will look when printed on paper.

Using Print Preview

Before you print your document, preview it full-screen. Previewing a document gives you an idea of how layout settings, such as margins, will look on the printed page.

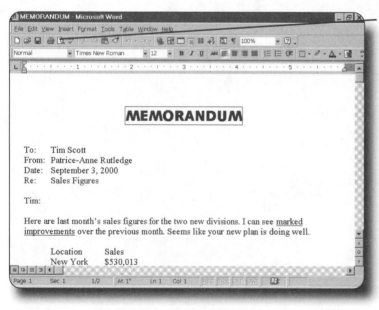

1. Click on the **Print Preview button**. The document will be sized so that an entire page is visible on the screen. You won't be able to edit the document from this screen.

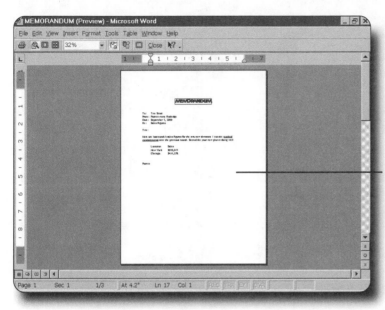

2. Press the **Page Down key.** The next page of the document will appear.

3. Press the **Page Up key.** The previous page of the document will appear.

4. Click on the **document body**. The text will become larger on the screen.

5. Click on the **document body** again. The text will become smaller on the screen.

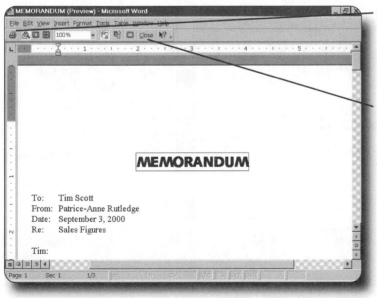

6. Optionally, **click** on **Print**. The document will automatically print with standard options.

7. Click on **Close**. The Print Preview window will close, and the document will return to the normal editing view.

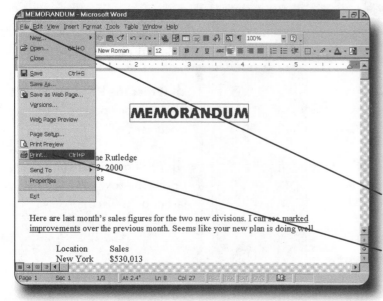

Printing Your Work

Typically, the end result of creating a document in Word is getting text onto paper. Word gives you a quick and easy way to do so.

1. **Click** on **File**. The File menu will appear.

2. **Click** on **Print**. The Print dialog box will open.

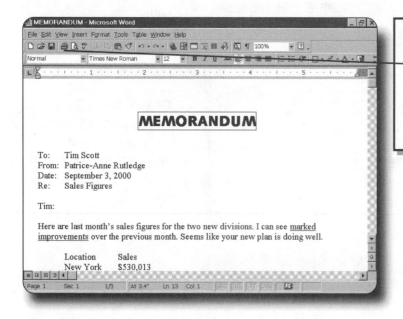

TIP

Alternatively, you can click on the Print button to print your document with default options.

3. **Click** on any desired **options**. The options will be activated. Many options are available, including:

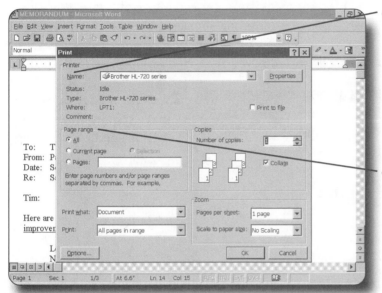

- **Name.** If you are connected to more than one printer, you can choose which one to use for this print job. Click on the Name drop-down arrow and make a selection.

- **Page range**. You can choose which pages of your document to print with the page-range options.

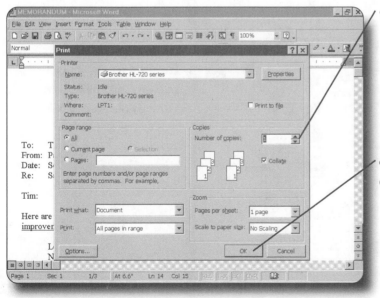

- **Number of copies**. Choose the number of copies to be printed by clicking on the up/down arrows at the right of the Number of copies drop-down list.

4. **Click** on **OK**. The document will print.

Creating an Envelope

With a laser or inkjet printer and Microsoft Word, you can easily print a professional-looking envelope.

1. Click on **Tools**. The Tools menu will appear.

2. Click on **Envelopes and Labels**. The Envelopes and Labels dialog box will open.

3. Click on the **Options button**. The Envelopes Options dialog box will open.

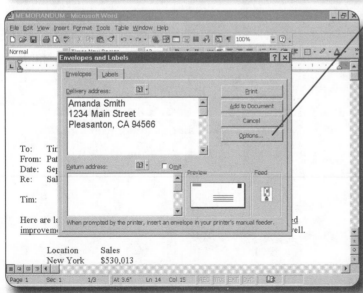

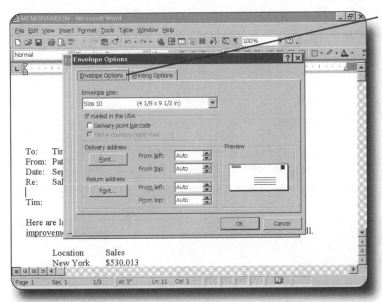

4. **Click** on the **Envelope Options tab.** The tab will display.

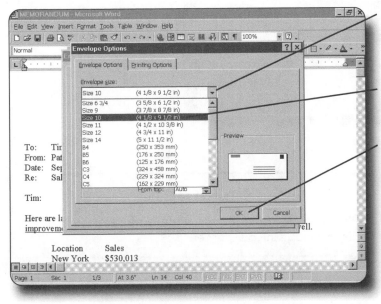

5. **Click** on the **Envelope size drop-down arrow.** A list of envelope sizes will appear.

6. **Click** on the **envelope size** you want.

7. **Click** on **OK.** The Envelope Options dialog box will close and you will return to the Envelopes and Label dialog box.

8. Type the **delivery address** in the Delivery address text box.

TIP

You can apply font styles to your delivery and return addresses in the Envelope Options dialog box. Simply click on the related Font button and then apply formatting options as you would for any other text.

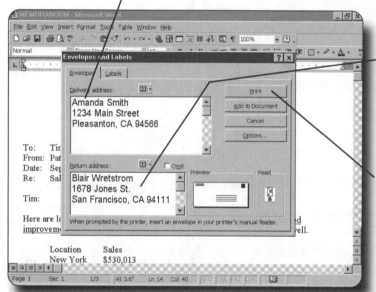

TIP

If you want the envelope to have a return address, enter one in the Return address text box.

9. Click on the **Print button**. The envelope will print.

NOTE

Refer to your printer manual for instructions on placing an envelope in your printer.

Opening an Existing Document

Once you've created a Word document, you'll probably want to open it again—for example, to modify it or print it. When you open a document, Word places a copy of that file into the computer's memory and onto your screen so that you can work on it again. If you make any changes, be sure to save the file again. See the section "Saving a Document" in Chapter 3, "Getting Started with Word," if you need help saving a file.

Opening a Document from the Task Launcher

You can open a document from the Works Task Launcher, which appears when you first start the Works Suite program.

1. Click on **History**. A listing of previously opened Works Suite documents will appear.

If the document you want to open is listed:

2. Click on the **name of the file** that you want to open. The filename will be highlighted, and the file will appear on your screen, ready for you to edit.

If the document you want to open is not listed:

3. Click on **Find Files or Folders**. The Find: All Files dialog box will open.

4. Type the **name of the file** you want to open. If you don't know the entire filename, type any portion of it. The text will appear in the Named text box.

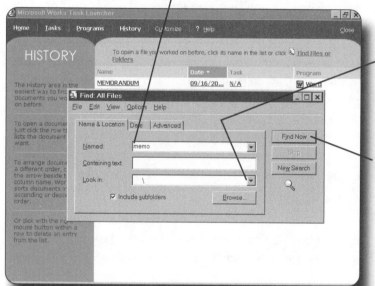

TIP

Click on the Look in drop-down arrow and choose a location to search.

5. Click on **Find Now**. The computer will search for any files whose names contain the text you specified.

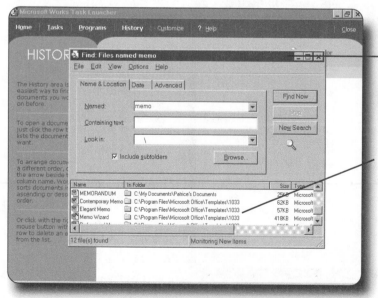

TIP

To better see the results, double-click on the title bar to enlarge the dialog box.

Any filenames containing the letters you specified will appear.

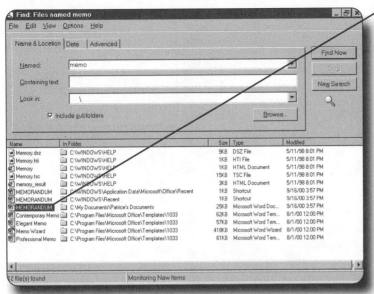

6. Double-click on the **name of the file** you want to open. The file will display on your screen, ready for you to edit.

Opening Multiple Documents

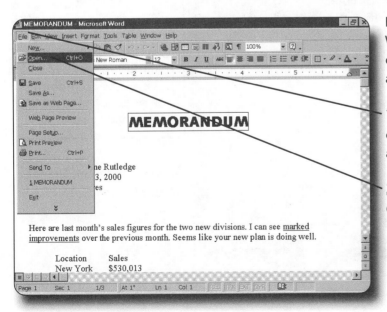

Even if you already have a Word document open onscreen, you can open another.

1. From within Word, **click** on **File**. The File menu will appear.

2. Click on **Open**. The Open dialog box will open.

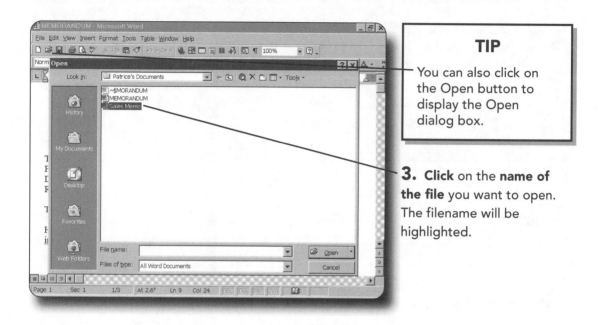

TIP

You can also click on the Open button to display the Open dialog box.

3. Click on the **name of the file** you want to open. The filename will be highlighted.

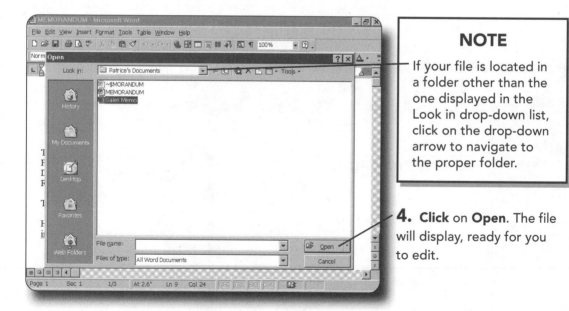

NOTE

If your file is located in a folder other than the one displayed in the Look in drop-down list, click on the drop-down arrow to navigate to the proper folder.

4. Click on **Open**. The file will display, ready for you to edit.

Working with Multiple Documents

Although multiple documents can be open, only one document can be edited at a time. Use the Windows Taskbar to locate and switch to a different open document. When more than one document is open at a time, one document will display on top of all the others.

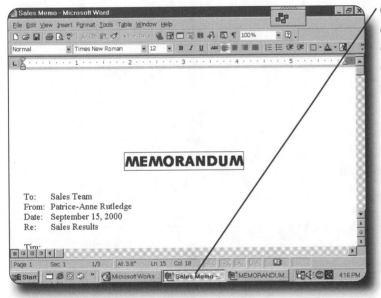

Click the name **of the document** that you want to edit. The document appears on top of the stack of open documents.

Closing a Document

When you are finished working on a document, you should close it. When you close a document, you are closing only the document itself—not the program. Word is still active and ready to work for you.

1. **Click** on **File**. The File menu will appear.

2. **Click** on **Close**. The document will close.

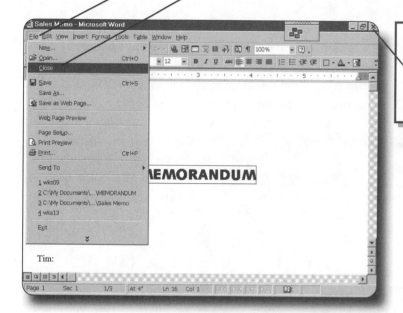

TIP

To combine this into one step, click on the Close button.

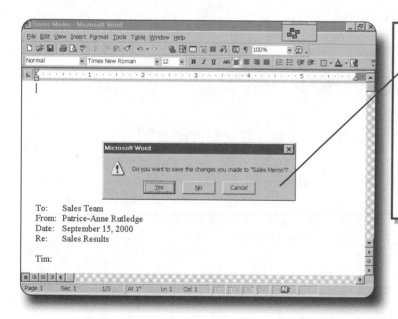

NOTE

If you close a document with changes that have not been saved, Word prompts you with a dialog box. Choose Yes to save the changes or No to close the file without saving the changes.

Part II Review Questions

1. What two keys can you press to quickly move to the beginning of a document? *See "Moving Around Using the Keyboard" in Chapter 3*

2. What feature will reverse the last step you performed? *See "Undoing Mistakes" in Chapter 3*

3. How often should you save a document? *See "Resaving a Document" in Chapter 3*

4. What are the four types of text alignment? *See "Setting Paragraph Alignment" in Chapter 4*

5. What should you display if you are going to be working with tabs? *See "Displaying the Ruler" in Chapter 4*

6. In a table, what key is used to move the insertion point from one cell to the next? *See "Entering Text into a Table" in Chapter 5*

7. What two areas of a document are reserved for repeating text? *See "Adding a Header or Footer" in Chapter 6*

8. Around which parts of your document can borders be placed? *See "Adding Borders" in Chapter 7*

9. When using Spell Check, what is the difference between the options Ignore and Ignore All? *See "Running a Spelling and Grammar Check" in Chapter 8*

10. What screen on the Task Launcher is used to open a previously created document? *See "Opening a Document from the Task Launcher" in Chapter 9*

PART III

Discovering Microsoft Works Suite

10

Creating a Spreadsheet

Works has a full-featured spreadsheet program that you can use to make calculations, create charts, and even sort data. In this chapter, you'll learn how to:

- Create a new spreadsheet
- Explore and move around in the spreadsheet screen
- Enter and edit labels and values
- Undo mistakes
- Save a spreadsheet

Opening a New Spreadsheet

Create a new spreadsheet from the Works Task Launcher.

1. Click on **Programs**. A list of Works programs will appear.

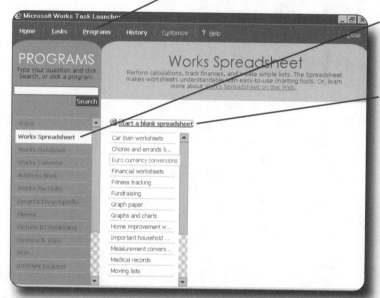

2. Click on **Works Spreadsheet**. A list of spreadsheet tasks will appear.

3. Click on **Start a blank spreadsheet.** A blank spreadsheet will appear on your screen.

NOTE

If the Help window is open, you might want to close it to better display your spreadsheet.

TIP

You can also start using the Works spreadsheet by clicking on one of the tasks that displays.

Exploring the Spreadsheet Screen

Many items that you see when you open a new spreadsheet are standard to most Windows 95 or Windows 98 programs. However, the following list illustrates a few elements specific to a spreadsheet program. These include

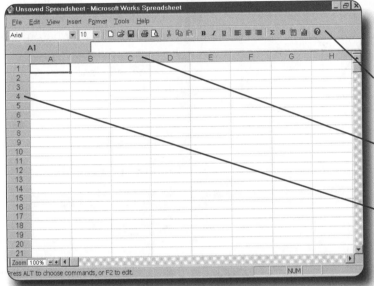

- **Toolbar.** A toolbar with a series of commonly used Works features.

- **Column headings.** Each spreadsheet has 256 columns.

- **Row headings.** Each spreadsheet has 16,384 rows.

- **Edit line.** This line consists of several parts:

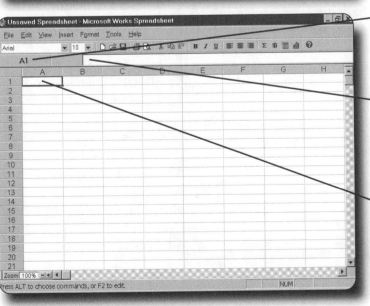

  - **Selection indicator.** This shows the address or name of the current selection.

  - **Contents box.** This area displays the entry you are typing or editing, or the contents of the selected cell.

  - **Cell.** An intersection of a column and row, sometimes called a *cell address*. A heavy border indicates the selected cell.

• **Status bar.** Gives you information about the current selection and tells you what Works is doing.

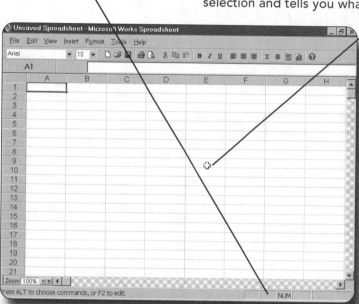

• **Mouse pointer.** Often, while you're using a spreadsheet, the mouse pointer will look like a white cross. You'll see in Chapter 11, "Editing a Spreadsheet," where the mouse pointer might change its shape.

Moving Around the Spreadsheet Screen

You can use your mouse or keyboard to quickly move around in a spreadsheet.

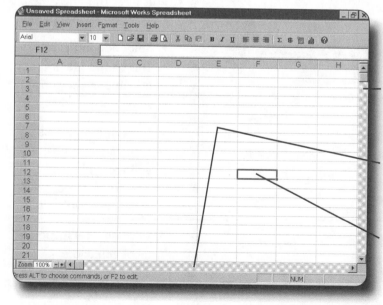

1. Click on the **vertical scroll bar** until the row you are looking for is visible.

2. Click on the **horizontal scroll bar** until the column you are looking for is visible.

3. Click on the **desired cell**. It will become the selected cell.

The following table describes keyboard methods for moving around in your spreadsheet:

Keystroke	Result
Arrow keys	Moves one cell at a time up, down, left, or right
Page Down	Moves one screen down
Page Up	Moves one screen up
Home	Moves to column A of the current row
Ctrl+Home	Moves to cell A1
F5	Displays the Find and Replace dialog box with the Go To tab selected, which enables you to specify a cell address

Entering Data

Spreadsheet data is made up of three components: labels, values, and formulas. *Labels* are traditionally descriptive pieces of information, such as names, months, or types of products.

Entering Labels into Cells

Works identifies a cell as a label if it begins with a letter or a prefix character.

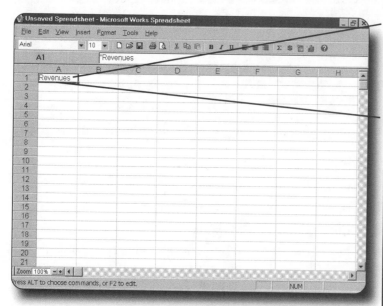

1. **Click** on the **cell** where you want to place the label. A border will appear around the selected cell.

2. **Type text**. The text will display in the cell.

TIP

If you make a mistake and you have not yet pressed Enter, press the Backspace key to delete characters and type a correction, or press the Escape key to cancel the typing.

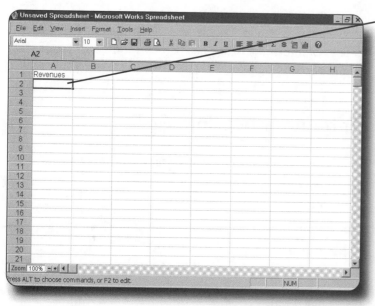

3. **Press Enter** to accept the label. The text will be entered and will align along the left edge of the cell. The next cell down will be selected.

4. **Repeat steps 1–3** for each label you want to enter.

NOTE

Optionally, you could press an arrow key instead of the Enter key. This not only accepts the text you typed in the selected cell, but also selects the next cell in the direction of the arrow key at the same time.

Entering Values into Cells

Values are the actual numbers that you track in a spreadsheet. There is no need to enter commas or dollar signs. Let Works do that for you later.

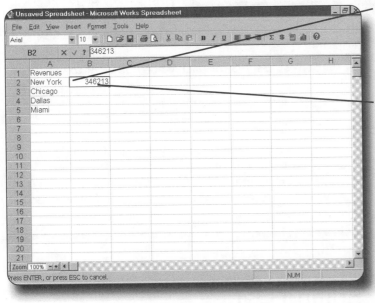

1. **Click** on the **cell** where you want to place the value. A border will appear around the selected cell.

2. **Type** a numerical **value**. The text will display in the cell.

3. **Press Enter** to accept the value. The number will be entered into the cell, and the next cell down will be selected.

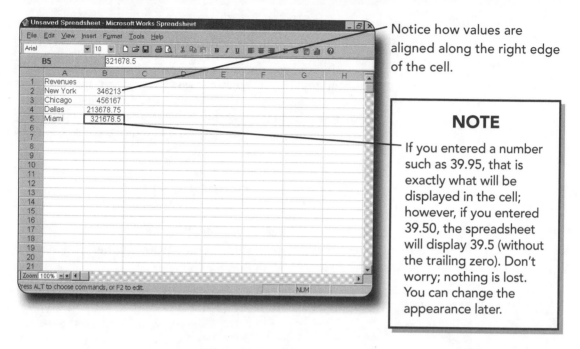

Notice how values are aligned along the right edge of the cell.

NOTE

If you entered a number such as 39.95, that is exactly what will be displayed in the cell; however, if you entered 39.50, the spreadsheet will display 39.5 (without the trailing zero). Don't worry; nothing is lost. You can change the appearance later.

4. **Repeat steps 1–3** for each value you want to enter.

TIP

To enter a number as a label, type a quotation (") character before the number, such as "2000. The quotation character tells Works that the information is a label. The quotation character won't display in your spreadsheet.

Editing Data

You can edit your data in a variety of ways. You might need to change the contents of a cell, or you might want to move the data to another part of the spreadsheet.

Replacing the Contents of a Cell

You can make changes to the contents of a cell in two ways. One is by typing over the contents of a cell.

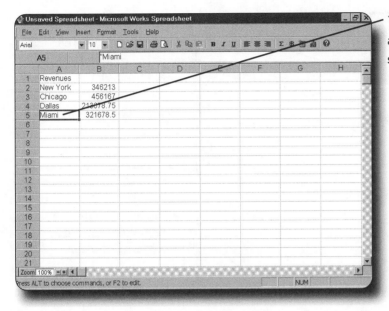

1. Click on a **cell**. The cell and its contents will be selected.

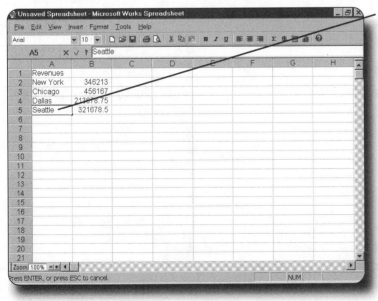

2. Type new **text**. The new text will appear in the cell.

3. Press Enter. The text will be entered in the selected cell.

Editing the Contents of a Cell

The other method to make changes to the contents of a cell is by using the Edit feature.

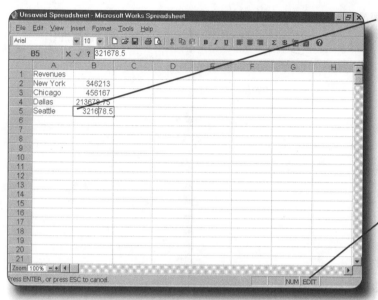

1. Double-click on the **cell** you want to edit. The insertion point will blink within the cell.

Edit mode is indicated on the status bar.

TIP

You can also press the F2 key to edit the contents of a cell.

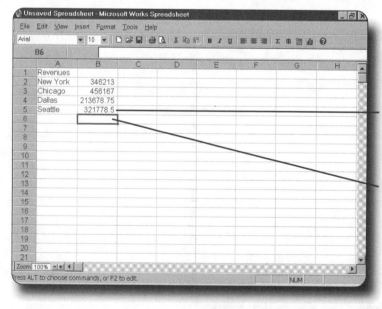

2. Press the **left arrow key**. The insertion point will be relocated within the current cell.

3. Type the **changes**. The changes will appear in the current cell.

4. Press Enter. The changes will be entered into the current cell and the next cell will be selected.

Undoing Mistakes

If you make a mistake while working in a spreadsheet, don't go any farther. Works can undo the last change you made.

1. Click on **Edit**. The Edit menu will appear.

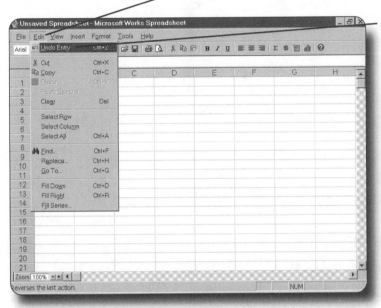

2. Click on **Undo Entry**. The last change you made will be undone.

TIP

You can also undo a mistake by pressing Ctrl+Z.

Saving a Spreadsheet

As you create a spreadsheet in Works, it is stored temporarily in the computer's memory. That memory is erased when you exit Works or when you turn off the computer. To prevent losing your work, you need to save it.

Saving a Spreadsheet the First Time

When you first create a spreadsheet, it is untitled. To save the spreadsheet for use again at a later date, you must give it a name. When you have saved a spreadsheet, the name appears at the top of the screen in the title bar.

1. Click on **File**. The File menu will appear.

2. Click on **Save**. The Save As dialog box will open.

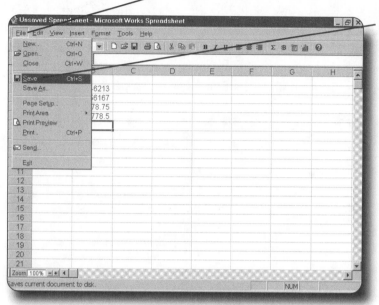

3. Type a **name** for your file in the File name text box. The file name will display.

The Save in drop-down list shows the folder where the file will be saved. The default folder that appears is My Documents. If you want to save to a different folder or disk, you can select another one. Click on the down arrow to browse.

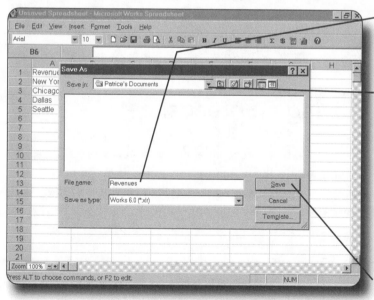

4. Click on **Save**. Your spreadsheet will be saved, and the name you specified will appear in the title bar.

NOTE

By default, Works will save your spreadsheet with the Works 6.0 file type. If you want to share your spreadsheet with someone who uses Microsoft Excel, you can choose Excel 97–2000 from the Save as type drop-down list.

Resaving a Spreadsheet

You should resave your spreadsheet every ten minutes or so to ensure that you do not lose any changes.

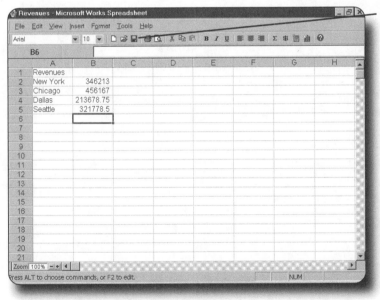

1. Click on the **Save button**. The spreadsheet will be resaved with any changes. No dialog box will appear because the spreadsheet is being resaved with the same name and in the same folder as previously specified.

TIP

If you want to save the spreadsheet with a different name or in a different folder, click on File, then choose Save As. The Save As dialog box prompts you for the new name or folder. The original document remains as well as the new one.

11

Editing a Spreadsheet

After you enter data into a spreadsheet, you might need to edit it. You can insert or delete rows or columns as needed or just move the data to a new location. In this chapter, you'll learn how to:

- Select cells, rows, and columns
- Insert and delete rows and columns
- Move data
- Use the Fill feature

Exploring Selection Techniques

To move, copy, delete, or change the formatting of data in the spreadsheet, you first must select the cells you want to modify. When cells are selected, they appear black onscreen—just the reverse of unselected text. An exception to this is if a block of cells is selected. In this case, the first cell won't be black—it will have a black border around it. The following table describes some of the different selection techniques.

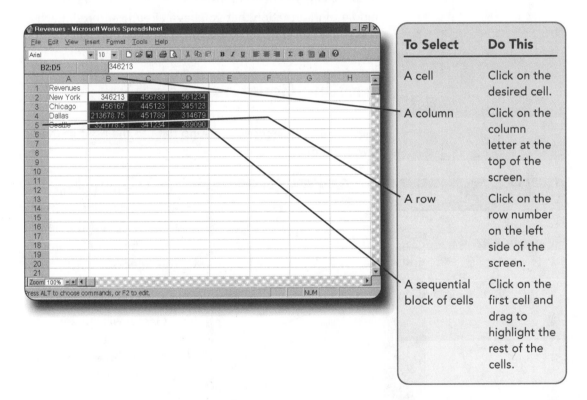

To Select	Do This
A cell	Click on the desired cell.
A column	Click on the column letter at the top of the screen.
A row	Click on the row number on the left side of the screen.
A sequential block of cells	Click on the first cell and drag to highlight the rest of the cells.

NOTE

Microsoft Works doesn't allow you to select a group of non-sequential cells.

> **TIP**
>
> To deselect a block of cells, click the mouse in any other cell.

Inserting Rows and Columns

Occasionally, you need to insert a column or a row into the middle of information that you have already entered. Each worksheet can contain 256 columns and 16,384 rows.

Inserting Columns

Inserting a column moves existing data to the right of the new column.

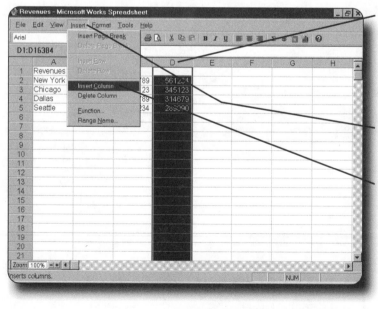

1. **Click** on the **Column Heading letter** before which you want to insert the new column. The entire column will be selected.

2. **Click** on **Insert.** The Insert menu will appear.

3. **Click** on **Insert Column.** A new column will be inserted.

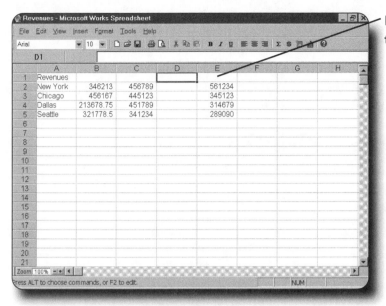

Existing columns move to the right.

Inserting Rows

Inserting a row moves existing data down one row.

1. **Click** on the **Row Heading number** before which you want to insert the new row. The entire row will be selected.

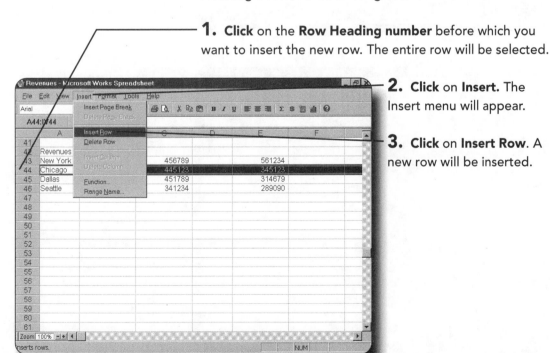

2. **Click** on **Insert.** The Insert menu will appear.

3. **Click** on **Insert Row.** A new row will be inserted.

Deleting Rows and Columns

Use caution when deleting a row or column. Deleting a row deletes it across all 256 columns; deleting a column deletes it down all 16,384 rows.

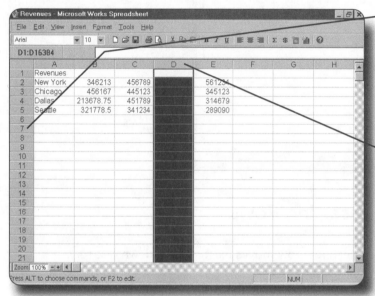

1a. **Select** the **Row Heading number** of the row that you want to delete. The row will be highlighted.

OR

1b. **Select** the **Column Heading letter** of the column that you want to delete. The column will be highlighted.

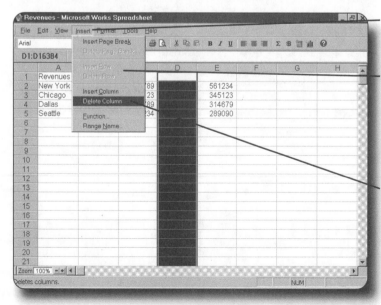

2. **Click** on **Insert**. The Insert menu will appear.

3a. **Choose Delete Row**. The highlighted row will be deleted.

OR

3b. **Choose Delete Column**. The highlighted column will be deleted.

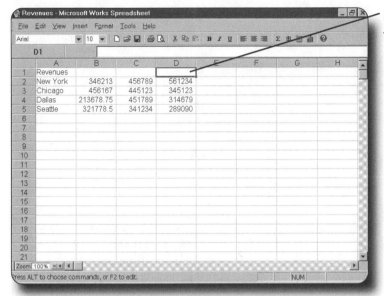

Remaining columns move to the left; remaining rows move up.

Moving Data Around

If you're not happy with the placement of data, you don't have to delete it and retype it. Works makes it easy for you to move it around.

Copying and Pasting Cells

Windows comes with a feature called the Clipboard. The Clipboard temporarily holds information in memory. It is helpful if you want to transfer information from one place to another. To copy information, Works uses the Copy and Paste features.

1. **Select** some **cells** to be duplicated. The cells will be highlighted.

2. **Click** on the **Copy button**. Although it won't look like anything happened, the text will be duplicated to the Clipboard.

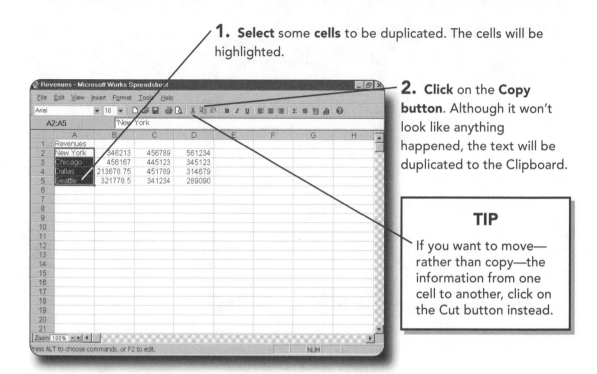

TIP

If you want to move— rather than copy—the information from one cell to another, click on the Cut button instead.

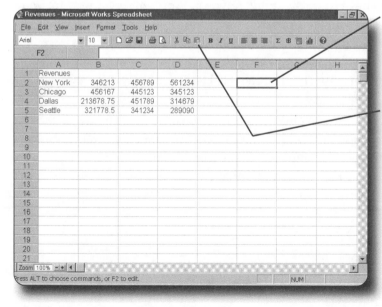

3. **Click** on the beginning **cell** where you want to place the duplicated information. The cell will be highlighted.

4. **Click** on the **Paste button**. The information will be copied to the new location.

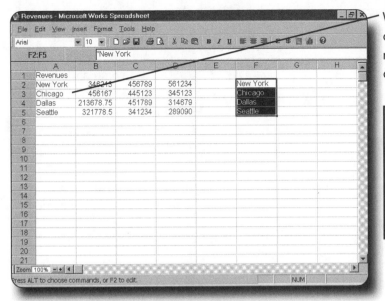

When you use the Copy command, the original cells retain the information you copied.

TIP

If you pasted the cells in the wrong area, click on the Edit menu and choose Undo Paste to undo the paste.

Using Drag-and-Drop to Move Cells

Another method that you can use to move information from one location to another is drag-and-drop.

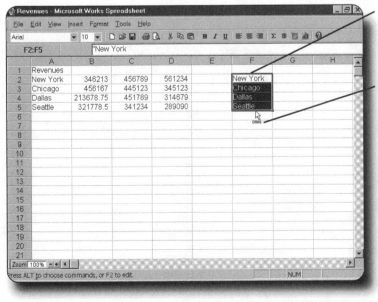

1. **Select** some **cells** to move. The cells will be highlighted.

2. **Position** the **mouse pointer** around one of the outside edges of the selection. The mouse pointer will become a small white arrow with the word "DRAG" displayed.

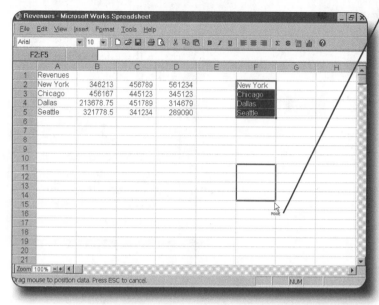

3. Press and **hold** the **mouse button** and **drag** the **cell** to a new location. The "DRAG" command changes to "MOVE." The second box represents where the moved cells will be located after the mouse button is released.

4. Release the **mouse button**. The cells will move.

Deleting Cell Contents

If you have data that you no longer want in cells, you can easily delete it.

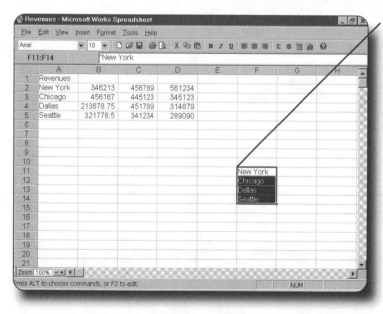

1. Select some **cells** to be cleared. The cells will be highlighted.

2. Press the **Delete key**. The contents of the cells will be removed.

Using the Fill Feature

Works has a great built-in time-saving feature called Fill. If you give Works the beginning month, day, season, or numbers, it can fill in the rest of the pattern for you. For example, if you type January, Works fills in February, March, April, and so on.

1. Type the **beginning month, day, or season** in the beginning cell. The text will display in the cell.

If you want Works to fill in numbers, you must first give it a pattern. For example, enter the value of "1" in the first cell and then enter "2" in the second cell. The sequential cells will fill with 3, 4, 5, and so on.

2. Position the **mouse pointer** on the lower-right corner of the beginning cell. The mouse pointer will become a small black cross with the word "FILL" displayed.

TIP

For numbers, select both the first and second cells before proceeding to step 3.

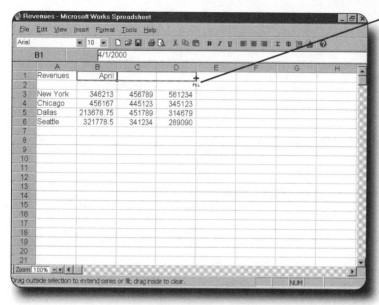

3. **Press** and **hold** the **mouse button** and **drag** to select the next cells to be filled in. The cells will have a gray border surrounding them.

4. **Release** the **mouse button**. The pattern will be repeated in the selected cells.

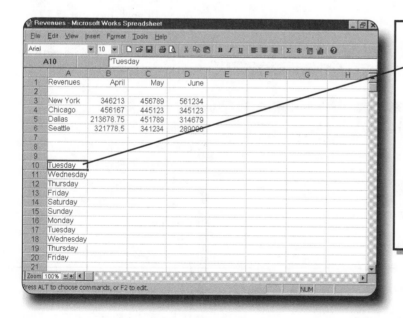

TIP

A pattern will begin with wherever you start and repeat if necessary. For example, if you fill up the cells with Tuesday, Wednesday, Thursday, all the way through Monday, and still have cells to fill, Works will begin with Tuesday again.

12

Working with Functions and Formulas

Formulas in a Works spreadsheet do calculations for you, such as adding, subtracting, averaging, or multiplying numbers. They're also dynamic—for example, if you reference a cell address in a formula, the formula will change if the data in the cell changes. In this chapter, you'll learn how to:

- Create simple and compound formulas
- Copy formulas
- Create an absolute reference
- Use functions

Creating Formulas

All formulas must begin with the equal (=) sign, regardless of whether the formula consists of adding, subtracting, multiplying, or dividing.

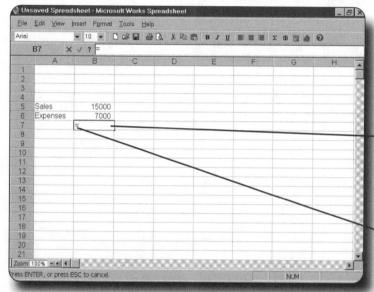

Creating a Simple Formula

An example of a simple formula might be =B5-B6.

1. **Click** on the **cell** in which you want to place the formula answer. The cell will be selected.

2. **Type** an **equal sign** to begin the formula. The symbol will appear in the cell.

3. **Type** the **cell address** of the first cell to be included in the formula. This is called the cell *reference*. In this example, the cell reference B5 is referring to the value of 15000.

NOTE

Spreadsheet formulas are not case sensitive. For example, B5 is the same as b5.

A formula needs an *operator* to suggest the next action to be performed.

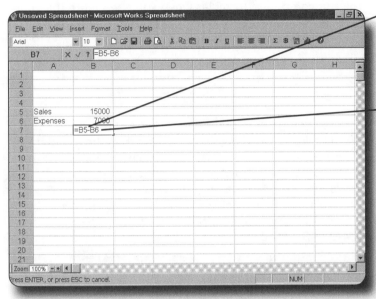

4. **Type** the **operator**: plus (+), minus (-), multiply (*), or divide (/). The operator will appear in the formula.

5. **Type** the **reference** to the second cell of the formula. The reference will appear in the cell.

6. **Press Enter**. The result of the calculation will appear in the cell.

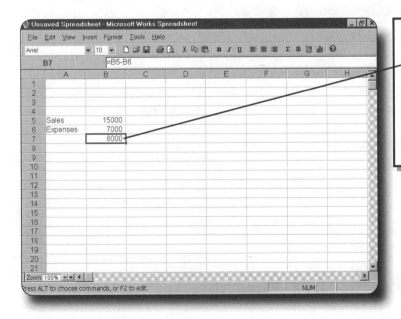

NOTE

Notice how the result appears in the cell, but the actual formula, =B5-B6, appears in the Contents box of the Edit line.

Creating a Compound Formula

You use compound formulas when you need more than one operator. Examples of a compound formula might be =B7+B8+B9+B10 or =B11-B19*A23.

NOTE

When you have a compound formula, Works does the multiplication and division first, and then the addition and subtraction. If you want a certain portion of the formula to be calculated first, put it in parentheses. Works does whatever is in the parentheses before calculating the rest of the formula. The formula =B11-B19*A23 gives a totally different answer than =(B11-B19)*A23.

---

1. **Click** on the **cell** in which you want to place the formula answer. The cell will be selected.

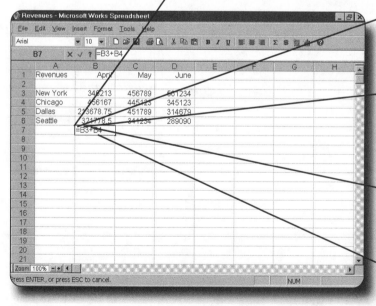

2. **Type** an **equal sign** to begin the formula. The symbol will appear in the cell.

3. **Type** the **reference to the first cell** of the formula. The reference will appear in the cell.

4. **Type** the **operator**. The operator will appear in the cell.

5. **Type** the **reference to the second cell** of the formula. The reference will appear in the cell.

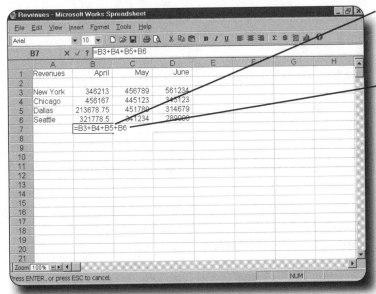

6. Type the **next operator**. The operator will appear in the cell.

7. Type the **reference to the third cell** of the formula. The reference will appear in the cell.

8. Repeat steps 6 and **7** until the formula is complete, adding parentheses wherever necessary.

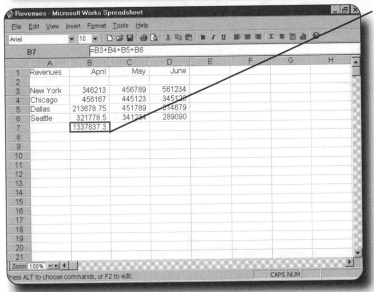

9. Press Enter to accept the formula. The calculation answer will appear in the cell, and the formula will appear in the content bar.

Try changing one of the values you originally typed in the spreadsheet and watch the answer to the formula change.

Copying Formulas

If you're going to copy a formula to a surrounding cell, you can use the Fill method. If the cells are not sequential, you can use Copy and Paste. Fill and Copy and Paste were discussed in Chapter 11, "Editing a Spreadsheet."

Copying Formulas Using Fill

Similar to filling a pattern of days, months, or seasons as you learned in the previous chapter, Works can also fill cells with the pattern of a formula. For example, say your spreadsheet contains a list of annual revenues for each of your 27 branches. You estimate that revenues should increase by 15% for the next year. Cell B7 contains the revenue amount for the first branch. In cell C7, you enter =SUM(B7*.15)+B7 to display the projected amount for the next year. Rather than manually entering this same formula for each of the 27 branches, you can simply copy this formula to the rest of column C using the fill feature.

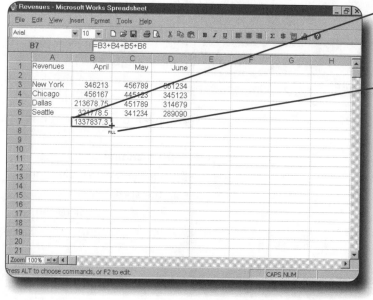

1. Click on the **cell** that has the formula. The cell will be selected.

2. Position the **mouse pointer** on the lower-right corner of the beginning cell. The mouse pointer will become a black cross with the word "FILL" below it.

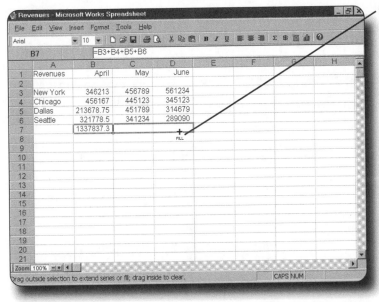

3. Press and hold the mouse button and drag to select the next cells to be filled in. The cells will be selected.

4. Release the mouse button. The formula will be copied.

When Works copies a formula, the references change as the formula is copied. If the original formula was =B11-B19 and you copied it to the next cell to the right, the formula would read =C11-C19. Then, if you copied it to the next cell to the right, it would be =D11-D19, and so on. This is because when you copy a formula, the concept behind it is actually copied, not the formula itself. For example, if the original formula is B5+B6 and the answer is to be placed in cell B7, Works is actually theorizing to add the two cells above the answer. When you copy that formula to cell C7, it's still theorizing to add the two cells above it, which would be C5 and C6.

Copying Formulas with Copy and Paste

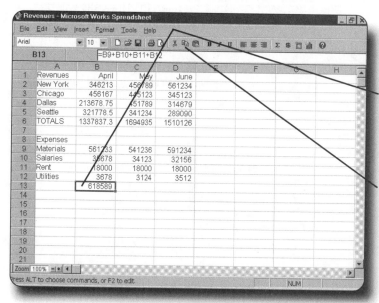

Another time-saving way to duplicate formulas is to use the Copy and Paste buttons.

1. **Click** the **cell or cells** with the formula that you want to duplicate. The cells will be selected.

2. **Click** on the **Copy button**. The formulas will be copied to the Clipboard.

3. **Highlight** the **cells** in which you want to place the duplicated formula. The cells will be selected.

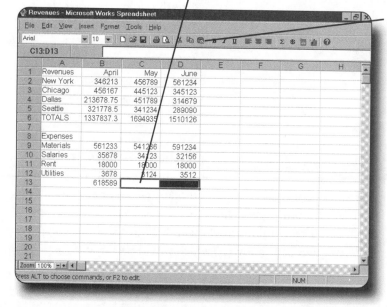

4. **Click** on the **Paste button**. The information will be copied to the new location.

Creating an Absolute Reference in a Formula

When you copy a formula, you might not want one of the cell references to change. That's when you need to create an absolute reference. An absolute reference never changes. You use the dollar sign ($) to indicate an absolute reference. An example of a formula with an absolute reference might be =B21*B23. The reference to cell B23 will not change when copied.

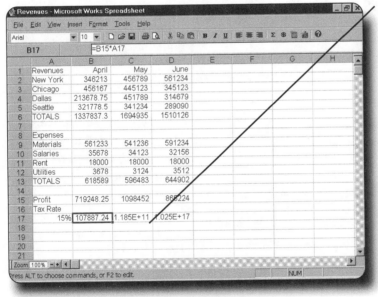

Notice the values in cells C17 and D17. The original formula was intended to multiply the profit figure of $719,248.25 in cell B15 by the tax rate of 15% in cell A17. That formula is fine for cell B17, but when copied to C17 and D17, the answers appear to be in error. Works read the copied formula in cell C17 as C15 times B17 instead of C15 times A17.

It's easy to create an absolute reference in a Works spreadsheet.

1. Click on the **cell** in which you want to place the formula answer. The cell will be selected.

2. Type an **equal sign** to begin the formula.

3. Type the **reference to the first cell** of the formula. If this reference is to be an absolute reference, add dollar signs in front of both the column reference and the row reference. In the example shown, the first cell does not need to be an absolute reference.

4. Type the **operator**.

5. Type the **reference to the second cell** of the formula. If this reference is to be an absolute reference, add dollar signs in front of both the column reference and the row reference.

6. Press Enter to complete the formula.

7. Copy the **formula** to the adjacent cells using one of the methods in the preceding sections.

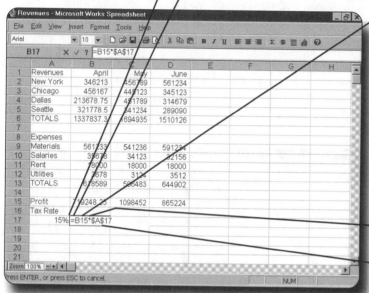

NOTE

Compound formulas can also have absolute references.

Viewing Formulas

When you create formulas, the result of the formula displays in the spreadsheet rather than the formula itself. Viewing the formula is a wonderful tool for troubleshooting formula errors in your spreadsheet.

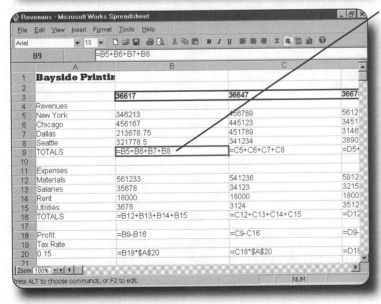

1. **Click** on **View**. The View menu will appear.

2. **Click** on **Formulas**. The option will be selected.

The spreadsheet formulas will display in each cell instead of the result of the formula.

3. **Repeat steps 1** and **2**. The formula results will reappear.

NOTE

If you print the spreadsheet while the formulas are displayed, the formulas will be printed, but the formula results will not be printed.

Using Functions

NOTE

There are two ways to reference a range of values. If the cells to be included are sequential, they are separated by a colon (:). If the range is non-sequential, the cells are separated by a comma (,). For example, the range (B7:D7) would include cells B7, C7, and D7; the range (B7:D7,F4) includes cells B7, C7, D7, and F4.

Sometimes formulas can be complex and time-consuming to build. To simplify things, you can create formulas that contain functions. A function is a ready-to-use formula that performs a specific calculation. Works has more than 70 different functions to assist you with your calculations. All Works functions begin with the equal sign and have the basis (arguments) for the formula in parentheses. SUM (which summarizes) and AVG (which averages) are two of the most common Works spreadsheet functions, but there are many others.

Using the SUM Function

The SUM function totals a range of values. The syntax for this function is =SUM(*range of values to total*). An example might be =SUM(B7:D7).

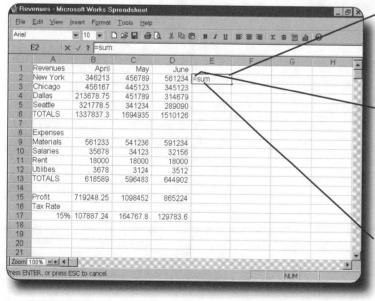

1. Click on the **cell** in which you want to place the sum of values. The cell will be selected.

2. Type the **equal sign**. The symbol will appear in the cell. Remember that functions are complex formulas and all formulas must begin with the equal sign.

3. Type the function name **sum**. The characters will appear in the cell.

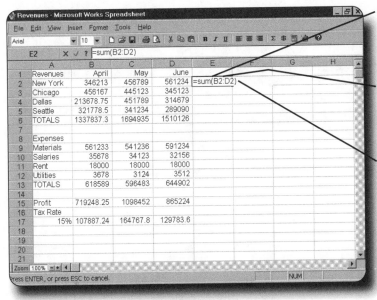

4. Type the **open parentheses** symbol. The symbol will appear in the cell.

5. Type the **range** to be totaled. The range will appear in the cell.

6. Type the **close parentheses** symbol. The symbol will appear in the cell.

7. Press **Enter**. The total of the range will appear in the selected cell.

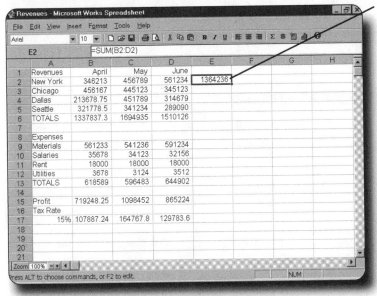

The result displays in the selected cell, and the formula appears in the contents box.

Using the AutoSum Button

Works includes the SUM function as a button on the toolbar. This makes creating a simple addition formula a mouse click away.

1. Click on the **cell** below or to the right of the values to be totaled. The cell will be selected.

2. Click on the **AutoSum button**. The cells to be totaled will be highlighted.

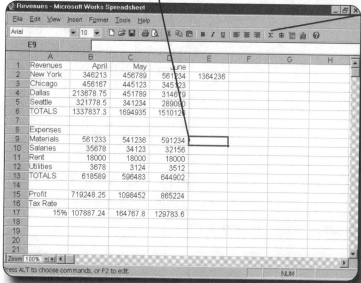

3. Press Enter. The sum of the values will appear above the selected cell or to the left of it.

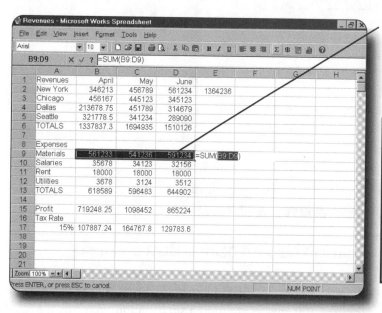

NOTE

Works will sum the values directly above the selected cell first. If no values are above it, Works will look for values in the cells to the left.

Using the AVG Function

The AVG function finds an average value of a range of cells. The syntax for this function is =AVG(*range of values to average*). An example might be =AVG(B7:D7).

1. Click on the **cell** in which you want to place the average. The cell will be selected.

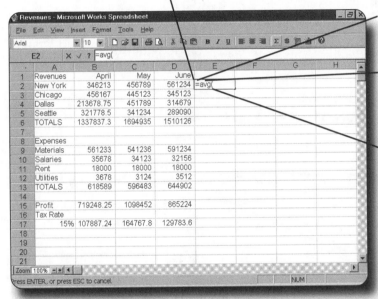

2. Type the **equal** sign. The symbol will appear in the cell.

3. Type the function name **AVG**. The characters will appear in the cell.

4. Type the **open parentheses** symbol. The symbol will appear in the cell.

TIP

Instead of typing the range as noted in step 4, you can highlight the range with the mouse. Works fills in the cell references for you.

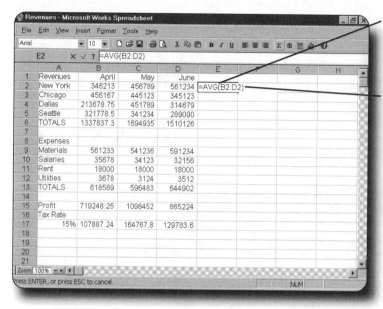

5. Type or **highlight** the **range** to be averaged. The range will appear in the cell.

6. Type the **close parentheses** symbol. The symbol will appear in the cell.

7. Press Enter. Works will average the values in the selected range.

NOTE

Other similar functions are the MAX, MIN, and COUNT functions. The MAX function finds the largest value in a range of cells. The MIN function finds the smallest value in a range of cells. The COUNT function counts the non-blank cells in a range of cells. Examples might include =MAX(B7:B15) or =COUNT(B7:B15).

13

Formatting Worksheets

The days of the dull spreadsheet are gone; you can liven up your spreadsheet by changing its appearance. In this chapter, you'll learn how to:

- Set number formatting
- Change alignment and column width
- Select fonts and cell borders
- Use AutoFormat
- Adjust the view of the spreadsheet

Formatting Numbers

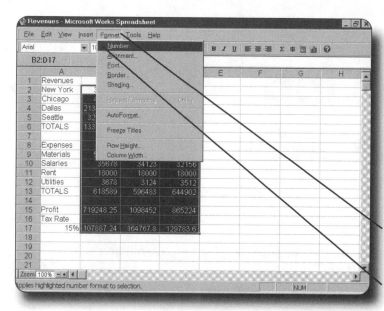

By default, values display as general numbers. You can, however, display values as currency, percentages, fractions, dates, or in many other formats.

1. **Select** some **cells** to be formatted. The cells will be highlighted.

2. **Click** on **Format**. The Format menu will appear.

3. **Click** on **Number**. The Format Cells dialog box will open with the Number tab in front.

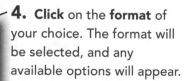

4. **Click** on the **format** of your choice. The format will be selected, and any available options will appear.

5. **Change** any desired **option**. The option will be selected.

6. **Click** on **OK**. The Format Cells dialog box will close.

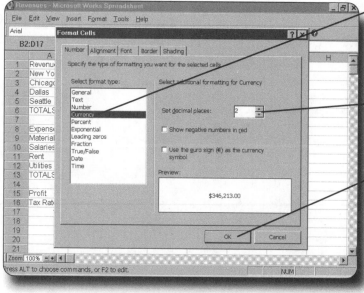

The new number format will be applied to the selected cells. Notice the dollar signs and two decimal points. These cells had the currency style applied to them.

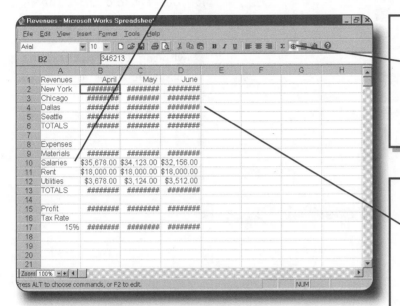

TIP

A quick way to apply currency style is to select the cells and click on the currency button.

NOTE

Don't be alarmed if some of the cells display a series of number signs (#####) or in scientific format (1E+08) instead of your values. This is because the column width is too small. You learn how to change this in the next section.

Adjusting Column Width

The default width of a column is nine characters, but each individual column can be from one to 240 characters wide.

A line located at the right edge of each column heading divides the columns. You use this line to change the column width.

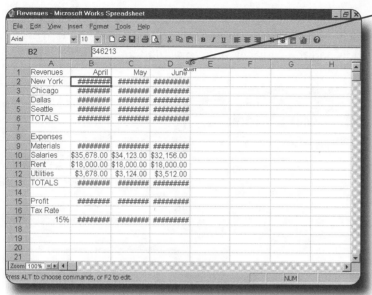

1. Position the **mouse pointer** on the right-hand column line for the column you want to change. The mouse pointer will become a double-headed white arrow with the word "ADJUST" displayed under it.

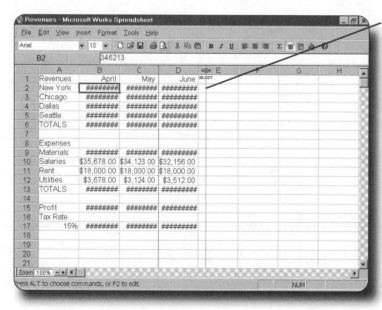

2. Press and **hold** the **mouse button** and **drag** the column line. If you drag it to the right, the column width will increase; if you drag it to the left, the column width will decrease.

3. Release the **mouse button**. The column width will be changed.

NOTE

Row height can be adjusted in a similar manner. Position the mouse pointer on the bottom edge of the row heading. Again, the mouse will change to a double-headed white arrow. Drag the line down to increase row height or up to decrease row height.

TIP

To automatically adjust column width or row height to exactly fit the contents of the cell, double-click the mouse after the pointer becomes a double-headed white arrow.

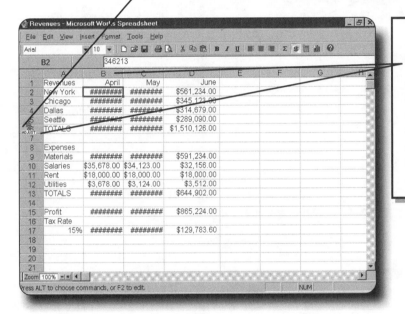

Setting Worksheet Alignment

Labels are left aligned, and values are right aligned by default; however, you can change the alignment of either one to be left, right, centered, or justified. Also by default, both are vertically aligned to the bottom of the cell.

Wrapping text in cells is useful when text is too long to fit in one cell, and you don't want it to overlap to the next cell.

Adjusting Cell Alignment

Adjust cells individually or adjust a block of cells at once.

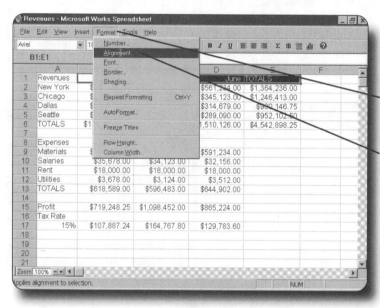

1. **Select** the **cells** you want to format. The cells will be highlighted.

2. **Click** on **Format**. The Format menu will appear.

3. **Click** on **Alignment**. The Format Cells dialog box will open with the Alignment tab in front.

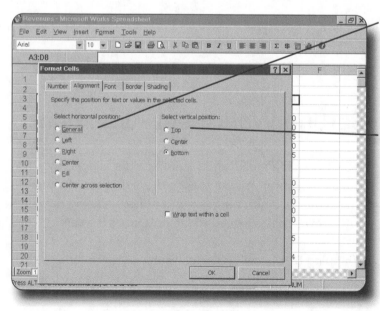

4. **Click** on an **option** under Select horizontal position. The horizontal alignment of the text in the cell will change.

5. **Click** on an **option** under Select vertical position. The vertical alignment of the text in the cell will change.

TIP

The wrap text feature treats each cell like a miniature word processor, with text wrapping around in the cell. For example, if you enter a lengthy description in a cell, it will spread across adjacent cells in the same row by default. By applying word wrap, the height of the cell expands to allow the text to flow downward, creating additional lines of text within that individual cell and eliminating overflow into other cells.

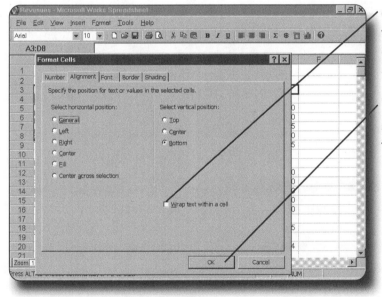

6. **Click** on the **Wrap text within a cell check box**, if desired. A check mark ✓ will appear in the selection box.

7. **Click** on **OK**. The selections will be applied to the highlighted cells.

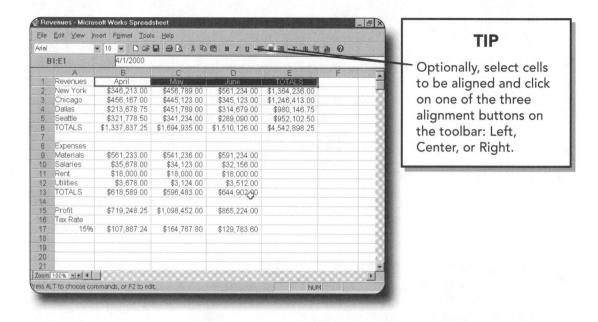

TIP

Optionally, select cells to be aligned and click on one of the three alignment buttons on the toolbar: Left, Center, or Right.

Centering Headings

Text also can be centered across a group of columns to create attractive headings.

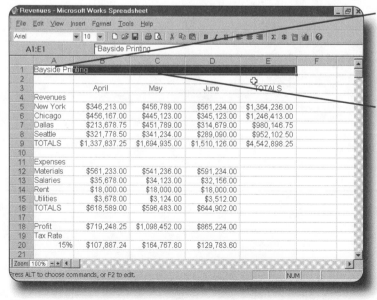

1. **Type** the **heading text** in the first column of the worksheet body. This is usually column A.

2. **Select** the **heading cell** and **the cells to be included** in the heading. The cells will be highlighted.

3. Click on **Format**. The Format menu will appear.

4. Click on **Alignment**. The Format Cells dialog box will open with the Alignment tab in front.

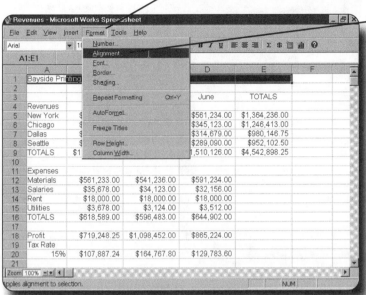

5. Click on **Center across selection**. The option will be selected.

6. Click on **OK**. The Format Cells dialog box will close, and the title will be centered.

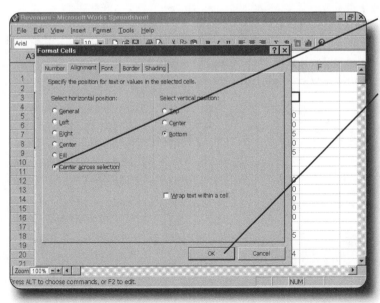

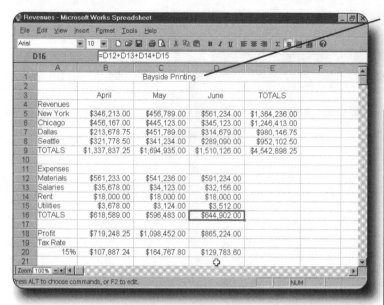

Notice the gridlines have disappeared, and the cells appear to be joined together.

NOTE

In this example, the headings appear to be located in column C; however, the text is still in column A. If you are going to make other changes, be sure to select column A, not column C.

Formatting with Fonts

The default font in a spreadsheet is Arial 10 points, but you can easily change both the typeface and the size.

Selecting a Font Typeface

Your font choices vary depending on the software installed on your computer.

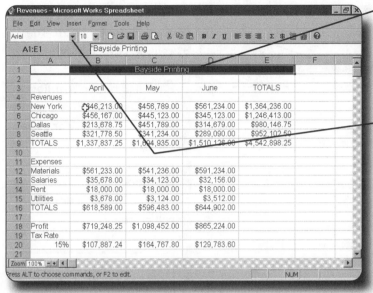

1. Select the **cells** that include the text whose typeface you want to change. The cells will be highlighted.

2. Click on the **Applies font drop-down arrow**. A list of available fonts will appear.

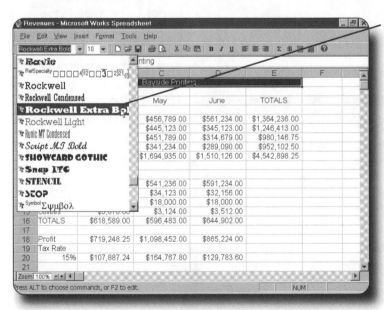

3. Click on the **font** of your choice. The selection list will close, and the new font will be applied to the selected cells.

Selecting a Font Size

The default font size in a Works spreadsheet is 10 points. There are approximately 72 points in an inch, so a 10-point font is slightly less than one-seventh of an inch tall.

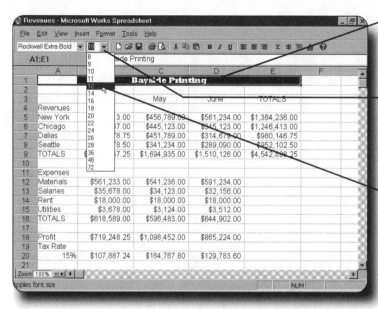

1. Select some **cells** to change the font size. The cells will be highlighted.

2. Click on the **Applies font size drop-down arrow**. A list of available font sizes will appear.

3. Click on the **size** of your choice. The selection list will close.

TIP

If the size you want is not listed, type in the desired size in the size text box.

The new font size will be applied to the selected cells.

Selecting a Font Style

Font styles include attributes such as **bold**, *italics*, and underlining.

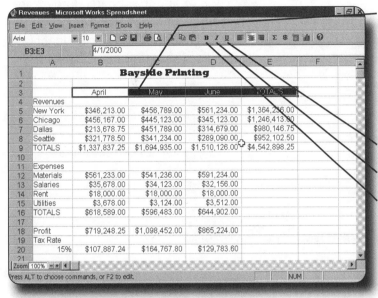

1. Select some **cells** to change the style. The cells will be highlighted.

2. Click on any of the following **buttons**:

- Underline button

- Italic button

- Bold button

The attributes will be applied to the text in the cell.

The Bold, Italic, and Underline buttons are like toggle switches. Click on them a second time to turn off the attribute.

TIP

Shortcut keys include Ctrl+B for Bold, Ctrl+I for Italic, and Ctrl+U for Underline.

NOTE

Underlining is not the same as adding a cell border. Cell borders are discussed in the next section.

Adding Borders

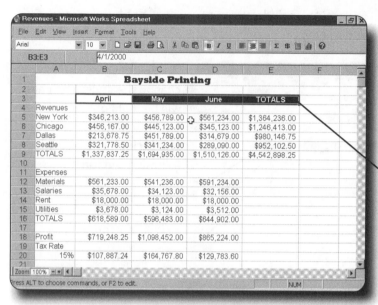

You can add borders or lines to cells to emphasize important data. Borders are different from the gridlines that separate cells in the sheet. You can change the style and color of borders.

1. **Select** the **cells** you want to have borders or lines. The cells will be highlighted.

2. **Click** on **Format**. The Format menu will appear.

3. **Click** on **Border**. The Format Cells dialog box will open with the Border tab in front.

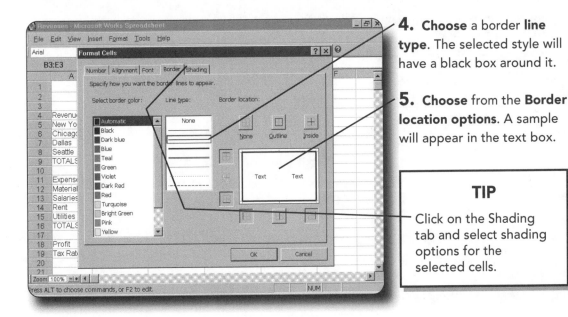

4. Choose a border **line type**. The selected style will have a black box around it.

5. Choose from the **Border location options**. A sample will appear in the text box.

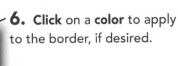

TIP

Click on the Shading tab and select shading options for the selected cells.

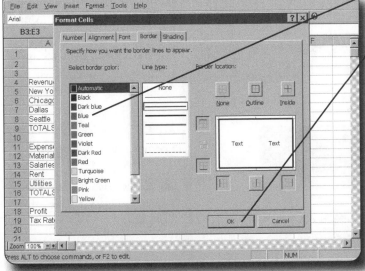

6. Click on a **color** to apply to the border, if desired.

7. Click on **OK**. The Format Cells dialog box will close.

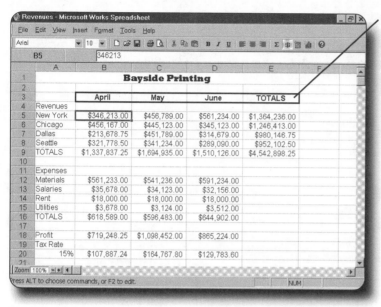

The border choices will be applied to the highlighted cells.

Saving Time with AutoFormat

Save time by letting Works format your spreadsheet using the AutoFormat feature. You can choose from 16 different styles.

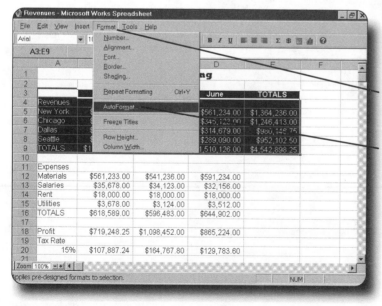

1. **Select** the **cells** to be formatted. The cells will be highlighted.

2. **Click** on **Format**. The Format menu will appear.

3. **Click** on **AutoFormat**. The AutoFormat dialog box will open.

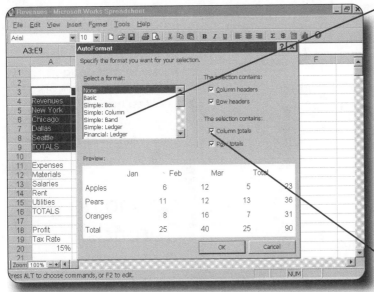

4. **Click** on a **format** from the Select a format drop-down list. A sample will appear in the Preview box.

Works assumes that the last row and column of your selection are totals and displays check marks ✓ in the Column totals and Row totals check boxes by default.

5a. Optionally, **click** on the **Column totals check box** to remove the Total column. The option will be deselected.

OR

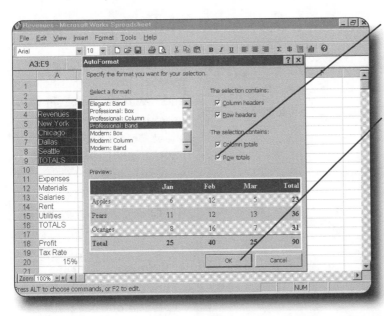

5b. Optionally, **click** on the **Row totals check box** to remove the Total row. The option will be deselected.

6. **Click** on **OK**. The AutoFormat dialog box will close, and the selected cells will be formatted.

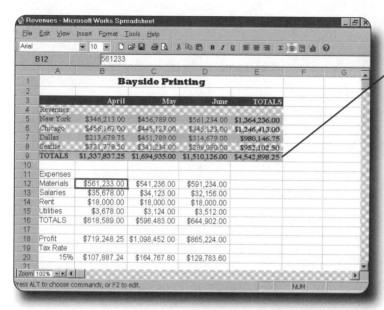

TIP

You can still change any format option (such as numbers or fonts) manually as necessary.

Changing the Spreadsheet Display

Works includes several options to modify the display of your spreadsheet. Most display options do not affect how the spreadsheet prints, only the way you see it on the monitor.

Freezing Spreadsheet Titles

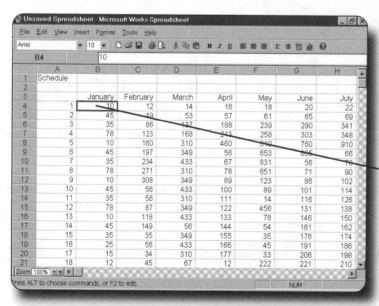

You can freeze columns, rows, or both so that column and row titles remain in view as you scroll through the sheet. This is particularly helpful with larger spreadsheets.

1. Click the **mouse** on the desired cell:

• To freeze columns, position the mouse pointer one cell to the right of the columns you want to freeze.

- To freeze rows, position the cell pointer one cell below the rows you want to freeze.

- To freeze both columns and rows, position the cell pointer in the cell below the rows and to the right of the columns you want to freeze.

2. **Click** on **Format**. The Format menu will appear.

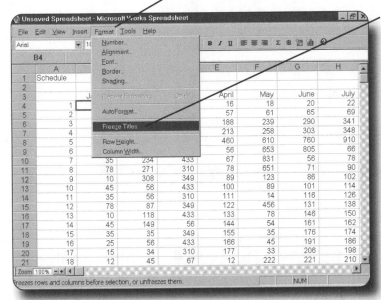

3. **Click** on **Freeze Titles**. Lines will appear on the document indicating the frozen areas.

As you scroll down or across in your document, the frozen part stays stationary on the screen while the rest of the text moves.

TIP

Repeat steps 2 and 3 to unfreeze the windows.

Using Zoom

Zoom enlarges or shrinks the display of your spreadsheet to enable you to see more or less of it. Zooming in or out does not affect printing. The normal display of your spreadsheet is 100%.

1. Click on **View**. The View menu will appear.

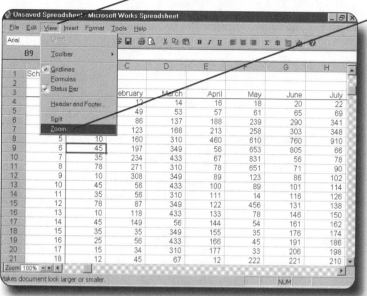

2. Click on **Zoom**. The Zoom dialog box will open.

3. Click on a **magnification percentage choice**. The higher the number, the larger the cells will appear onscreen. The option will be selected.

4. Click on **OK**. The Zoom dialog box will close, and the display of your screen will adjust according to your selection.

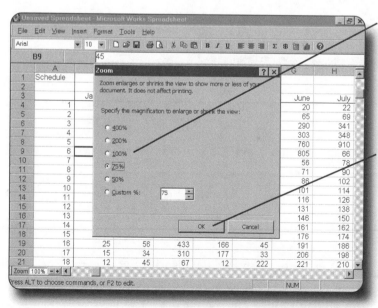

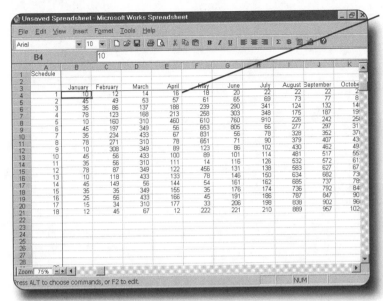

In this example, the zoom was set to 75%, which allowed more of the worksheet to display on the screen.

Hiding Gridlines

Gridlines are the light gray lines displayed on the screen that separate one cell from another. If you do not want the gridlines to display on the screen, you can easily turn them off.

1. Click on **View**. The View menu will appear.

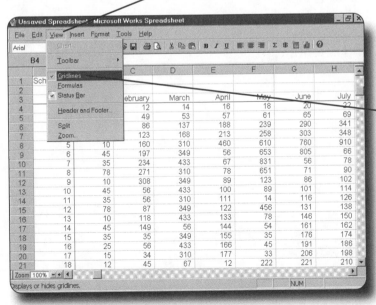

The check mark beside menu items indicates that these items are currently activated and in use.

2. Click on **Gridlines**. The option will be deselected, and the gridlines will (temporarily) disappear.

3. Repeat steps 1 and **2**. The gridlines will reappear.

By default, gridlines do not print, even if they are displayed on the spreadsheet. You have to select the option to print gridlines separately. See Chapter 14, "Printing Your Spreadsheet," for instructions on printing gridlines.

14

Printing Your Spreadsheet

Now that you have created your spreadsheet with all its text, values, and formulas, you'll want to prepare it for final output. You should proof its appearance as well as specify what area you want to print. In this chapter, you'll learn how to:

- Set page margins and orientation
- Use Print Preview
- Print a spreadsheet

Preparing to Print

Before you print your spreadsheet, you might want to tell Works what size paper you'd like to use, how large the margins should be, and whether to print the gridlines. These options and others are selected from the Page Setup feature of Works.

Setting Up Margins

By default, the top and bottom margins are set at 1 inch, and the left and right margins are set at 1.25 inch. You can change these margins.

1. **Click** on **File**. The File menu will appear.

2. **Click** on **Page Setup**. The Page Setup dialog box will open.

	B	C	D	E	F
	Bayside Printing				
	April	May	June	TOTALS	
	46,213.00	$456,789.00	$561,234.00	$1,364,236.00	
	56,167.00	$445,123.00	$345,123.00	$1,246,413.00	
	13,678.75	$451,789.00	$314,679.00	$980,146.75	
	21,778.50	$341,234.00	$289,090.00	$952,102.50	
	37,837.25	$1,694,935.00	$1,510,126.00	$4,542,898.25	
	61,233.00	$541,236.00	$591,234.00	$1,693,703.00	
	35,678.00	$34,123.00	$32,156.00	$101,957.00	
14 Rent	$18,000.00	$18,000.00	$18,000.00	$54,000.00	
15 Utilities	$3,678.00	$3,124.00	$3,512.00	$10,314.00	
16 TOTALS	$618,589.00	$596,483.00	$644,902.00	$1,859,974.00	
17					
18 Profit	$719,248.25	$1,098,452.00	$865,224.00	$2,682,924.25	
19 Tax Rate					
20 15%	$107,887.24	$164,767.80	$129,783.60	$402,438.64	
21					

Revenues - Microsoft Works Spreadsheet

File Edit View Insert Format Tools Help

New...   Ctrl+N
Open..   Ctrl+O
Close   Ctrl+W

Save   Ctrl+S
Save As...

Page Setup...
Print Area
Print Preview
Print...   Ctrl+P

Send...

Exit

1 Schedule
2 Revenues

Zoom 100%

Specifies page size, margins, and first page number.

NUM

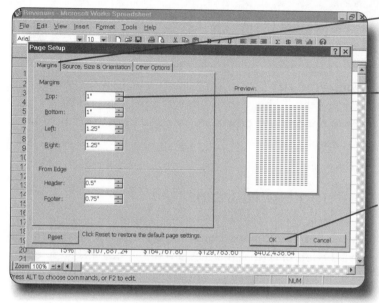

3. If necessary, **click** on the **Margins tab**. The tab will display.

4. Click on the **up/down arrows** next to each margin you want to change. The effects of the change will appear in the Sample box.

5. Click on **OK**. The Page Setup dialog box will close.

Setting Up Page Orientation and Size

If your spreadsheet uses many columns, you might want to change the orientation or paper size. The default size is 8½-by-11-inch paper in portrait orientation—the short side at the top. Changing to landscape orientation prints with the long edge of the paper at the top.

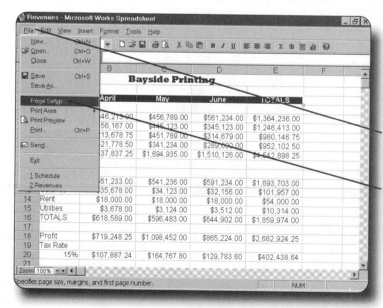

1. Click on **File**. The File menu will appear.

2. Click on **Page Setup**. The Page Setup dialog box will open.

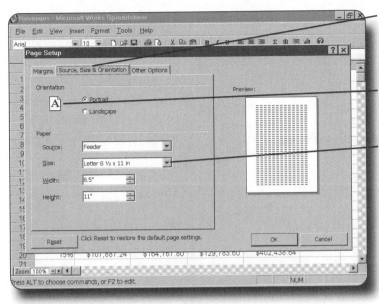

3. If necessary, **click** on the **Source, Size & Orientation tab**. The tab will display.

4. **Click** on an **Orientation**. The option will be selected.

5. **Click** on the **Size drop-down arrow**. The list of available paper-size options will appear.

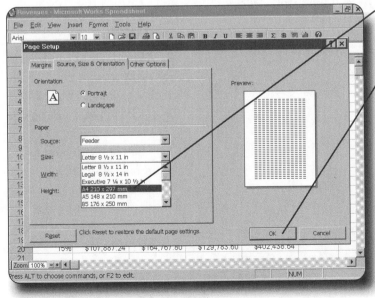

6. **Click** on a **paper size**. The paper size will be selected.

7. **Click** on **OK**. The Page Setup dialog box will close.

Setting Other Printing Options

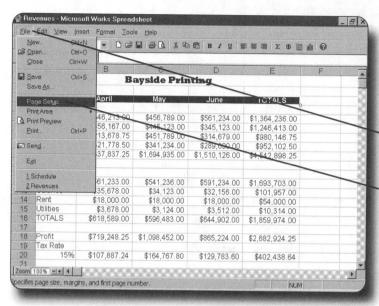

You might want to consider other options for your worksheet, such as whether to print the gridlines or the row and column headings.

1. Click on **File**. The File menu will appear.

2. Click on **Page Setup**. The Page Setup dialog box will open.

3. If necessary, **click** on the **Other Options tab**. The tab will display.

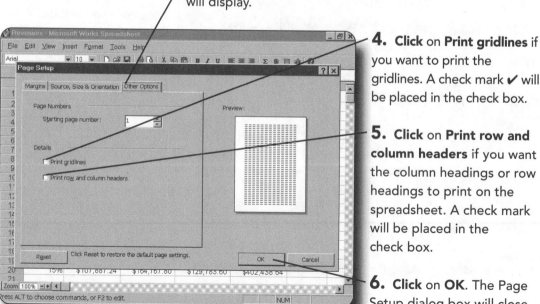

4. Click on **Print gridlines** if you want to print the gridlines. A check mark ✔ will be placed in the check box.

5. Click on **Print row and column headers** if you want the column headings or row headings to print on the spreadsheet. A check mark will be placed in the check box.

6. Click on **OK**. The Page Setup dialog box will close.

Printing a Spreadsheet

After you have created your spreadsheet, you can print a hard copy for your records or to send to someone else.

Printing a Range

By default, Works assumes that you want to print the entire spreadsheet. If this is not the case, you need to specify the area you want to print.

1. Select the **cells** you want to print if you do not intend to print the entire spreadsheet. The cells will be highlighted.

2. Click on **File**. The File menu will appear.

3. Click on **Print Area**. The Print Area submenu will appear.

4. Click on **Set Print Area**. A confirmation dialog box will open.

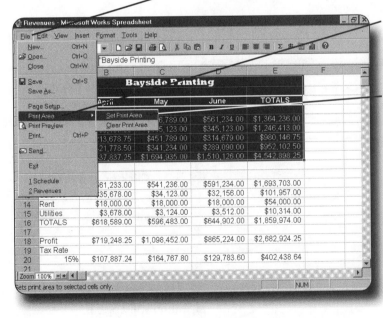

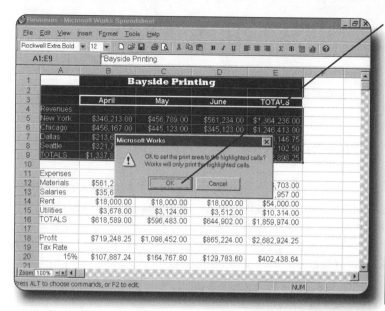

5. Click on **OK**. The dialog box will close.

Now when you print your spreadsheet, only the cells you selected in step 1 will print.

TIP

If you later want to print the entire spreadsheet, choose File, Print Area, Clear Print Area.

Printing Your Work

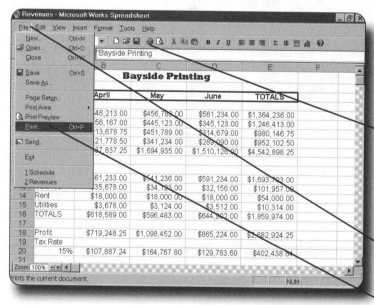

Typically, the end result of creating a Works document is getting text onto paper. Works gives you a quick and easy way to get that result.

1a. Click on the **Print button**. The spreadsheet will print with standard options.

OR

1b. Click on **File**. The File menu will appear.

2. Click on **Print**. The Print dialog box will open.

Many options are available from the Print dialog box, including:

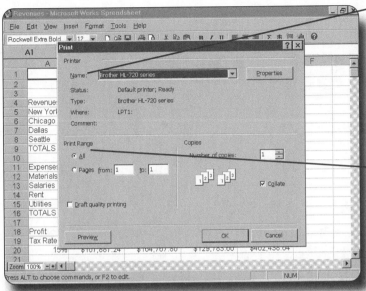

- **Printer name**. If you are connected to more than one printer, you can choose the name of the printer to use for this print job. Click on the Name drop-down arrow and make a selection.

- **Print range**. Choose which pages of your document to print in the Print range box.

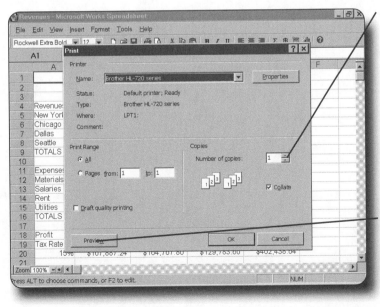

- **Number of copies**. Choose the number of copies to be printed by clicking on the up/down arrows in the Number of copies spin box.

3. **Click** on any desired **option**. The option will be selected.

4. **Click** on **OK** after you have made your selections. The document will print on your printer.

15

Creating Charts

A chart is an effective way to illustrate the data in your spreadsheet. It can make relationships between numbers easier to see because it turns numbers into shapes, which can then be compared to one another. In this chapter, you'll learn how to:

- Create a chart
- Modify a chart
- Delete a chart

Creating a Chart

Creating a chart is a simple process using the Works Chart Wizard. You first decide what you want to chart and how you want it to look.

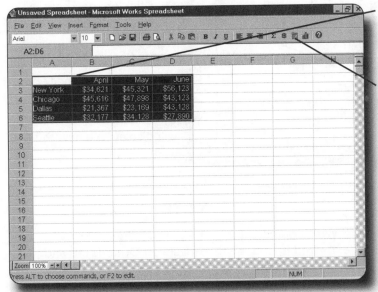

1. **Select** the **range** that you want to chart. The range will be highlighted.

2. **Click** on the **New Chart button**. The New Chart Wizard will display onscreen.

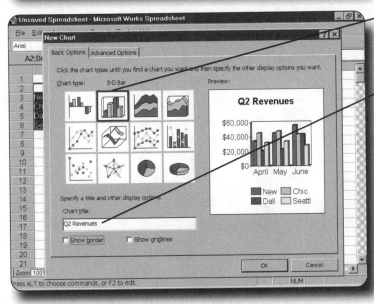

3. **Click** on a **Chart type**. A sample will display in the Preview area.

4. **Type** a **title** for your chart in the Chart title text box.

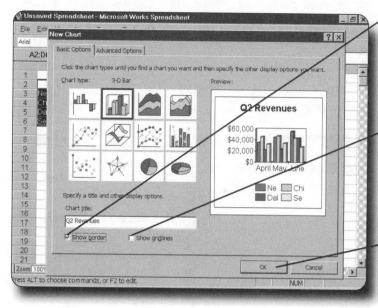

5. **Click** on the **Show border check box** if you want a border around the entire chart. A check mark ✔ will be placed in the check box.

6. **Click** on the **Show gridlines check box** if you want gridlines to display in your chart. A check mark will be placed in the check box.

7. **Click** on **OK**. The chart will display as a new window.

NOTE

If Works doesn't display the data in the order you expected it, click on the Advanced Options tab and experiment with the options listed.

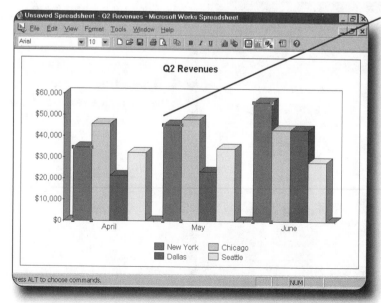

The data from the selected cells of the spreadsheet is plotted out in a chart. If the data in the spreadsheet changes, the chart also changes.

Switching Views

After creating the chart, you may need to return to the spreadsheet window to edit the data.

1. Click on **View**. The View menu will appear.

2. Click on **Spreadsheet**. The spreadsheet will display.

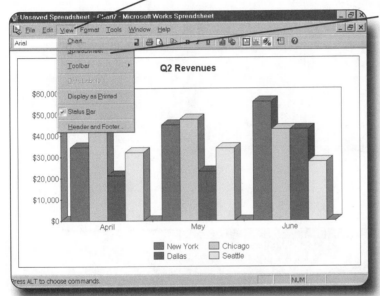

3. Click on **View** to return to the chart window. The View menu will appear.

4. Click on **Chart**. The View Chart dialog box will open.

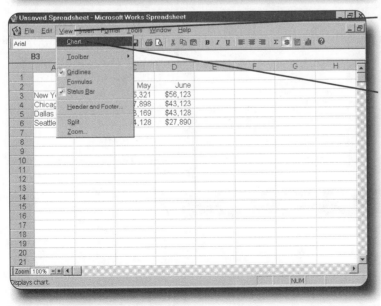

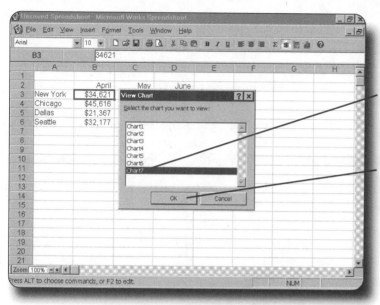

A spreadsheet can have many different charts associated with its data.

5. Click on the **chart** to display. The option will be highlighted.

6. Click on **OK**. The chart window will display.

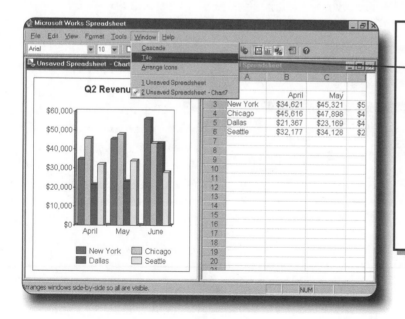

TIP

To view both the spreadsheet and chart at the same time, click on Window and then click on Tile. The two windows will display side by side. Double-click on the title bar of either window to maximize it to a full screen.

Modifying a Chart

You may want to enhance a chart to improve its appearance. You can change the style, make it 3-D, or add titles to the chart to further explain its use.

Changing a Chart Style

If you want to change the style of the chart, you can select a bar, area, pie, or line chart, as well as make it 3-D.

1. Display the **chart**. The chart window will be active.

2. Click on **Format**. The Format menu will appear.

3. Click on **Chart Type**. The Chart Type dialog box will open with the Basic Types tab selected.

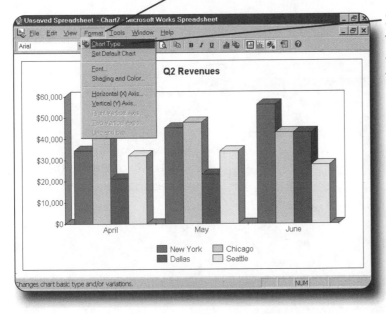

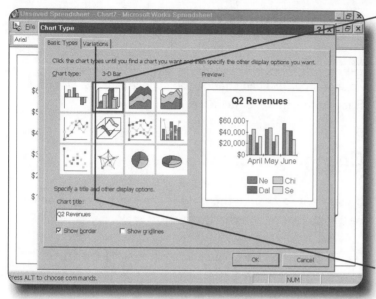

4. **Click** on a **chart type**. A sample will display.

NOTE

Traditionally, bar charts compare an item to an item, pie charts compare parts of a whole item, and line charts show a trend over a period of time.

---

5. **Click** on the **Variations tab**. Options for each chart type will display.

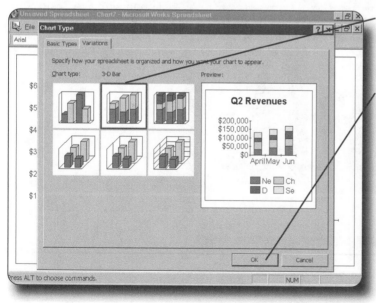

6. **Click** on any desired **variation**. A sample will display.

7. **Click** on **OK**. The chart will change to the selected style.

Adding Chart Titles

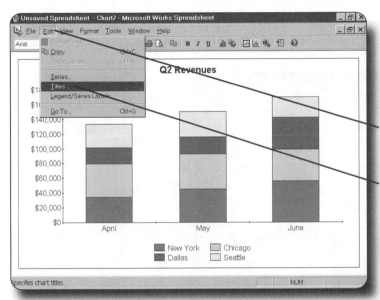

When you first created the chart, you had an option to give the chart a title. You can edit or delete that title, or assign other types of titles.

1. Click on **Edit**. The Edit menu will appear.

2. Click on **Titles**. The Titles dialog box will open.

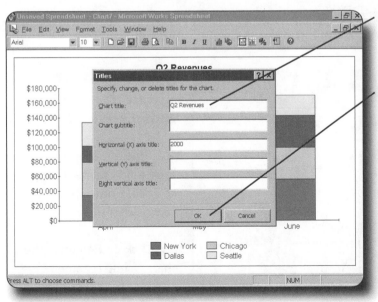

3. Type or modify the **text** for any title. The title will appear in the text box.

4. Click on **OK**. The chart titles will change.

NOTE

Note that a chart title is a label that displays on the actual chart. It's not the same thing as the filename of the chart itself.

Naming a Chart

It's possible to have many charts associated with a single spreadsheet. Identify the charts by assigning them a name other than the default name—Chart1, Chart2, and so on.

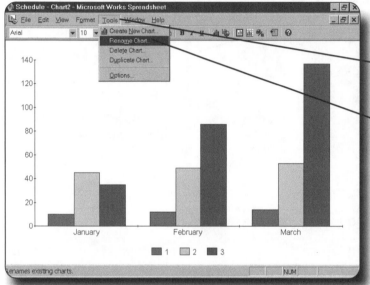

1. **Click** on **Tools**. The Tools menu will appear.

2. **Click** on **Rename Chart**. The Rename Chart dialog box will open.

3. **Click** on the **chart** to be renamed. The chart name will be highlighted.

4. **Type** a new **name** in the Type a new name for the chart text box. The new name will display.

5. **Click** on **Rename**. The chart will be renamed.

6. **Click** on **OK**. The Rename Chart dialog box will close.

Changing the Chart Series

If you do not like the default colors assigned to a chart, you can change them for any series.

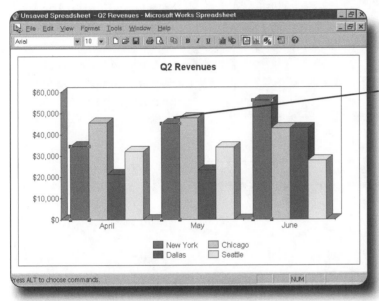

1. Display the **chart** to be modified. The chart will display.

2. Click on any colored **bar, line, or series** item. Four white handles will appear around all items in the selected series.

3. Click on **Format**. The Format menu will appear.

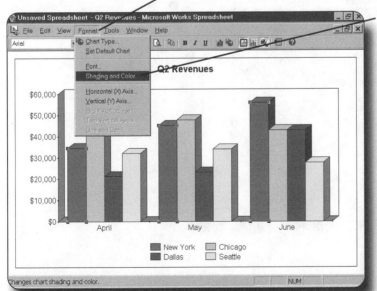

4. Click on **Shading and Color**. The Shading and Color dialog box will open.

TIP

Alternatively, double-click on any bar, line, or series item to open the Shading and Color dialog box.

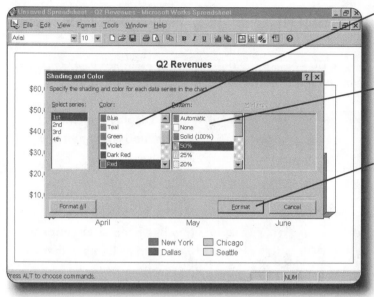

5. Click on a **color** for the selected series. The color will be highlighted.

6. Click on a **pattern** for the selected series. The pattern will be highlighted.

7. Click on **Format**. The chart will be updated with the new options.

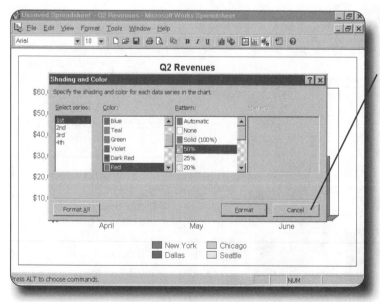

8. Repeat steps 3–5 for each series to be changed.

9. Click on **Cancel**. The Shading and Color dialog box will close.

Printing a Chart

A chart generally takes a little longer to print than other types of documents. Be patient.

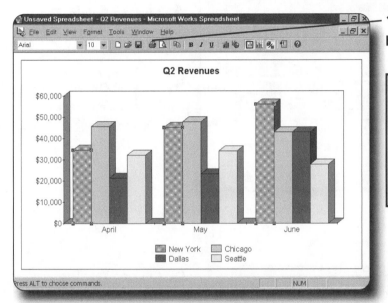

1. **Click** on the **Print button**. The chart will print.

TIP

Set up the page size and orientation by selecting File, Page Setup before clicking the Print button.

Deleting a Chart

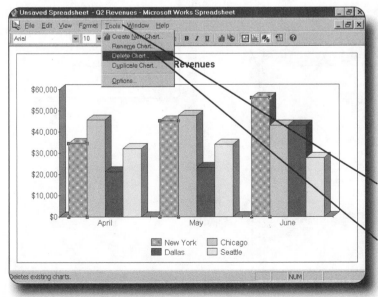

If you no longer want the chart created from your spreadsheet, you can delete it.

1. **Click** on **Tools**. The Tools menu will appear.

2. **Click** on **Delete Chart**. The Delete Chart dialog box will open.

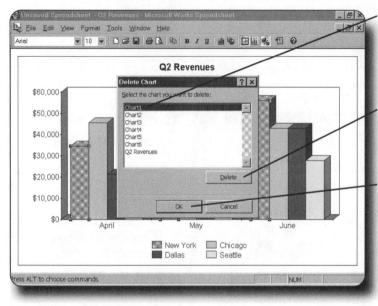

3. Click on the **chart** that you want to delete. The chart name will be highlighted.

4. Click on **Delete**. The chart will be deleted from the dialog box.

5. Click on **OK**. A confirmation message will appear.

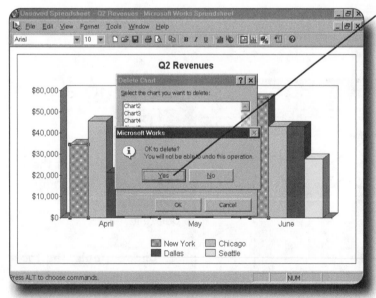

6. Click on **Yes**. The chart will be permanently deleted.

NOTE

All charts are saved with their corresponding spreadsheet.

Part III Review Questions

1. Spreadsheet data is made up of what three components? *See "Entering Data" in Chapter 10*

2. What character should you type first to enter a value as a label? *See "Entering Values" in Chapter 10*

3. What function key can be pressed to edit the contents of a cell? *See "Editing the Contents of a Cell" in Chapter 10*

4. When deleting a spreadsheet column, where do the remaining columns move? *See "Deleting Rows and Columns" in Chapter 11*

5. What does the Fill feature do when you type the word January in a cell and drag across to other cells? *See "Using the Fill Feature" in Chapter 11*

6. With what character must all spreadsheet formulas begin? *See "Creating Formulas" in Chapter 12*

7. What character is used in a formula to designate an absolute reference? *See "Creating an Absolute Reference in a Formula" in Chapter 12*

8. How can you center heading text across a group of columns? *See "Centering Headings" in Chapter 13*

9. How do you tell Works you want to print a specific area of the spreadsheet? *See "Printing a Range" in Chapter 14*

10. What styles of charts can Works create? *See "Changing a Chart Style" in Chapter 15*

PART IV

Working with Databases

16

Creating a Database

Whether you realize it or not, you use databases every day. Your phone book is a database; your television show listing is a database; even a cookbook is a database. A database in its simplest form is an organized list of information. Works provides a simple database application that enables you to create and manage your own databases. In this chapter, you'll learn how to:

- Understand fields and records
- Create a new database
- Look at different database views
- Move, add, or delete fields
- Save a database

Understanding Fields and Records

Information in a database is grouped into records and fields.

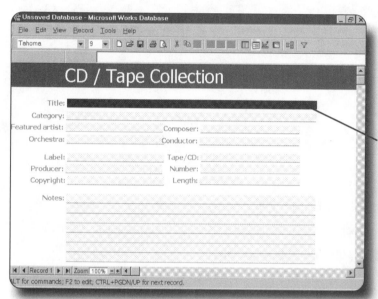

- A *record* is all the information about one person, product, event, and so on. Every record in a database contains the same fields.

- A *field* is one item in a record, such as a name or address. You can enter text, numbers, dates, or formulas in a field.

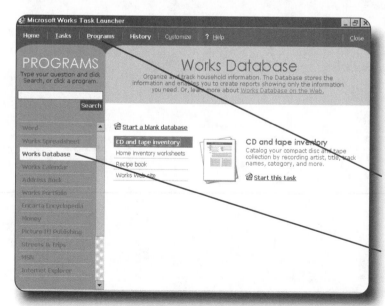

Creating a New Database

Create a new database by using the Works Task Launcher.

1. **Click** on **Programs**. A listing of the Works components will appear.

2. **Click** on **Works Database**. A listing of database tasks will appear.

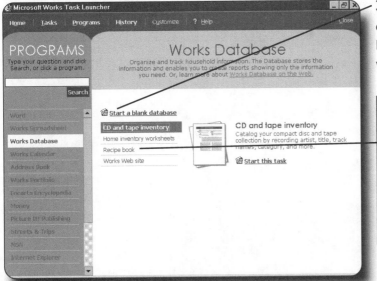

3. **Click** on **Start a blank database**. The Create Database dialog box will open.

TIP

You can also click on a database task to start a database Task Wizard. See Appendix B, "Using Task Wizards" to learn more.

Adding Fields

The first thing you must do when creating a new database is name your fields. If you are creating an address database, you might include fields such as name, address, phone number, and birth date. If you are creating a database to track your CD collection, you might include fields such as title, artist, and date purchased.

TIP

Before creating a database from scratch, you should study an existing database to learn more about how it's structured. Also, designing your database structure on paper first can help you avoid having to redesign it later.

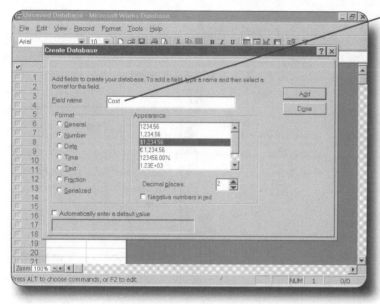

1. Type a **name** for the first field in the Field name text box in the Create Database dialog box.

Fields can be in a variety of formats such as General, Number, or Date. Items such as a name, address, or telephone number would be in General (text) format, whereas data such as age might be in Number format, and a hire date might be in Date format.

2. Click on a **format type** for the field. The option will be selected.

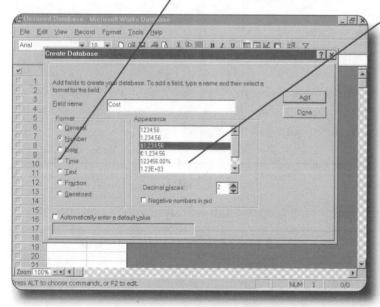

3. Select any **Appearance options**. The options will be selected.

Works can automatically enter field data. For example, if you are creating an address book where most entrants reside in California, Works can automatically enter CA or California. It is then easy to change it for the few records of people who do not reside in California.

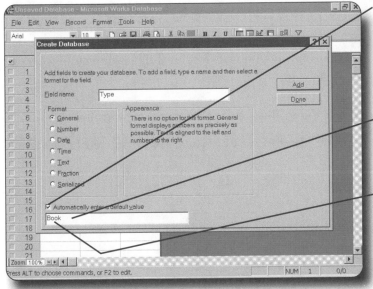

4. Optionally, **click** on **Automatically enter a default value**. A check mark ✔ will be placed in the check box.

5. Click in the **default value text box**. A blinking insertion point will appear.

6. Enter the **default value**. The text will appear in the default value text box.

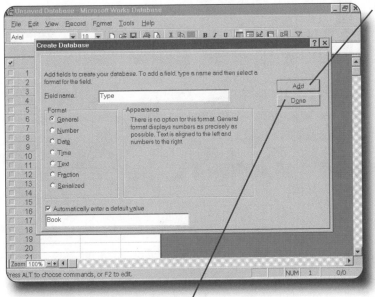

7. Click on **Add**. The field is added, and you are prompted for the name of the next field.

8. Repeat steps 1–7 until all fields have been added.

TIP

You can edit fields, add fields, or delete unwanted fields later.

---

9. Click on **Done**. The Create Database dialog box will close.

Looking at the Different Views

You can view a database in several different ways, including the following:

- **List View.** This view is similar to a spreadsheet.

- **Form View.** In this view, you can view one record at a time.

- **Form Design View.** Here you can make design changes to a form.

Your database will initially display in List view.

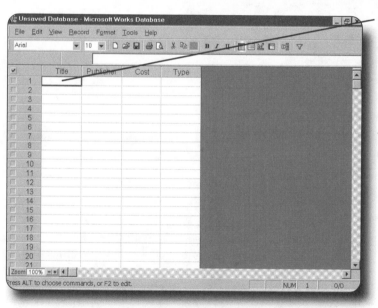

List view is similar to looking at a spreadsheet. The field names display as column headings. As you enter each record, the information displays in the rows. In List view, you can see multiple records at the same time.

1. **Click** on **View**. The View menu will appear.

2. **Click** on **Form**. The database will appear in Form view.

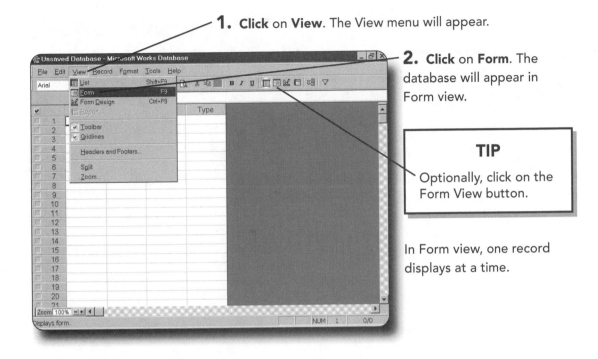

TIP

Optionally, click on the Form View button.

In Form view, one record displays at a time.

3. **Click** on **View**. The View menu will appear.

4. **Click** on **Form Design**. The database will appear in Form Design view. You can edit the database design in this view.

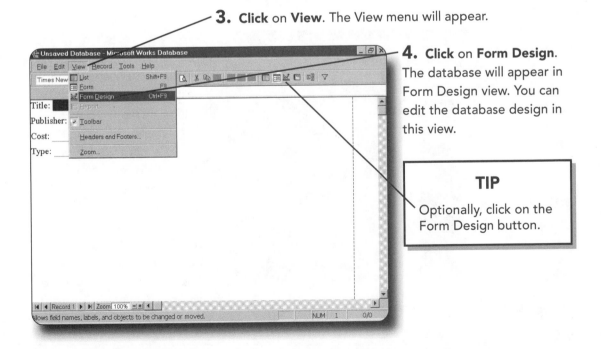

TIP

Optionally, click on the Form Design button.

5. **Click** on **View**. The View menu will appear.

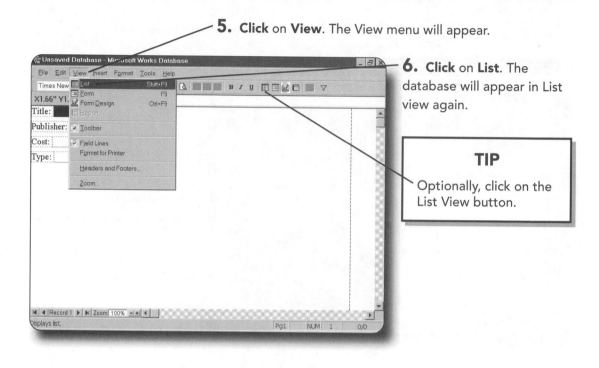

6. **Click** on **List**. The database will appear in List view again.

TIP

Optionally, click on the List View button.

Adding Fields

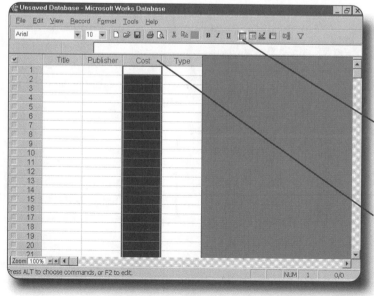

After you create a database, you can still add as many fields as you need. The easiest way to add fields is using List view.

1. If necessary, **click** on the **List View button**. The database will appear in List view.

2. **Click** on the **field heading** located at the position where you want to add the new field. The field column will be highlighted.

3. Click on **Record**. The Record menu will appear.

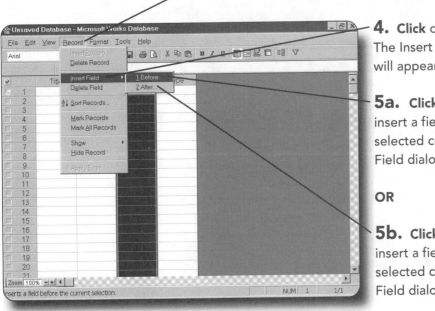

4. Click on **Insert Field**. The Insert Field submenu will appear.

5a. Click on **Before** to insert a field before the selected column. The Insert Field dialog box will open.

OR

5b. Click on **After** to insert a field after the selected column. The Insert Field dialog box will open.

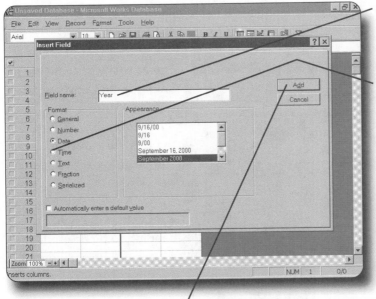

6. Type a **name** in the Field name text box. The text will appear in the text box.

7. Click on a **Format** type. The option will be selected.

TIP

Optionally, click on the Automatically enter a default value check box and enter the default value in the text box.

8. Click on **Add**. The field will be added.

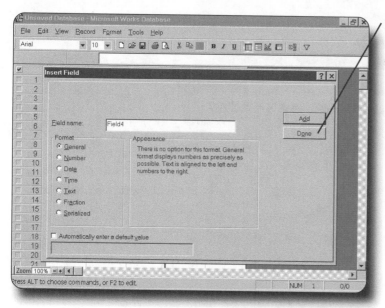

9. Click on **Done**. The Insert Field dialog box will close.

Deleting a Field

If you no longer need a field, you can delete it. When you delete a field, any data for that field is also deleted.

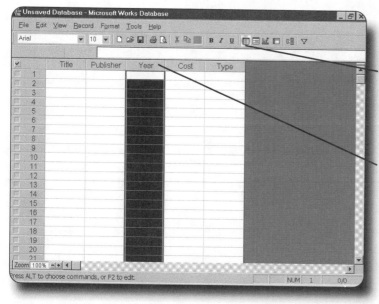

The easiest way to delete a field is using List view.

1. If necessary, **click** on the **List View button**. The database will appear in List view.

2. Click on the **field heading** to be deleted. The column will be highlighted.

3. Click on **Record**. The Record menu will appear.

4. Click on **Delete Field**. A confirmation message will appear.

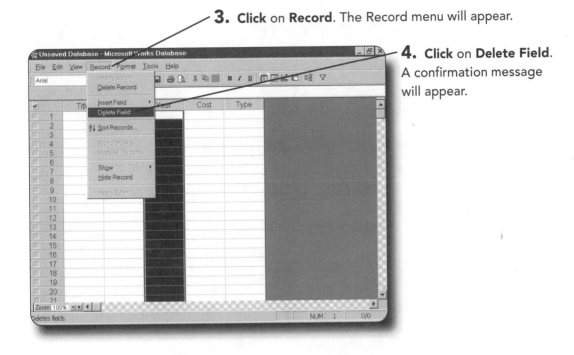

5. Click on **OK**. The field will be deleted.

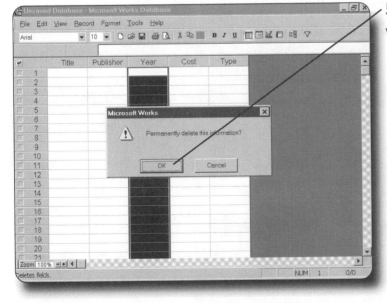

Moving a Field

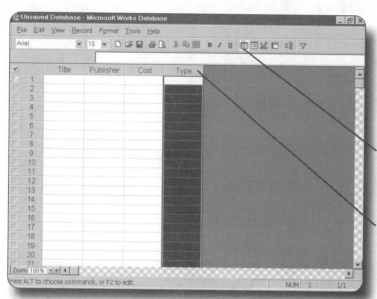

If you place a field in the wrong position, you can move it. The easiest way to move a field is to use the Cut and Paste commands in List view.

1. **Click** on the **List View button**. The database will appear in List view.

2. **Click** on the **field name** to be moved. The column will be highlighted.

3. **Click** on **Edit**. The Edit menu will appear.

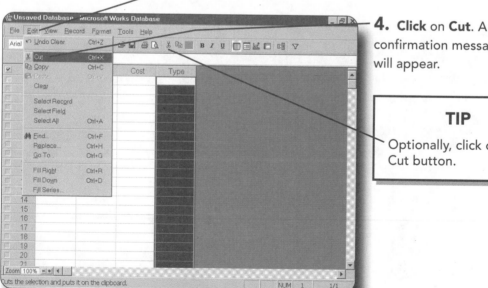

4. **Click** on **Cut**. A confirmation message box will appear.

TIP

Optionally, click on the Cut button.

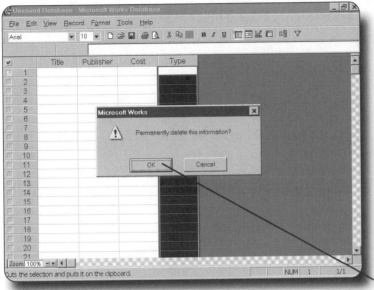

NOTE

Although this message box asks whether you want to permanently delete this information, don't be alarmed. You are not going to *permanently* delete the information. Instead, you are going to temporarily place the information on the Windows Clipboard.

5. Click on **OK**. The column/field will be deleted.

6. Click on the **field heading** before which you want the field in the Clipboard to be positioned. The current field will be highlighted.

7. Click on **Edit**. The Edit menu will appear.

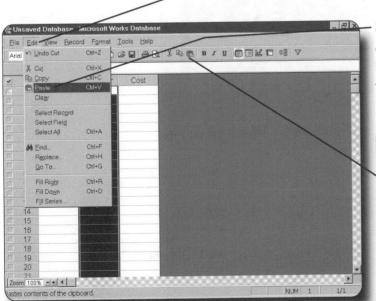

8. Click on **Paste**. The existing field (and data) will be moved to the right, and the field that you put in the Clipboard will be inserted.

TIP

Optionally, click on the Paste button.

Saving a Database

As with the other components of Microsoft Works, when you create a file, you should save it for future use.

Saving a Database the First Time

When you first create a document, it has no name. If you want to use that document later, it must have a name so that Works can find it.

1. **Click** on **File**. The File menu will appear.

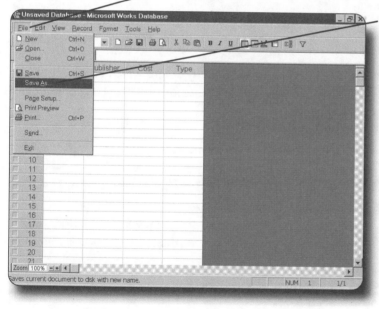

2. **Click** on **Save As.** The Save As dialog box will open.

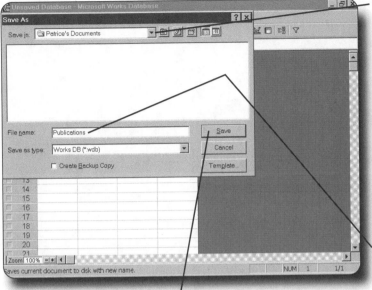

The Save in drop-down list specifies the folder where the file will be saved. The default folder that appears is My Documents. If you don't want to save the database in this folder, or if you want to save your database to another disk, you can select the disk or folder here. Click on the drop-down arrow to browse.

3. **Type** a **name** for your file in the File name text box. The file name will display.

4. **Click** on **Save**. Your database will be saved, and the name you specified will appear in the title bar.

Resaving a Database

As you continue to work on your database, you should resave it every ten minutes or so. This ensures that you do not lose any changes.

Click on the **Save button**. The database will be resaved with any changes. No dialog box will open because the database is resaved with the same name and in the same folder as previously specified.

17

Working with Data

After you create an initial database, you're ready to add and work with data. In this chapter, you'll learn how to:

- Enter data
- Move around the database
- Edit records
- Find and sort records
- Delete records

Working with Data

You can enter data in either List view or Form view. The number of records you can enter is limited only by the size of your hard drive.

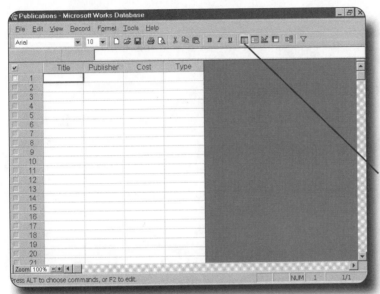

Entering Data in List View

If you are working in List view, you'll see all the records together as you enter them.

1. Click on the **List View button**. The database will appear in List view.

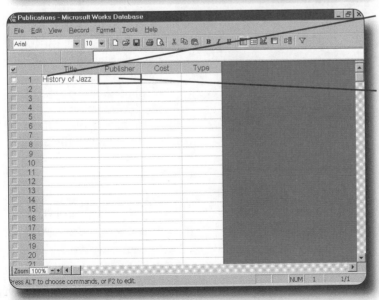

2. Type the **data** for the first field. The data will be entered.

3. Press the **Tab key**. The next field will be selected.

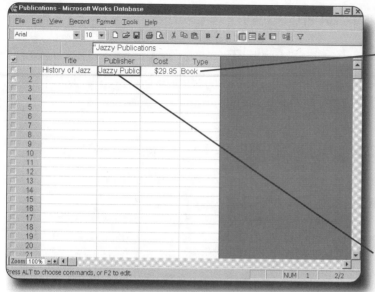

NOTE

As you access fields that you designed with a default value, the value will be automatically entered for you. If you need a different value, highlight the default value and replace it with the new one.

4. Type the **data** for the next field. That data will be entered.

5. Repeat steps 3 and **4** until you have entered all the data for the current record.

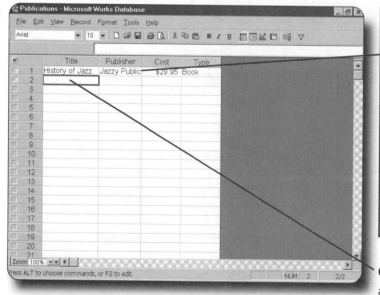

NOTE

If the data you are typing is larger than the field size, you might not see all the data displayed or you might see #### displayed. In Chapter 18, "Formatting a Database," you'll learn how to change the size of a field.

6. When you are ready to add another record, **press** the **Tab** key in the last field of the current row. Works will automatically move to the first field of the next record.

Entering Data in Form View

When entering data in Form view, one record at a time will display. Form view is usually the easiest view to use if you have many fields in your database.

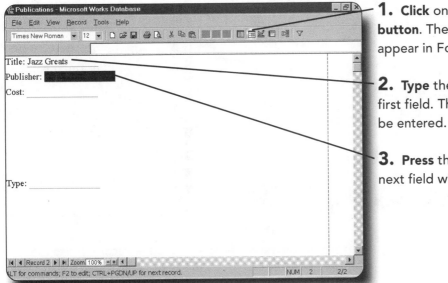

1. Click on the **Form View button**. The database will appear in Form view.

2. Type the **data** for the first field. The data will be entered.

3. Press the **Tab key**. The next field will be selected.

NOTE

If the data you are typing is larger than the field size, you might not see all the data displayed or you might see a series of #### displayed. In Chapter 18, "Formatting a Database," you'll learn how to change the size of a field.

4. **Type** the **data** for the next field. That data will be entered.

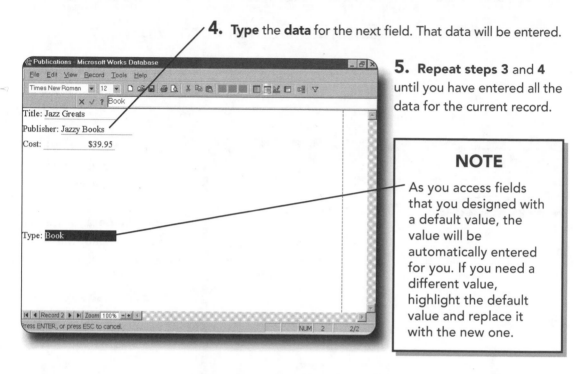

5. **Repeat steps 3** and **4** until you have entered all the data for the current record.

NOTE

As you access fields that you designed with a default value, the value will be automatically entered for you. If you need a different value, highlight the default value and replace it with the new one.

6. When you are ready to add another record, **press** the **Tab** key in the last field of the current row. Works will automatically display a blank record, ready for entering data.

Moving Around in the Database

After several records are in the database, you might need to return to a specific record to review it.

Moving Around in List View

Moving around the database in List view is similar to moving around in a Works spreadsheet. You can use your mouse or keyboard to quickly move around your database in List view.

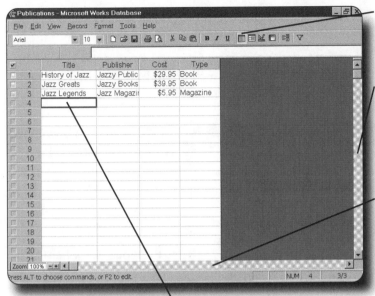

1. **Click** on the **List View button**. The database will appear in List view.

2a. **Click** on the **vertical scroll bar** until the record you are looking for is visible.

OR

2b. **Click** on the **horizontal scroll bar** until the field you are looking for is visible.

3. **Click** anywhere on the **desired record**. The field you click within that record will be selected.

The following table describes keyboard methods for moving around in your database in List view:

Keystroke	Result
Up/down arrow keys	Moves one record at a time up or down
Left/right arrow keys	Moves one field at a time left or right
Page Down	Moves one screen of records down
Page Up	Moves one screen of records up
Home	Moves to the first field of the current record
Ctrl+Home	Moves to the first field of the first record
F5	Displays the Go To dialog box

Moving Around in Form View

If you are working in Form view, you can display different records one at a time. A movement bar is displayed at the bottom of the Form view window.

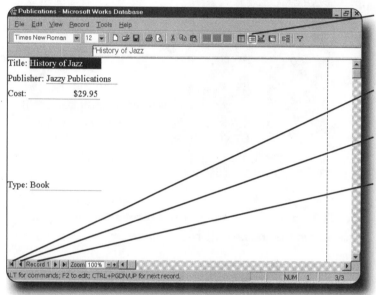

1. Click on the **Form View button**. The database will appear in Form view.

- **First**. Click here to go to the first record.

- **Previous**. Click here to go to the previous record.

- **Current**. Double-click here to open the Go To dialog box. Using the Go To dialog box is discussed in the next section.

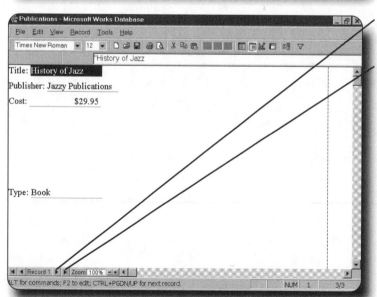

- **Next**. Click here to go to the next record.

- **Last**. Click here to go to the last record.

Using the Go To Dialog Box

Use the Go To dialog box to quickly jump to a specific
record or field.

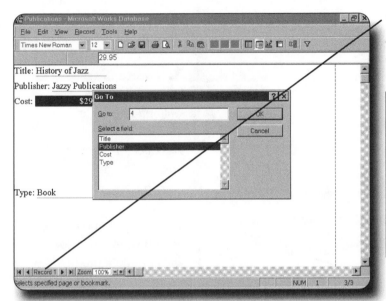

1. Double-click on the
current record number. The
Go To dialog box will open.

TIP

Other ways to open
the Go To dialog box
include pressing
Ctrl+G, pressing the F5
key, or clicking on the
Edit menu and
selecting Go To.

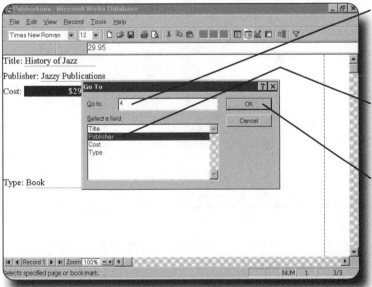

2a. Enter a **record number**
in the Go To text box.

OR

2b. Click on a **field name**.
The field name will appear in
the Go To text box.

3. Click on **OK**. The Go To
dialog box will close, and
the specified record or field
will appear.

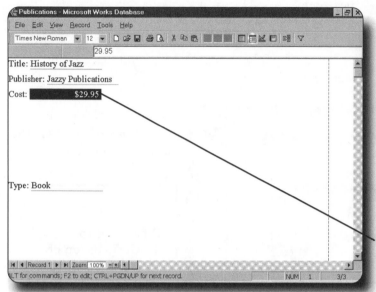

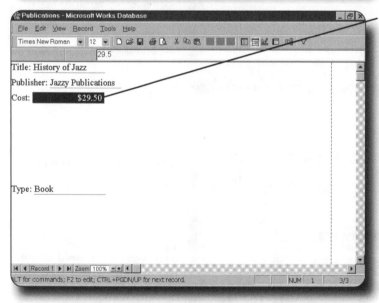

Editing Records

Editing data is the same whether you are in Form view or List view.

1. Locate the **record** to be edited. The record will appear.

2. Click on the **data** to be edited. The data will be highlighted.

3. Type the **corrected information**. The new data will appear in the field.

4. Press Enter. The existing data will be replaced with the new data.

Finding Records

Need to locate a specific record? Let Works do the searching for you. An example might be to search for anyone who lives in Chicago. Finding records is slightly different from filtering records, which you learn to do in Chapter 19, "Working with Filters."

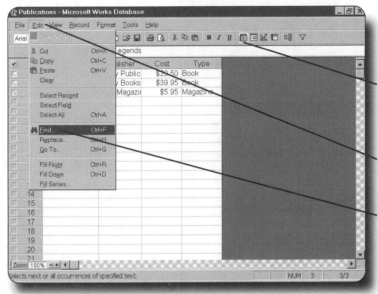

List view is easy to work with when searching for specific records.

1. **Click** on the **List View button**. The database will appear in List view.

2. **Click** on **Edit**. The Edit menu will appear.

3. **Click** on **Find**. The Find dialog box will open.

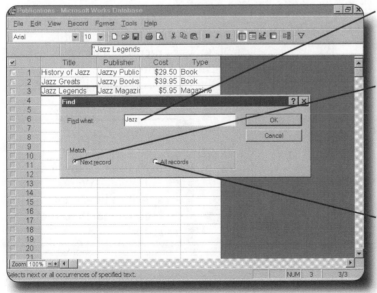

4. **Type** the **characters** you want to locate in the Find what text box.

5a. **Click** on **Next Record** to find the next occurrence of the specified characters but not search any further.

OR

5b. **Click** on **All records** to find all records in the database that contain the specified characters.

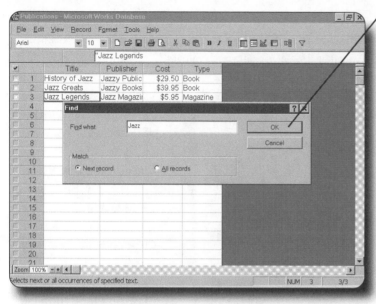

6. Click on **OK**. If you selected Next record, the next field that contains the specified text will be highlighted. If you chose All records, the records matching the criteria will appear.

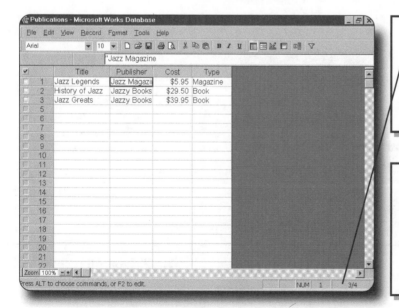

NOTE

Notice in this example that three out of four records match the criteria.

TIP

In both List view and Form view, Works specifies how many records matched the criteria.

Redisplaying Records

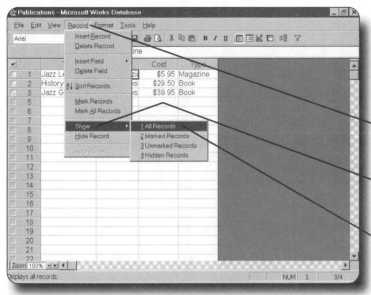

If you chose to find all records, only the records that matched your selection display. You can easily redisplay all records.

1. Click on **Record**. The Record menu will appear.

2. Click on **Show**. The Show submenu will appear.

3. Click on **All Records**. All records in the database will appear.

Sorting Records

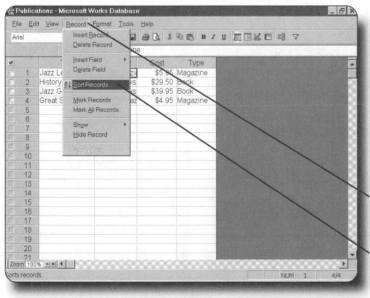

By default, the records are listed in the order that you entered them. You can, however, sort them by any field. If multiple records have the same data in the specified field, you also can specify a second or third sorting method.

1. Click on **Record**. The Record menu will appear.

2. Click on **Sort Records**. The Sort Records dialog box will open.

NOTE

Records can be sorted in either List view or Form view.

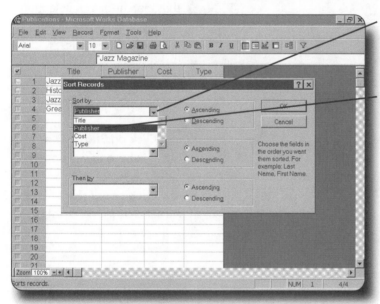

3. **Click** on the **Sort by drop-down arrow.** A list of fields will appear.

4. **Click** on the first **field** to sort by. The field name will appear.

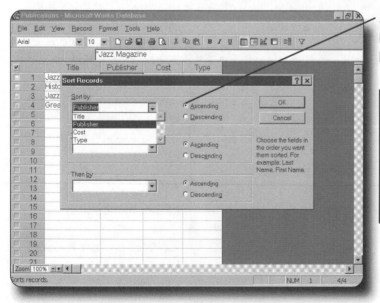

5. **Click** on **Ascending** or **Descending.** The option will be selected.

NOTE

Ascending order will sort from A to Z if the field is alphabetical or from smallest to largest if the field is numerical.

If multiple records have the same data in the specified field, you can also specify a second or third sorting method.

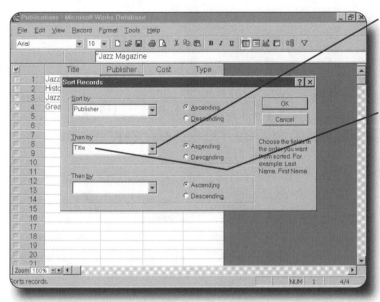

6. **Click** on the **down arrow** in the first Then by drop-down list. A list of fields will appear.

7. **Click** on the second **field** to sort by. The field name will appear in the first Then by drop-down list.

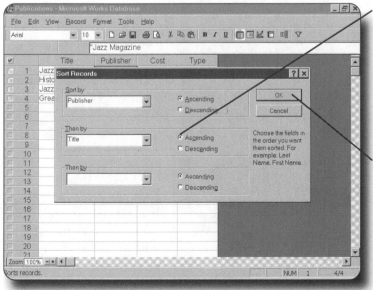

8. **Click** on **Ascending** or **Descending**. The option will be selected.

9. Optionally, **repeat steps 6–8** for the second Then by drop-down list.

10. **Click** on **OK**. The Sort dialog box will close.

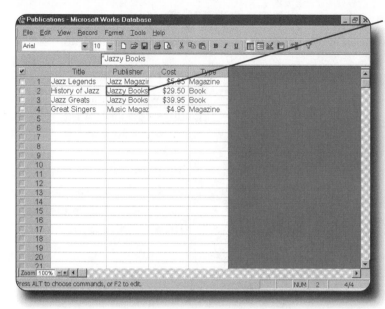

The records will sort and display in the order specified.

Deleting Records

It is simple to delete a record. Deleting a record erases all data from all fields of the selected record only. The procedure for deleting a record is the same in List view and Form view.

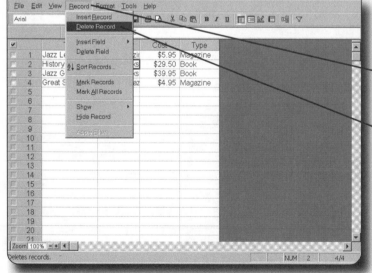

1. **Click** anywhere on **the record** to be deleted. The selected record will appear.

2. **Click** on **Record**. The Record menu will appear.

3. **Click** on **Delete Record**. The selected record will be deleted.

TIP

If you delete a record in error, immediately go to the Edit menu and click on Undo.

18

Formatting a Database

You've learned how to create database fields and enter records. Now it's time to make your database more noticeable. You can modify and enhance its appearance by changing the look or size of fields or even adding a company logo. In this chapter, you'll learn how to:

- Change the field type
- Change the alignment or size of a field
- Rename a field
- Add non-field text
- Add artwork to a database

Formatting Fields

When you format fields, you change the appearance of your field data. Formatting options include field type as well as the alignment, font, border, or shading options of field data.

Changing the Field Type

When you first created your database, Works offered you several options to set the format type of the field. You can change the format of a field at any later time as well.

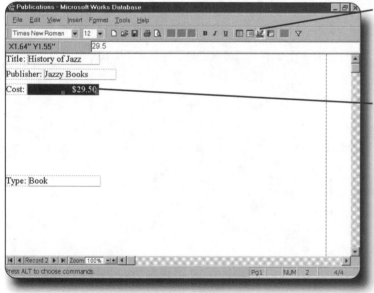

1. **Click** on the **Form Design button**. The database will appear in Form Design view.

2. **Click** on the **field** to be modified. The field will be highlighted.

NOTE

In Form Design view, you can edit the design and appearance of your form, but you can't enter data.

3. Click on **Format**. The Format menu will appear.

4. Click on **Field**. The Format dialog box will open with the Field tab displayed.

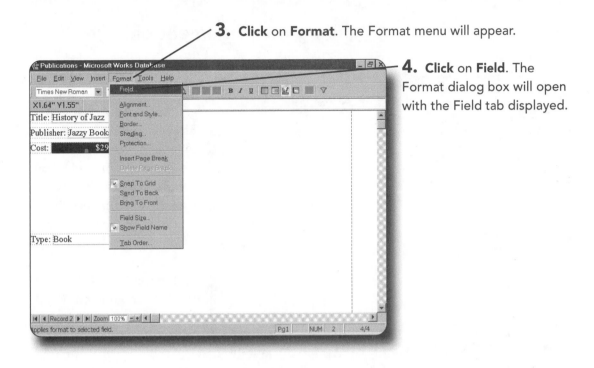

5. Click on a **format**. The option will be selected, and any appearance options will display.

6. Click on an **Appearance option**. The option will be selected.

7. Click on **OK**. The Format dialog box will close.

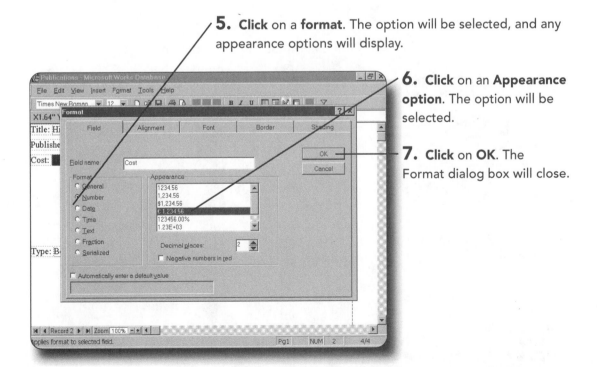

Changing the Alignment of a Field

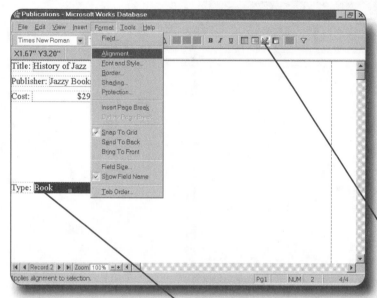

The default alignment of field contents is General. Text items are aligned to the left, whereas dates and numerically formatted fields are aligned to the right. You can override the default alignment and set any field to line up on the right, left, or center of the field.

1. If necessary, **click** on the **Form Design button**. The database will be in Form Design view.

2. Click on the **field** to be modified. The field will be highlighted.

3. Click on **Format**. The Format menu will appear.

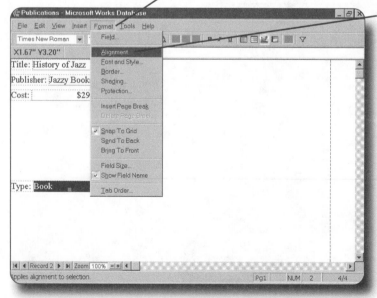

4. Click on **Alignment**. The Format dialog box will open with the Alignment tab displayed.

5. **Click** on a **Horizontal alignment option**. The option will be selected.

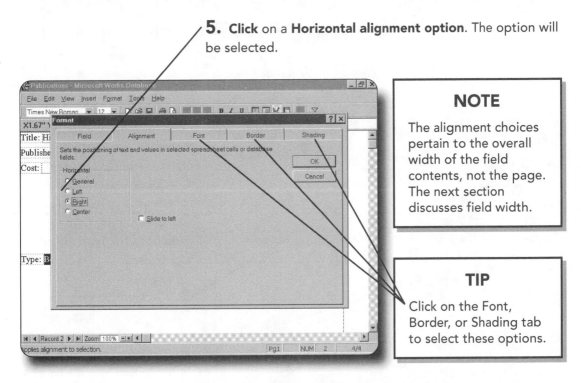

NOTE

The alignment choices pertain to the overall width of the field contents, not the page. The next section discusses field width.

TIP

Click on the Font, Border, or Shading tab to select these options.

6. **Click** on **OK**. The Format dialog box will close. The field alignment will be modified to your specifications.

Changing the Size of a Field

When the fields are first created, Works makes each field the same size: 20 characters. Depending on your needs, that might be too much or not enough. For example, only two characters might be needed for a State field, whereas you might need 40 for an Address field. If you've included a field to store miscellaneous information, such as a Note field, you might even want the data to consume several lines of text. When a field height is set to more than one line, Works wraps the text to the next line when the text is longer than the field width.

Changing Field Size Using the Menu

Fields can be a maximum of 325 characters wide and 325 lines long.

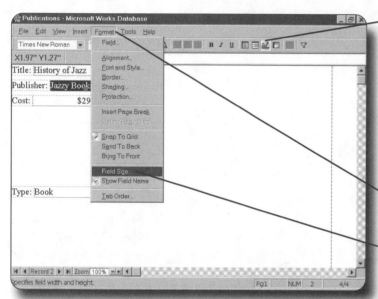

1. If necessary, **click** on the **Form Design button**. The database will be in Form Design view.

2. **Click** on the **field** to be modified. The field will be highlighted.

3. **Click** on **Format**. The Format menu will appear.

4. **Click** on **Field Size**. The Format Field Size dialog box will open.

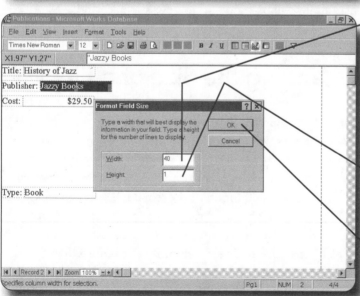

5. **Type** a **size** in the Width text box. The new value will appear.

6. **Press** the **Tab** key. The Height text box will be highlighted.

7. **Type** a **size** for the field height. The new value will appear.

8. **Click** on **OK**. The Format Field Size dialog box will close, and the field will change to the specified width and height.

Changing Field Size by Dragging

Visually resize the field by using the mouse.

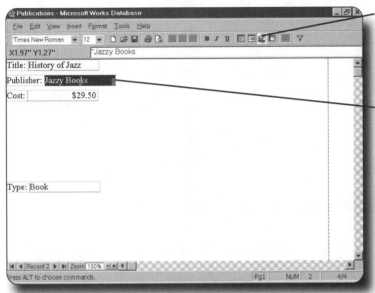

1. If necessary, **click** on the **Form Design button**. The database will be in Form Design view.

2. Click on the **field** to be modified. The field will be highlighted.

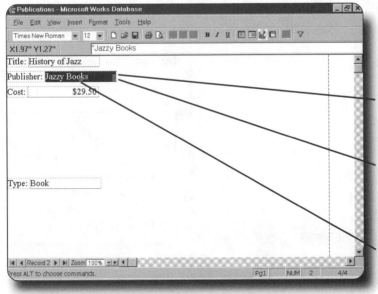

Notice the three size boxes that appear around the perimeter of a field when it is highlighted:

- The top box on the right is used to change the field width.

- The bottom box on the right is used to change both the height and width at the same time.

- The box at the bottom is used to change the field height.

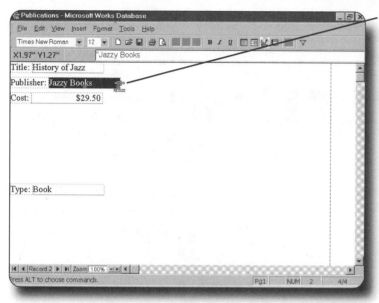

3. Position the **mouse pointer** on one of the size boxes. The mouse pointer will change to an arrow with the word "RESIZE" displayed.

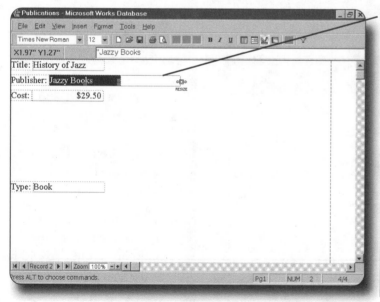

4. Drag the **box** to the desired size. A dotted box will indicate the new size.

5. Release the **mouse button**. The field will be resized.

NOTE

Field text that previously did not display because the field size was too small may now appear.

Renaming a Field

The name originally assigned to a field can be changed. Field names can be up to 15 characters including spaces and punctuation.

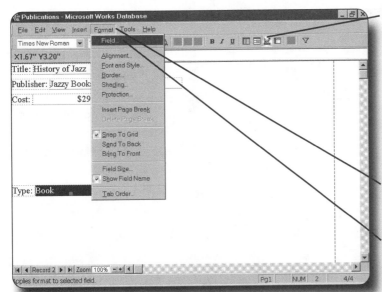

1. If necessary, **click** on the **Form Design button**. The database will be in Form Design view.

2. Click on the **field** to be modified. The field will be highlighted.

3. Click on **Format**. The Format menu will appear.

4. Click on **Field**. The Format dialog box will open with the Field tab displayed.

5. Type a new **field name** in the Field name text box.

6. Click on **OK**. The field name will be changed.

NOTE

No data changes when a field is renamed.

Adding Non-Field Text

Text that is not related to a field can be added. Add items such as your company name or a description of the information you're storing in the database.

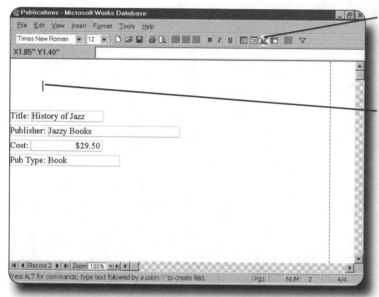

1. If necessary, **click** on the **Form Design button**. The database will be in Form Design view.

2. Click the **mouse** where you want the text to be located. A blinking insertion point will appear.

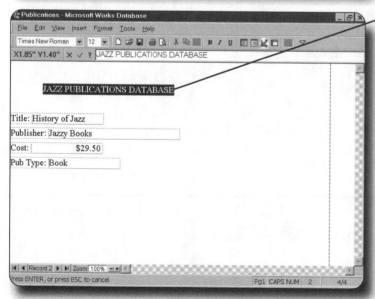

3. Type text. The text will be displayed and highlighted.

4. Click anywhere in the database. The text will be deselected.

NOTE

Do not type any colons (:) in the text. Works treats an item with a colon as a new field.

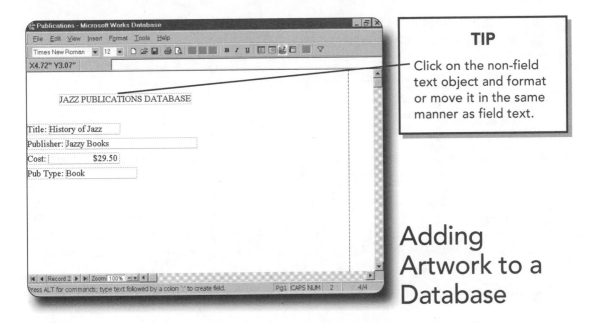

TIP

Click on the non-field text object and format or move it in the same manner as field text.

Adding Artwork to a Database

Improve the appearance of your database by adding artwork to the design. Any artwork added appears on each record in the database. One of the easiest ways to enhance your database is by adding one of the many pieces of clip art or photographs supplied with Microsoft Works.

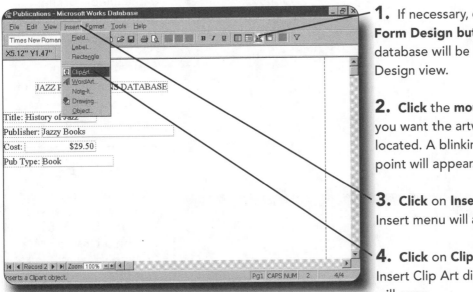

1. If necessary, **click** on the **Form Design button**. The database will be in Form Design view.

2. Click the **mouse** where you want the artwork to be located. A blinking insertion point will appear.

3. Click on **Insert**. The Insert menu will appear.

4. Click on **ClipArt**. The Insert Clip Art dialog box will open.

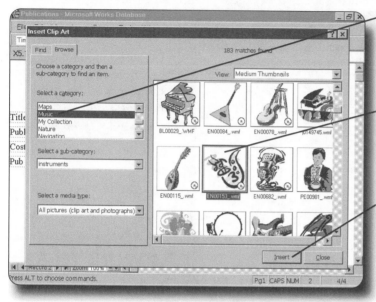

5. **Click** on the **category** of images that you want to use. The selection of available artwork will appear.

6. **Click** on the **image** you want to insert. The selection will be surrounded by a black box.

7. **Click** on **Insert**. The clip art image or picture will be inserted into your database.

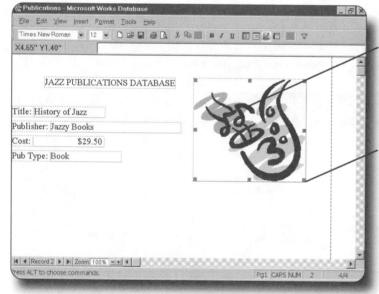

You can now

- Move the artwork by placing the mouse pointer in the middle of the artwork and dragging it to the desired location.

- Resize the artwork by clicking and dragging on one of the eight handles surrounding the image.

NOTE

You can also add your own artwork, such as a logo or WordArt, by clicking on Insert, Drawing or Insert, WordArt.

19

Working with Filters

Filtering information enables you to select which records you want to work with. Based on conditions you specify, you can tell Works which records to display. In this chapter, you'll learn how to:

- Create filters
- Apply a filter
- Rename or delete filters

Filtering Records

Filtering records is the process of letting Works know which records to select from the database. For example, you could create a filter named "Chicago Smiths" that includes only the people named Smith who live in Chicago. You could create another filter named "Youth" that includes only the people under 21 years of age.

Creating a Filter the First Time

The first time you create a filter in the database, a Filter Name box appears. This box does not appear on subsequent filters.

1. Click on **Tools**. The Tools menu will appear.

2. Click on **Filters**. The Filter Name dialog box will open.

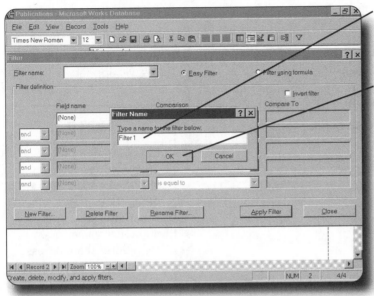

3. Enter a **name** for the filter. The default name is Filter 1.

4. Click on **OK**. The Filter Name dialog box will close, revealing the Filter dialog box.

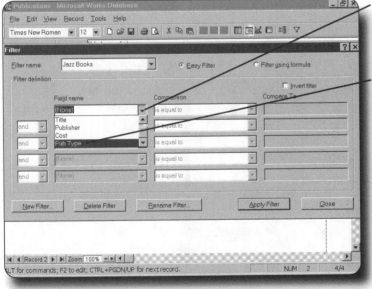

5. Click on the **Field name drop-down arrow**. A list of field names will appear.

6. Click on the first **field name** that you want to filter. The name will appear in the Field name text box.

7. Press the **Tab key**. The Comparison text box will be highlighted.

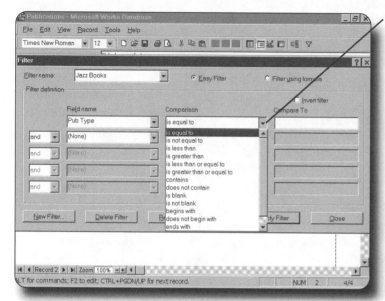

8. Click on the **Comparison drop-down arrow**. A list of comparison types will appear.

NOTE

Comparison types enable you to filter on either numerical or text data. For example, you could filter on numerical values equal to, greater than, or less than the number you enter in the Compare To text box. Or you could filter on specific words or partial words. You can also filter on what's not there—a blank field, for instance.

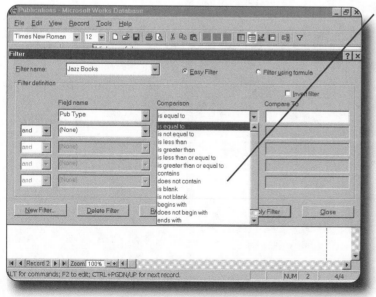

9. Click on the desired **option**. The option will appear in the Comparison text box.

10. Press the **Tab key**. The Compare To text box will be highlighted.

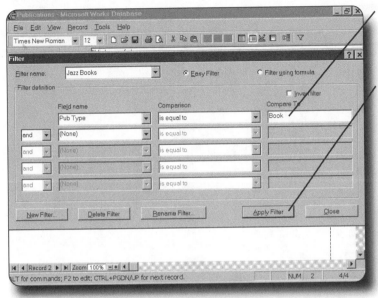

11. **Type** the **value or criterion** to compare. You can type text or numbers.

12. **Click** on **Apply Filter**. The Filter dialog box will close, and only records that match the filter will display.

Creating Additional Filters

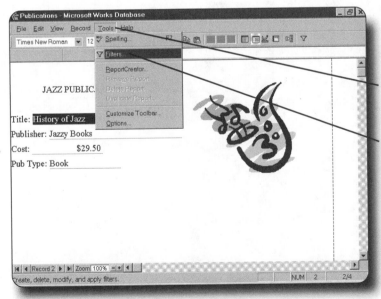

You can create filters in List view or Form view—up to eight in a database.

1. **Click** on **Tools**. The Tools menu will appear.

2. **Click** on **Filters**. The Filter dialog box will open with the last filter you created.

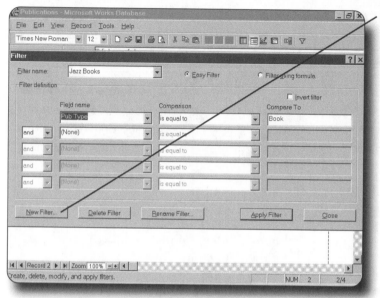

3. Click on **New Filter**. The Filter Name dialog box will open.

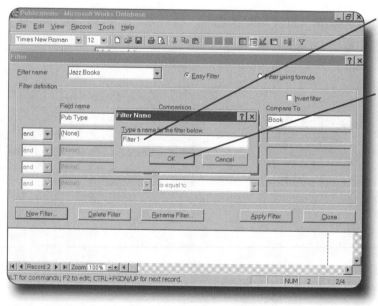

4. Enter a **name** for the new filter. The name will appear in the dialog box.

5. Click on **OK**. The Filter Name dialog box will close.

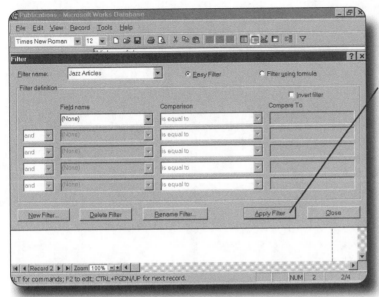

6. Apply the **filter information** as you learned in the previous section.

7. Click on **Apply Filter**. The Filter dialog box will close, and only records that match the filter will display.

Selecting Multiple Filter Criteria

You can define up to five criteria for Works to match. Each additional criterion will use the logical operators AND or OR. For example, you could choose the last name Smith AND they must live in the City of Chicago. This would exclude a person named Smith who lives in San Francisco. If you use OR in the preceding example, the criteria would include anyone named Smith (regardless of where they lived), and it would include anyone who lives in Chicago, regardless of whether their last name was Smith, Jones, Williams, or whatever.

1. Click on **Tools**. The Tools menu will appear.

2. Click on **Filters**. The Filter dialog box will open with the last filter you created.

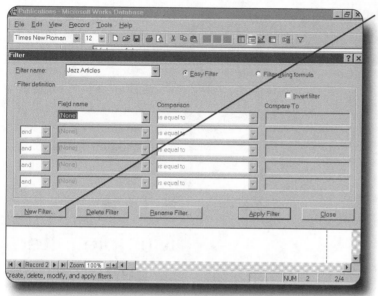

3. Click on **New Filter**. The Filter Name dialog box will open.

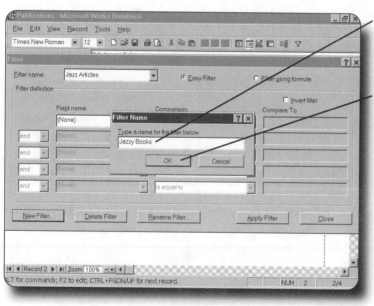

4. Enter a **name** for the new filter. The name will appear in the dialog box.

5. Click on **OK**. The Filter Name dialog box will close.

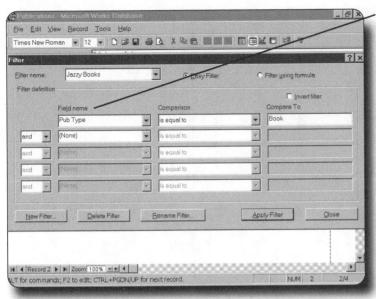

6. Set the **Field name, Comparison, and Compare To information** for the first criterion. The settings will display.

7. Press the **Tab key**. The second criterion line will be highlighted.

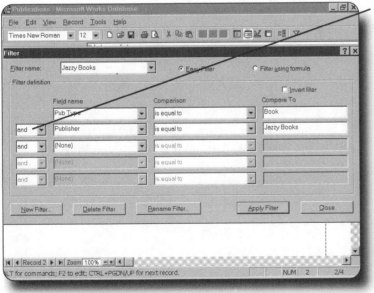

8. Click on **and** or **or** from the and/or drop-down list.

TIP

Choose the AND option to include this criterion as well the previous criterion, or choose the OR option to include *either* this criterion or the previous criterion, but not necessarily both.

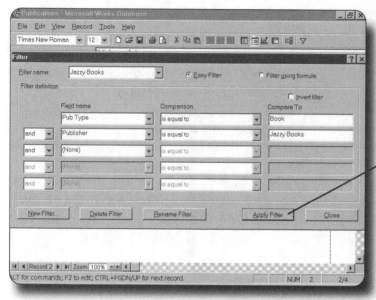

9. **Press** the **Tab key**. The second Field name text box will be highlighted.

10. **Repeat steps 6–8** for each criterion that you want to specify.

11. **Click** on **Apply Filter**. The Filter dialog box will close, and only records that match the filter will display.

Applying a Filter

If you want to reuse a filter that you previously created, Works enables you to select the filter from a list.

NOTE

The figures in this section show the filters from the List view; however, you can apply filters from either List view or Form view.

1. Click on **Record**. The Record menu will appear.

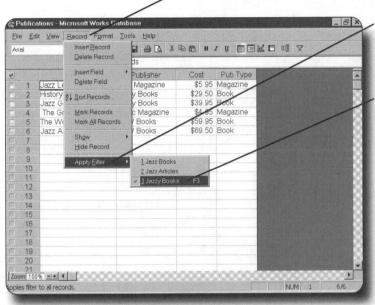

2. Click on **Apply Filter**. The Apply Filter submenu will appear.

3. Click on the **filter name** to apply. The filter will be applied.

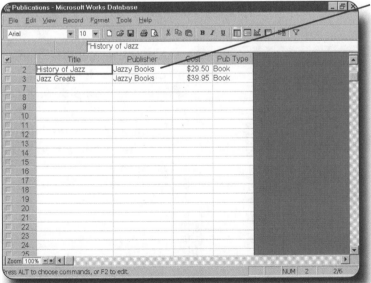

The records that match the filtered criteria will display.

TIP

To redisplay all records, choose Record, Show, All Records from the menu.

Renaming a Filter

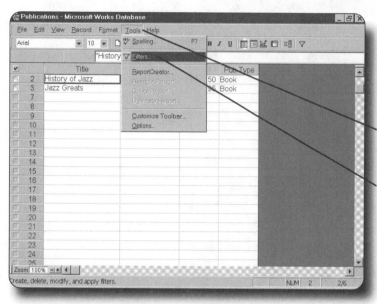

If the name you originally selected for your filter doesn't seem appropriate, rename it. You can rename a filter at any time.

1. Click on **Tools**. The Tools menu will appear.

2. Click on **Filters**. The Filter dialog box will open.

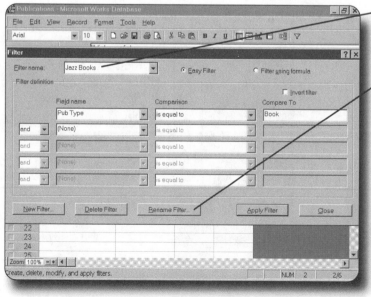

3. Click on the **filter name** you want to change in the Filter name drop-down list.

4. Click on **Rename Filter**. The Filter Name dialog box will open.

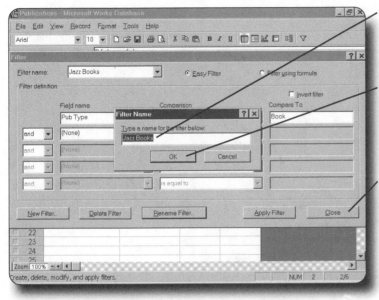

5. Type a **new name** for the filter. The text will appear in the text box.

6. Click on **OK**. The Filter Name dialog box will close, and the filter will be renamed.

7. Click on **Close**. The Filter dialog box will close.

Deleting a Filter

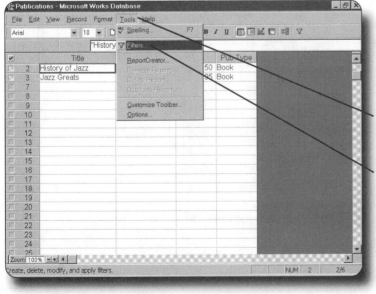

You can easily delete filters. When you delete a filter, you are not deleting any records or fields, only the instructions to filter it.

1. Click on **Tools**. The Tools menu will appear.

2. Click on **Filters**. The Filter dialog box will open.

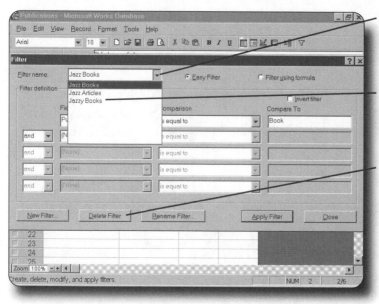

3. **Click** on the **Filter name drop-down arrow**. A list of current filters will appear.

4. **Click** on the **filter name** to be deleted. The filter information will display.

5. **Click** on **Delete Filter**. A confirmation box will open.

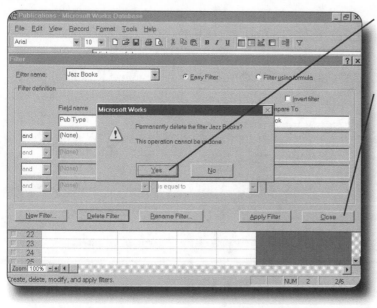

6. **Click** on **Yes**. The filter will be removed from the filter list.

7. **Click** on **Close**. The Filter dialog box will close.

20

Using Reports

Works enables you to decide how to display your printed data by letting you design reports. You can control the format of the report, which fields and records are included, and whether you want totals. In this chapter, you'll learn how to:

- Use the ReportCreator
- Modify reports
- Delete reports
- Print reports

Creating a Report

Reports organize and summarize database information. When you create a report, you specify which fields to print and where on the page to print them. You can also sort and group information as well as include calculations such as totals or averages.

Each database can include up to eight reports.

Using the ReportCreator

Use the ReportCreator to guide you through the creation of a report that you can sort and format.

1. **Click** on **Tools**. The Tools menu will appear.

2. **Click** on **ReportCreator**. The Report Name dialog box will open.

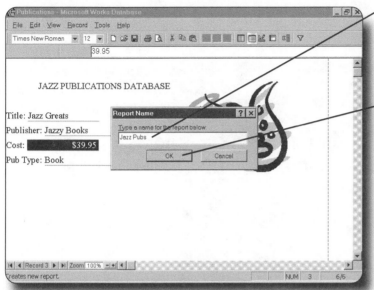

3. Enter a **name** for the report. Report names can be up to 15 characters in length, including spaces.

4. Click on **OK**. The ReportCreator Wizard will open.

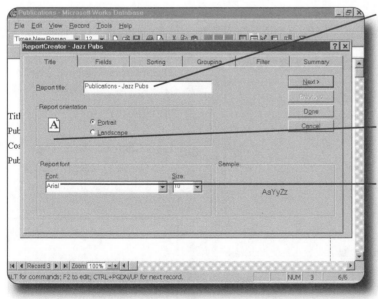

5. Type a **title** for your report in the Report title text box. The title will print on the report and can be up to 255 characters, including spaces.

6. Click on an **orientation**. The option will be selected.

7. Click on a **font** from the Font drop-down list. The font name will display.

8. **Click** on the **Size drop-down arrow**. A list of available font sizes will appear.

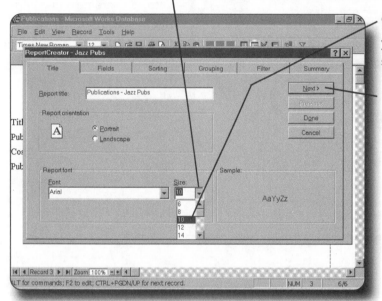

9. **Click** on the **size** that you want for your font. The size will display.

10. **Click** on **Next**. The Fields tab will display.

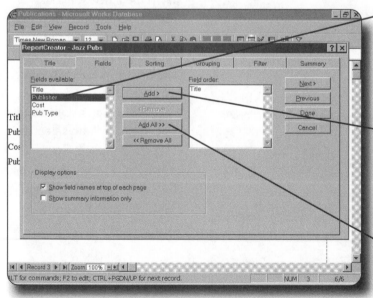

11. **Click** on the **first field name** that you want to display in the report. The field name will be highlighted.

12. **Click** on **Add**. The field name will be added to the Field order list.

TIP

To include all database fields in your report, click on Add All.

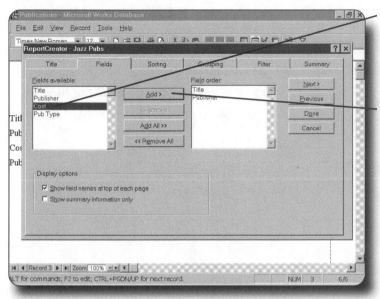

13. Click on the **next field name** to include in the report. The field name will be highlighted.

14. Click on **Add**. The field name will be added to the Field order list.

15. Repeat steps 13 and **14** for each field to be included in the report.

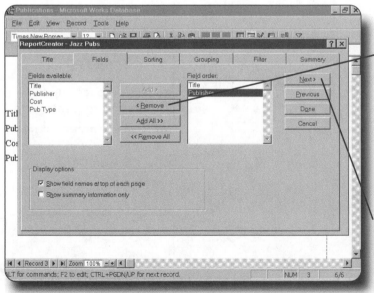

TIP

To remove a field from the report, click on the field name in the Field order list, and then click on Remove. The field is only removed from the report, not from the database.

16. Click on **Next**. The Sorting tab will display.

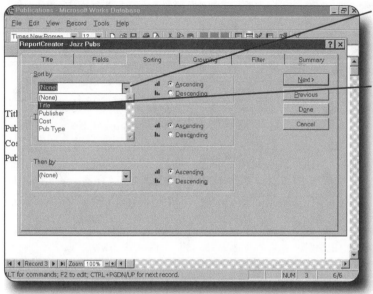

17. **Click** on the **Sort by drop-down arrow**. A list of field names will appear.

18. **Click** on the **field** to sort by. The field name will appear.

19. **Click** on **Ascending** or **Descending**. The option will be selected.

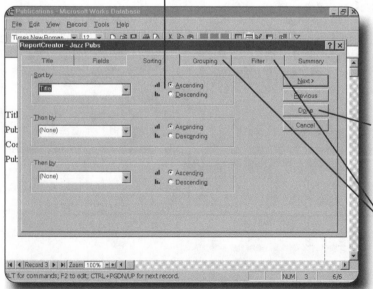

NOTE

You can specify up to three sort requests.

20. **Click** on **Done**. A message box will appear.

TIP

You can also continue to the Grouping and Filter tabs to set more advanced report options.

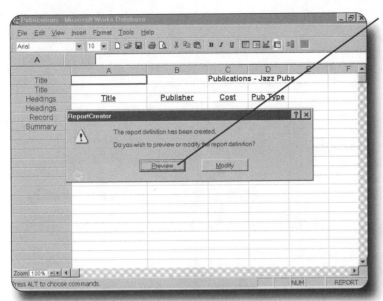

21. Click on **Preview**. The report will display with the data as specified.

TIP

Click the mouse on the report to zoom in and take a closer look.

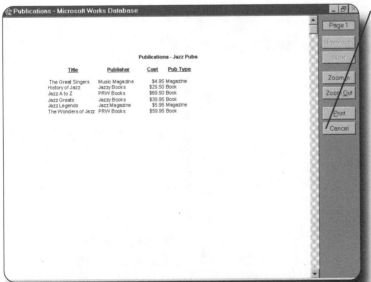

22. Click on **Cancel**. The report will display in Report view.

TIP

You can also click on Print to print the report.

You can later modify your report in this view.

Creating Summary Reports

Let a Works report summarize your data with totals, averages, or other statistical information.

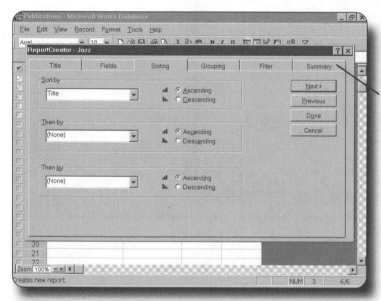

1. Create a **report** following steps 1 through 20 of the previous section.

2. Click on the **Summary tab**. The tab will display.

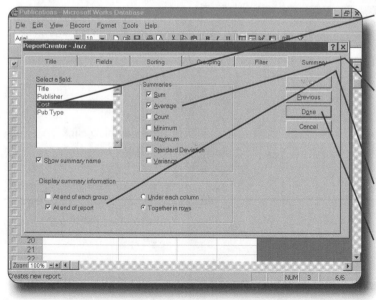

3. Click on the **field name** to summarize by. The field name will be highlighted.

4. Click on the **summary types** that you want in your report. Selected options will display a check mark ✔.

5. Click on a **location** for the summary information.

6. Click on **Done**. A message box will appear.

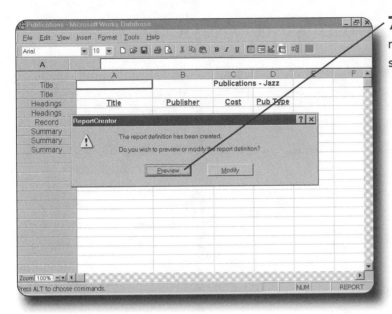

7. Click on **Preview**. The report will appear with the specified data.

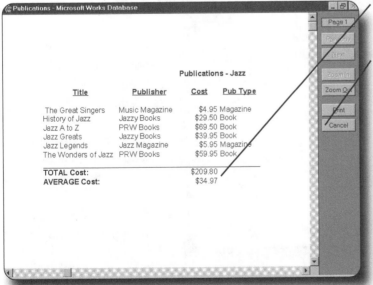

The summarized fields display.

8. Click on **Cancel**. The report will display in Report view.

TIP

You can also click on Print to print the report.

Modifying a Report

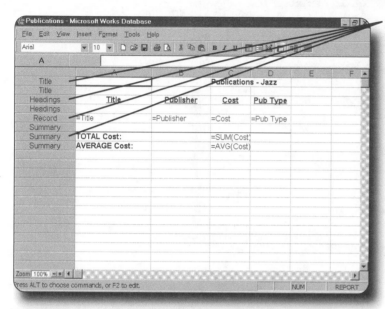

You might want to modify the appearance of the report data. Working in Report view is similar to working with a Works spreadsheet except that instead of row numbers, the rows are named with the type of data to display, such as a title, headings, record, or summary. This record band is where the records in your database will display in an actual report.

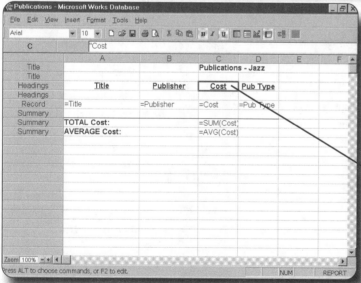

Editing Report Column Headings

By default, each column in a report displays with the field name, which you can easily edit.

1. Click on the **heading** that you want to modify. The cell will be selected.

2. Type a **new heading**. The new text will appear.

3. Press Enter. The new heading will replace the old heading. The field heading in the database will remain the same; only the heading for the report will be changed.

Changing Column Width

Use your mouse to widen a column. A line located at the right edge of each column heading divides the columns. Use this line to change the column width.

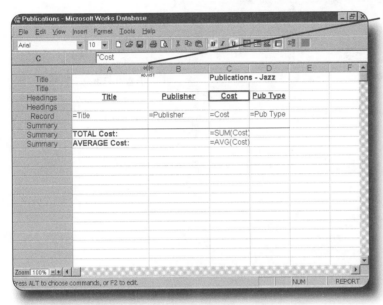

1. Position the **mouse pointer** on the right-hand column line for the field that you want to change. The mouse pointer will become a double-headed white arrow with the word "ADJUST" displayed under it.

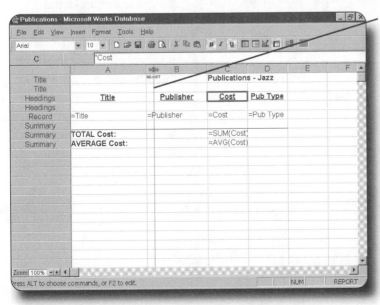

2. Press and **hold** the **mouse button** and **drag** the column line. If you drag it to the right, the column width will increase; if you drag it to the left, the column width will decrease.

3. Release the **mouse button**. The column width will be changed.

Increasing Row Height

Add more room between each record in your report by increasing row height.

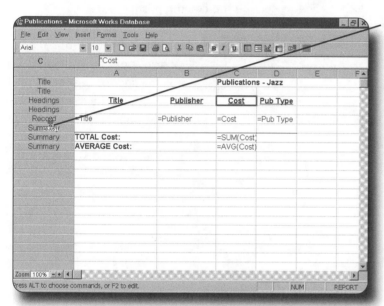

1. Position the **mouse pointer** on the lower row line for the row that you want to change. The mouse pointer will become a double-headed white arrow with the word "ADJUST" displayed under it.

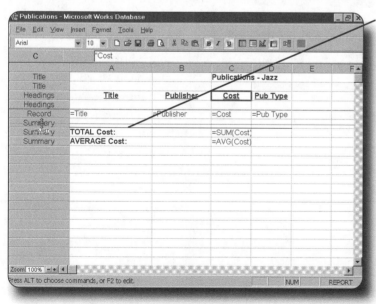

2. Press and **hold** the **mouse button** and **drag** the row line. If you drag it down, the row height will increase; if you drag it up, the row height will decrease.

3. Release the **mouse button**. The row height will be changed.

Modifying Alignment

Change the alignment of any field column, row, or individual field data.

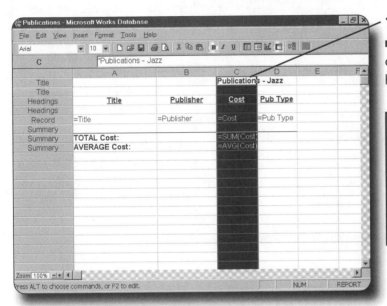

1. **Click** on a **field column, row, or cell** to modify. The column, row, or cell will be highlighted.

NOTE

To select an entire row, click on the row description; to select an entire column, click on the column letter.

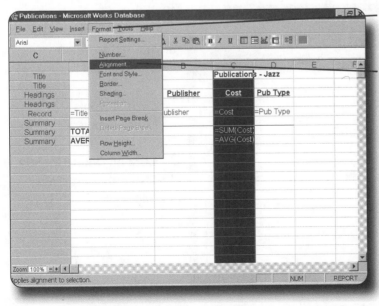

2. **Click** on **Format**. The Format menu will appear.

3. **Click** on **Alignment**. The Format dialog box will open with the Alignment tab in front.

4. Click on an **Alignment** option. The option will be selected.

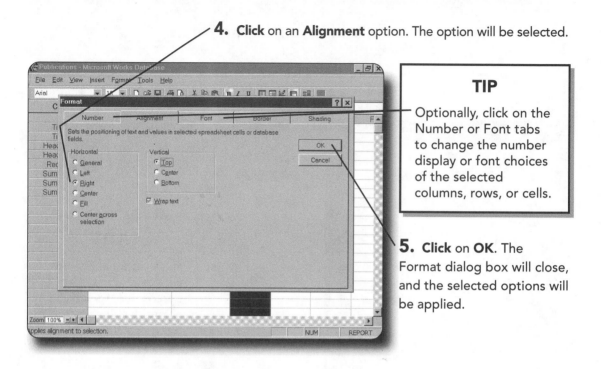

TIP

Optionally, click on the Number or Font tabs to change the number display or font choices of the selected columns, rows, or cells.

5. Click on **OK**. The Format dialog box will close, and the selected options will be applied.

Deleting a Report

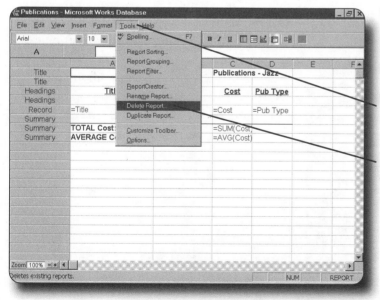

Works has a limit of eight reports per database. You might need to delete unwanted or old reports.

1. Click on **Tools**. The Tools menu will appear.

2. Click on **Delete Report**. The Delete Report dialog box will open.

3. Click on the **report name** to delete. The report name will be highlighted.

4. Click on **Delete.**

5. Click on **OK**. A confirmation message will appear.

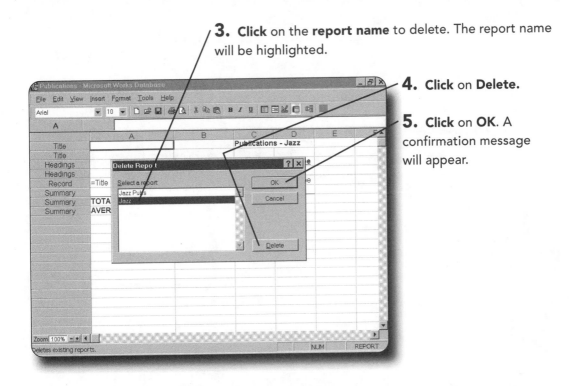

6. Click on **OK**. The report will be deleted.

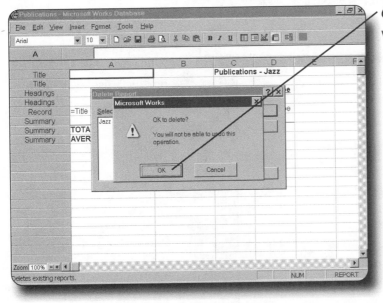

Previewing a Report

Before you print a report, you can preview it first and then make additional modifications if desired.

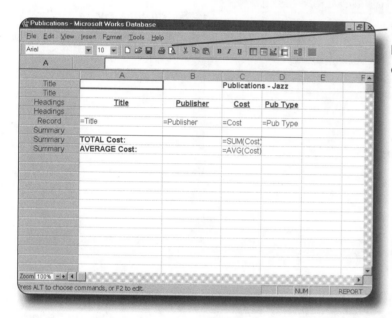

1. **Click** on the **Print Preview button**. The complete report will appear.

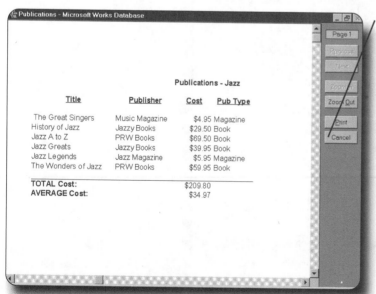

2. **Click** on **Cancel**. The report will display in Report view again.

Printing a Report

Print a hard copy of your report for your files or to distribute to others.

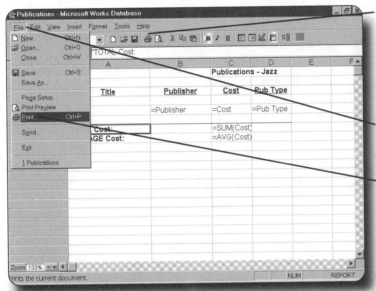

1a. **Click** on the **Print button**. The report will print with standard options.

OR

1b. **Click** on **File**. The File menu will appear.

2. **Click** on **Print**. The Print dialog box will open.

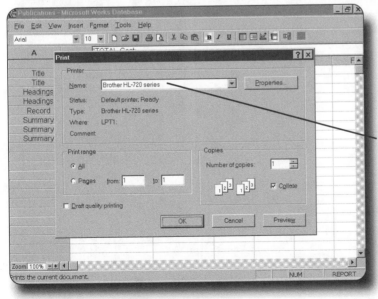

Many options are available from the Print dialog box.

3. **Click** on any desired **option**. The option will be activated.

- **Printer name**. If you are connected to more than one printer, you can choose the name of the printer to use for this print job. Click on the Name drop-down arrow and make a selection.

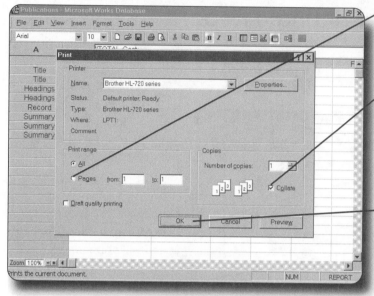

• **Print range**. Choose which pages of your report to print in the Print range group box.

• **Copies**. Choose the number of copies to print by clicking on the up/down arrows in the Number of copies box.

4. Click on **OK** after you have made your selections. The report will print to your printer.

Part IV Review Questions

1. In a database, what is a record? *See "Understanding Fields and Records" in Chapter 16*

2. What view must be active to change the design of a form? *See "Looking at the Different Views" in Chapter 16*

3. How many records are displayed when using Form View? *See "Entering Data in Form View" in Chapter 17*

4. How many ways can records be sorted? *See "Sorting Records" in Chapter 17*

5. What is the maximum size of a field? *See "Changing Field Size by Using the Menu" in Chapter 18*

6. When adding graphics to a database, on what records will the graphic display? *See "Adding Artwork to a Database" in Chapter 18*

7. How many filters can a database have? *See "Creating Additional Filters" in Chapter 19*

8. What do reports do to database information? *See "Creating a Report" in Chapter 20*

9. What feature does Works provide to assist you in creating a report? *See "Using the ReportCreator" in Chapter 20*

10. How can a report summarize your data? *See "Creating Summary Reports" in Chapter 20*

PART V

Managing Your Finances with Money

21

Getting Started with Money

Works Suite includes the Standard edition of Microsoft Money 2001, a powerful personal financial-management system. With Money, you can enter and track your income and expenses, track your investments, budget, plan for your financial future, estimate taxes, and much more. In this chapter, you'll learn how to:

- Set up your finances with the Setup Assistant
- Navigate Money
- Back up your data files

Exploring What You Can Do with Money

Money is a powerful, yet flexible program that enables you to track your finances whether you have an extensive portfolio of investments or are just getting started and have few assets—for now. Before you actually set up Money, you should first gather the latest statements from all your accounts (bank, credit card, investment, loan, and others) and then study them to get a clear understanding of your current financial picture. You'll need these documents during the setup process.

Opening Money

You can open Money from the Works Task Launcher.

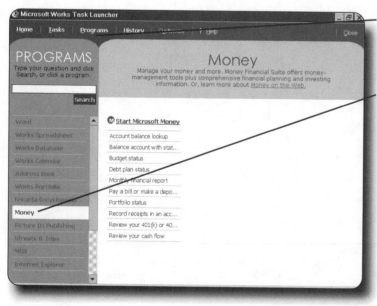

1. Click on **Programs.** A list of Works Suite programs will appear.

2. Click on **Money.** A list of Money tasks will appear.

3. Click on **Start Microsoft Money.** The initial Money screen will appear.

NOTE

After you set up Microsoft Money for the first time, the Your Money Home Page displays when you click on Start Microsoft Money rather than the initial screen.

Using the Money Setup Assistant

1. Click on **Start Here.** The Money Setup Assistant will open.

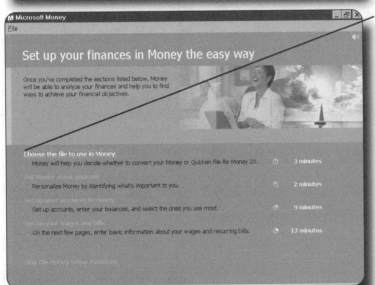

2. Click on **Choose the file to use in Money.** The next step in the Money Setup Assistant will appear.

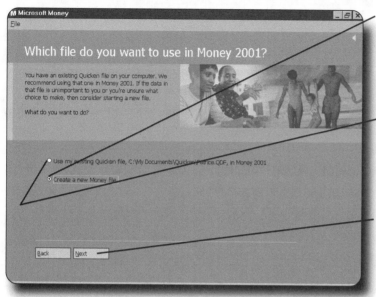

3. Click on **Create a new Money file.**

TIP

If you currently use Quicken, Money can find your Quicken file and convert it for you.

4. Click on **Next.** The Money Setup Assistant will display again.

Entering Personal Information

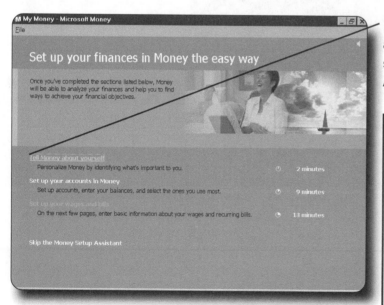

1. Click on **Tell Money about yourself.** The next step in the Money Setup Assistant will appear.

TIP

Because there are numerous options from which to choose when setting up Money, the scenario this book uses to illustrate setup most likely won't exactly match your personal situation. Be sure to view all options and choose those that reflect your needs.

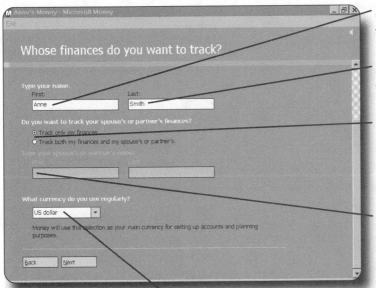

2. **Enter** your **first name** in the First text box.

3. **Enter** your **last name** in the Last text box.

4. **Choose** to **track** either your own finances or the joint finances of you and your spouse/partner.

You'll need to enter your spouse/partner's name if you choose the second option.

5. **Click** on a **currency** from the currency drop-down list. US dollar is the default.

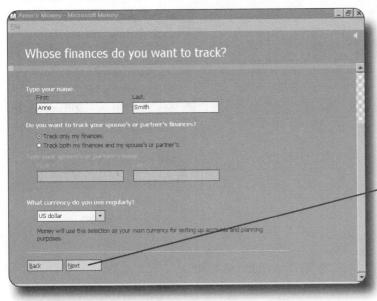

TIP

Throughout the Money Setup Assistant, you might need to scroll down to view additional options and buttons.

6. **Click** on **Next.** Money will ask you about your financial priorities.

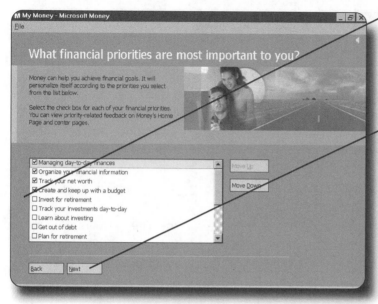

7. Click on the **financial goals** that are priorities. Money will customize based on your answers to these questions.

8. Click on **Next.** Money will ask about your Internet connection.

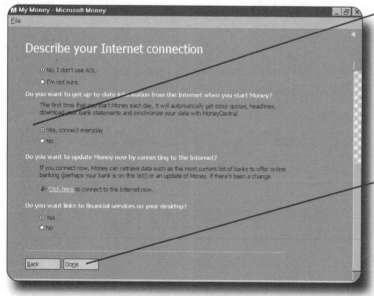

9. Answer the **questions about your Internet connection** and what Internet options you want to set. Chapter 32, "Connecting to the Internet" covers this topic in more detail.

10. Click on **Done.** The Money Setup Assistant initial screen will appear again.

Setting Up Your Accounts

Next, you can start setting up actual accounts, such as a bank checking or savings account.

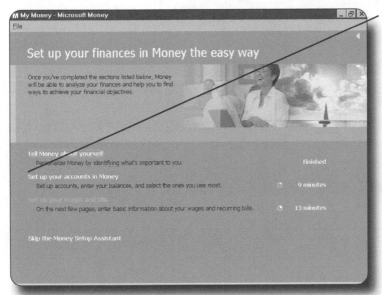

1. Click on **Set up your accounts in Money.** Money will proceed to the next step.

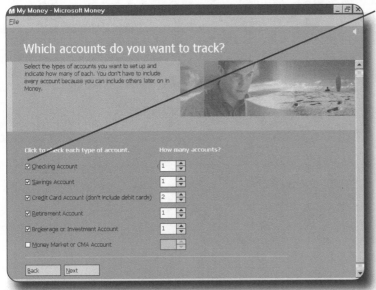

2. Click on each **type of account** you have. Options include

- Checking accounts

- Savings accounts

- Credit-card accounts

- Retirement accounts

- Brokerage or investment accounts

- Money market or CMA accounts

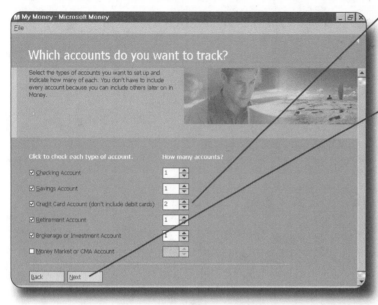

3. Click on the **number of accounts** you have for each type selected using the up/down arrows.

4. Click on **Next.**

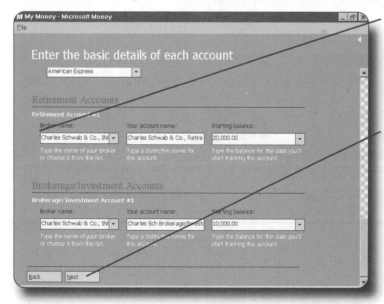

5. Enter basic **information about each account** you specified. You'll need to know account names, numbers, and balances.

6. Click on **Next.**

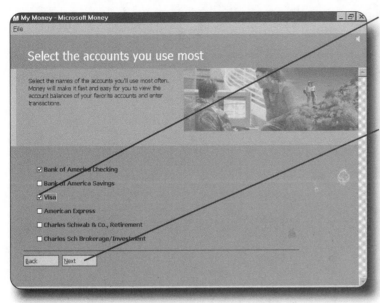

7. Click on the **accounts you use most.** Money will make it easier for you to view information about these favorite accounts.

8. Click on **Next.** Money will ask you to verify what you've entered.

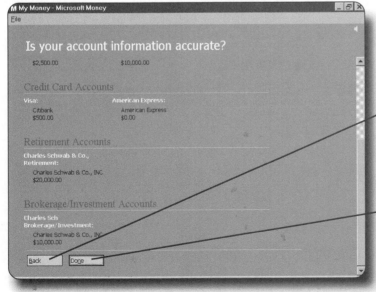

9. Verify that your **account information** is accurate.

TIP

If your information isn't accurate, click on Back to revise your entries and selections.

10. Click on **Done.** Money will display a warning dialog box asking if you're sure you're done setting up accounts. You can always modify account information later, but it's easier to set things up using the Money Setup Assistant when you start.

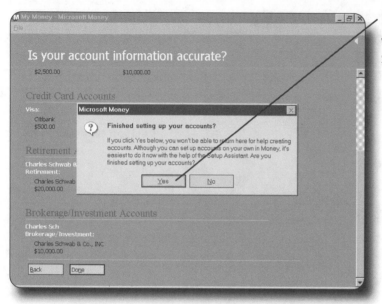

11. Click on **Yes.** Money will return to the initial Money Setup Assistant screen.

Setting Up Your Paycheck and Bills

You can also set up Money to track your paycheck and bills.

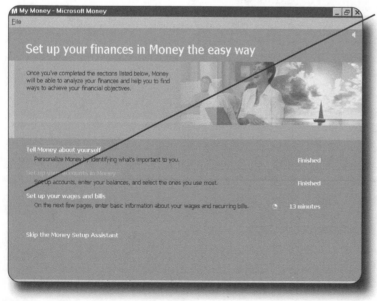

1. Click on **Set up your wages and bills.** The next step of the assistant will appear.

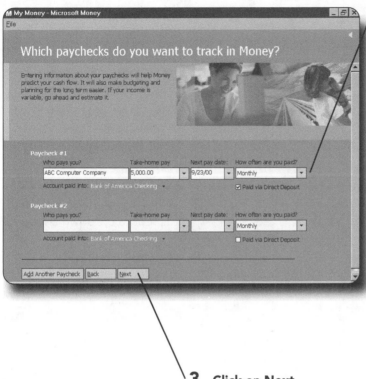

2. Enter information about your paycheck including

- Who pays you

- Your take-home pay

- Your next pay date

- How often you're paid

- Where to deposit your pay

- Whether you use direct deposit

Your company payslip should provide all the required information, so be sure to have it handy during this step.

3. Click on **Next.**

TIP

Click on Add Another Paycheck if there are more than two wage earners in your family or if you have more than one job.

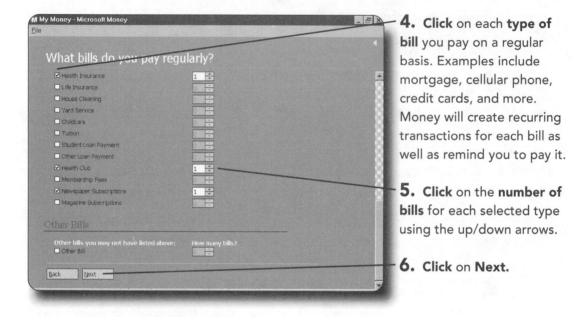

4. Click on each **type of bill** you pay on a regular basis. Examples include mortgage, cellular phone, credit cards, and more. Money will create recurring transactions for each bill as well as remind you to pay it.

5. Click on the **number of bills** for each selected type using the up/down arrows.

6. Click on **Next.**

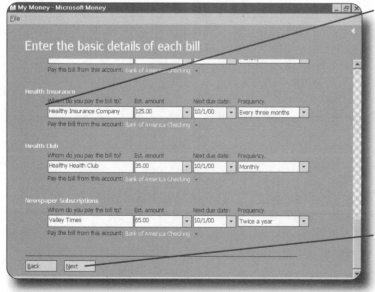

7. **Enter details** for each bill you selected in the last step including the

- Payee

- Amount

- Due date

- Frequency

- Account paid from

8. Click on **Next.** Money will ask you to verify what you've entered.

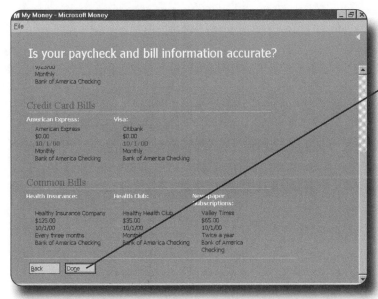

9. Verify that your **paycheck and bill information** is accurate.

10. Click on **Done.** Money will display a warning dialog box asking if you're sure you're finished setting up your pay and bills.

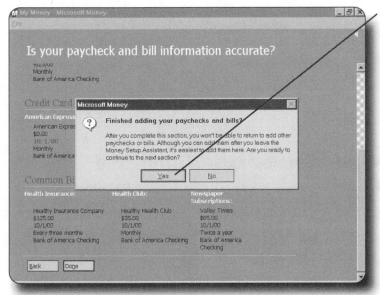

11. Click on **Yes.** Money will return to the initial Money Setup Assistant screen.

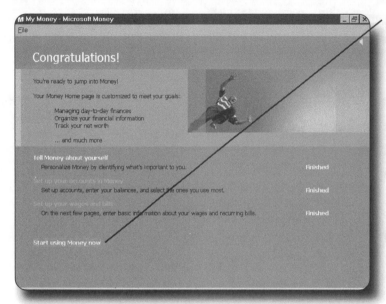

12. **Click** on **Start using Money now.** The Your Money Home Page will display.

Navigating Money

Money offers an intuitive navigation system that is similar to other Windows programs, with an emphasis on menus and links for navigation. There are several ways you can use and navigate Money:

- **Home Page.** The Your Money Home Page is the most frequent starting point for Money. From this home page, you have access to the most commonly used Money features. For example, you can

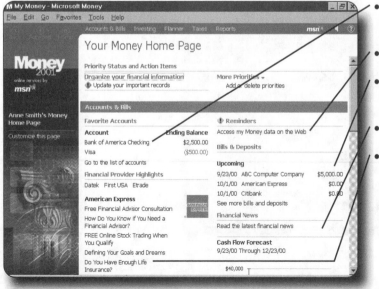

- Open the register for your favorite accounts

- View reminders

- Handle upcoming bills and deposits

- Read financial news

- Access financial information on the Web

You can also access information about your investments, plan your financial future, and analyze your tax situation from this page.

- **Money centers.** Money offers several centers, similar to Your Home Page, that provide details about a special financial activity such as accounts, investing, taxes, and your house as well as links to related information both within Money and on the Web.

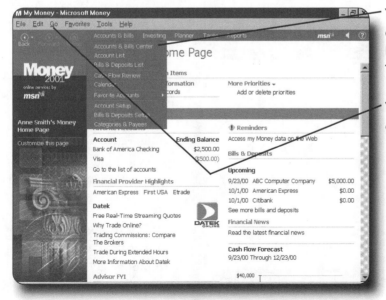

You can access Money centers from the Accounts & Bills, Investing, Planner, and Taxes menus.

You can also access money centers from the Go menu.

- **Buttons.** Money includes Back, Forward, and Home buttons in the upper left corner of the screen that help you return to previous tasks and then go forward again. The Home button takes you to Your Home Page.

Getting Help with Money

The Money Help menu provides several options for getting help with using Money. You can click on one of several menu choices:

- **Help Topics.** Displays a Help window, common to most Windows applications.

- **Online Guide to Money.** Opens the Online Guide to Money 2001, which provides further explanation on how to use this program.

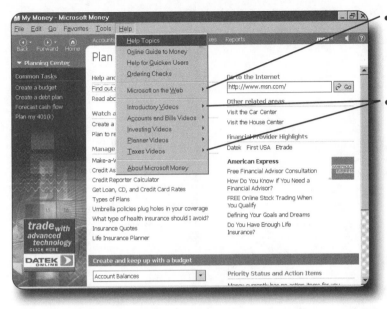

- **Microsoft on the Web.** Displays a submenu that links you to several areas on Microsoft's Web site.

- **Introductory, Accounts and Bills, Investing, Planner, and Taxes Videos.** Links you to educational videos on a variety of financial topics.

Exiting Money

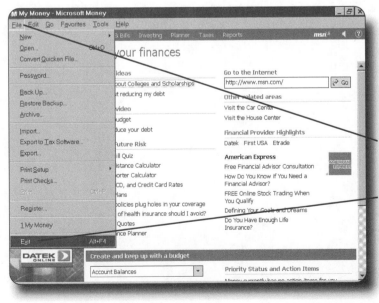

When you're finished with Money, you need to exit the program. You'll also want to back up your Money file, just in case it ever becomes damaged or corrupted.

1. **Click** on **File.** The File menu will appear.

2. **Click** on **Exit.** The Backup to Floppy dialog box will open.

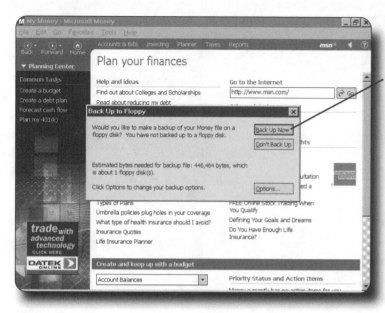

3. **Place** a **floppy disk** into your disk drive.

4. **Click** on **Back Up Now.** Money will compress your data file and back it up to the disk.

In the event something happens to your original data file, you can restore it from this backup.

22

Categorizing Your Financial Activities

Now that you've set up your basic Money file, it's time to prepare to enter data. One of the first steps is to verify that you have an adequate system for categorizing and classifying your transactions. Fortunately, Money already delivers many common categories. All you need to do is modify those that don't exactly suit your needs and add a few of your own. In this chapter, you'll learn how to:

- Understand categories and classifications
- Set up categories and subcategories
- Set up classes and subclasses

Understanding Categorization and Classification

Money enables you to categorize your income and expenses to give you a better understanding of—and more control over—your financial activities. A *category* is basically a type of income or expense, such as Food or Wages. In addition, Money provides several other "layers" of categorization:

- **Subcategory.** A category can contain several subcategories, to even further identify a type of income or expense. For example, under the category Food, you might have subcategories for Dining Out and Groceries.

- **Category Group.** A category group contains several categories and provides a broader way to identify transactions. For example, under the category group of Entertainment, you could include the Leisure and Vacation categories and their subcategories.

- **Classification.** A classification is a further layer of identifying and grouping transactions at a higher level. For example, you might want to identify sets of transactions that include multiple categories such as everything pertaining to a particular family member, a home business, or a rental property.

By using categories, subcategories, and classifications you can more easily

- Determine how much you're spending on what

- Define the sources of various forms of income

- Understand how taxes will affect your finances

- Create and stick to a budget

For convenience, Money already delivers many common categories and subcategories that you can immediately start using. From there, you can customize the program to suit your needs—adding, modifying, and deleting categories and subcategories as needed.

Before you start entering transactions, you should review Money's existing category information, determine whether you need to modify it, and consider any classifications you might want.

Viewing Categories

First, you'll want to view Money's existing categories and subcategories. This will give you a better idea of how categorization works and how well the existing structure suits your financial needs.

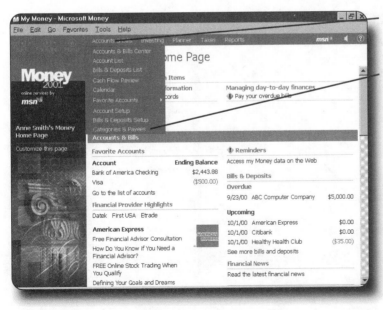

1. **Click** on **Accounts & Bills.** A submenu will appear.

2. **Click** on **Categories & Payees.** The Set up your categories page will appear.

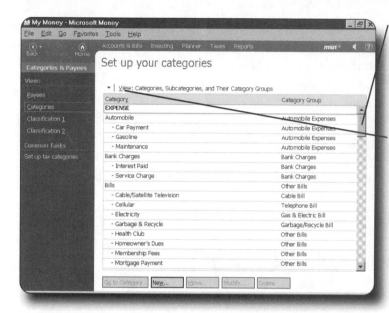

Scroll down the list of categories and subcategories to review what Money automatically delivers.

Click on View to display a menu of viewing options. By default, Money displays categories, subcategories, and their category groups.

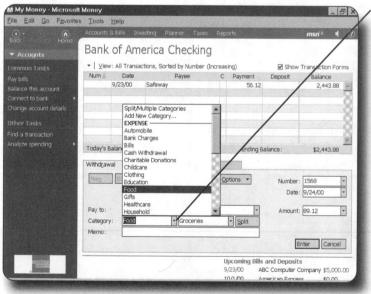

You can assign a category to a transaction in any register. For example, if you enter a transaction for purchases at a grocery store in your checkbook register, you could assign it to the Food category and Groceries subcategory.

Adding a Category

You might decide you want to add a category that doesn't already exist. This is probably the most common category modification you'll make.

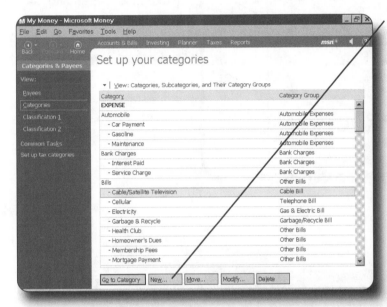

1. Click on **New.** The New Category dialog box will open.

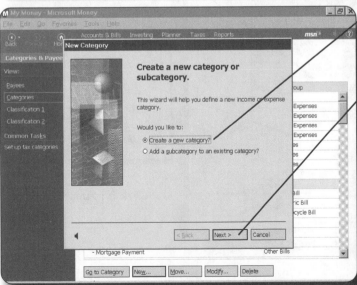

2. Click on **Create a new category**. The option will be selected.

3. Click on **Next.**

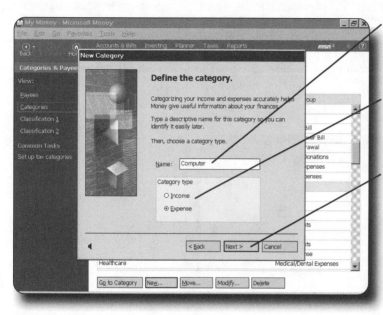

4. Enter a **name** for the category in the Name text box.

5. Click on either **Income** or **Expense**, depending on the type of category this is.

6. Click on **Next**.

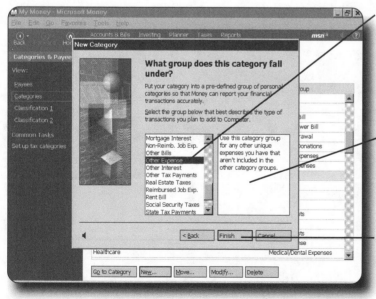

7. Click on the **category group** that best describes your category.

TIP

The box to the right describes each category group in more detail.

8. Click on **Finish**.

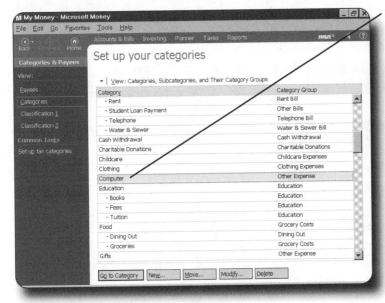

Your new category appears in the list of categories.

Modifying a Category

You might decide you need to change an existing category. For example, you can rename one of the categories Money provides to something else you prefer, such as renaming Clothing to Apparel. You can also change the type of category (such as changing from an income category to an expense category if you made a mistake when you set it up). Be careful, though, about changing category types because Money handles income very differently than an expense and you want to be sure all the reports you create by category are accurate.

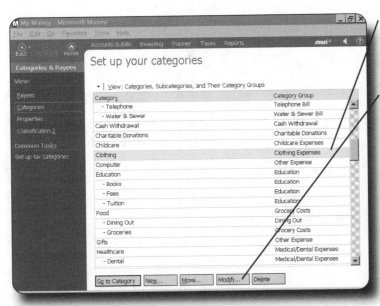

1. Click on the **category** in the list. It will be highlighted.

2. Click on **Modify.** The Modify Category dialog box will open.

3. **Enter** a **new name** for the category in the New name text box.

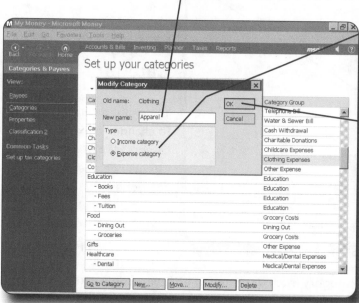

4. **Click** on either **Income category** or **Expense category** if the type of category is changing.

5. **Click** on **OK.** The category will be modified.

Deleting a Category

If you decide that you no longer need a category, you can delete it.

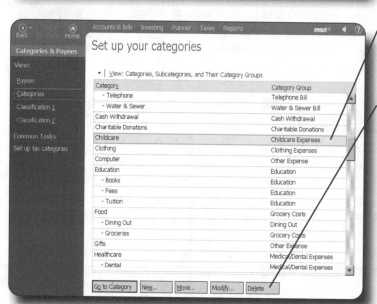

1. **Click** on the **category** you want to delete. It will be highlighted.

2. **Click** on **Delete.** The category will be deleted.

CAUTION

Money immediately deletes a category without a warning notice if you've never assigned the category to a transaction. Undo doesn't work with a deleted category, so if you delete a category by accident, you must add it again.

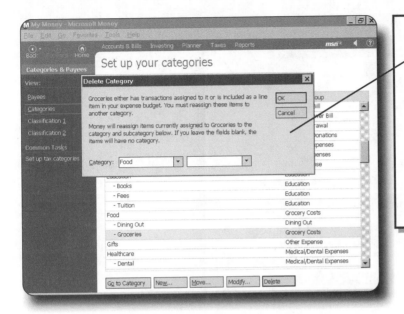

NOTE

If you've already assigned the category you're deleting to transactions in an account register, a warning dialog box will open, prompting you to assign another category to these transactions.

Adding a Subcategory

If you want to further define an existing category, you can add subcategories to it.

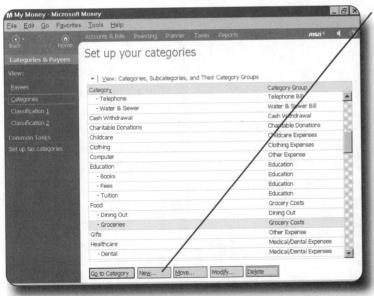

1. Click on **New.** The New Category dialog box will open.

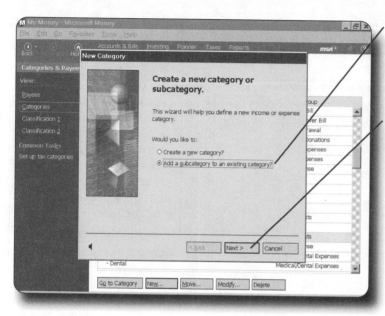

2. **Click** on **Add a subcategory to an existing category?**. The option will be selected.

3. **Click** on **Next**. The next step of the dialog box will appear.

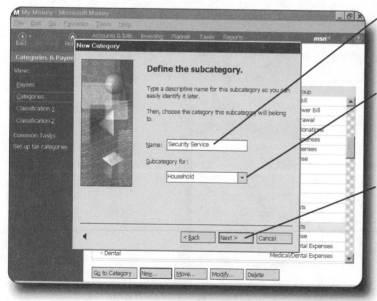

4. **Enter** a **name** for the category in the Name text box.

5. **Click** on the related **category** from the Subcategory for drop-down list.

6. **Click** on **Next**. The next step of the dialog box will appear.

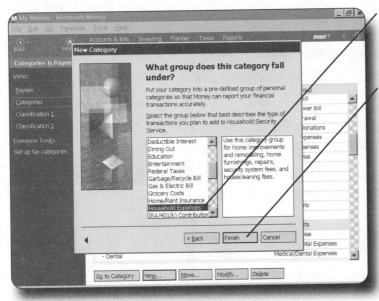

7. **Click** on the **category group** that best describes your category.

8. **Click** on **Finish.** Your new subcategory will appear beneath its master category.

TIP

You can modify and delete subcategories just like you do categories.

Viewing Category and Subcategory Details

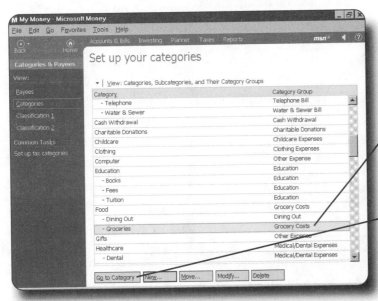

After you create categories and subcategories, you can view and add additional details, such as an abbreviation or related tax information.

1. **Click** on the **category or subcategory** you want to view. It will be highlighted.

2. **Click** on **Go to Category.** The category page for this category or subcategory will open.

On this page, you can

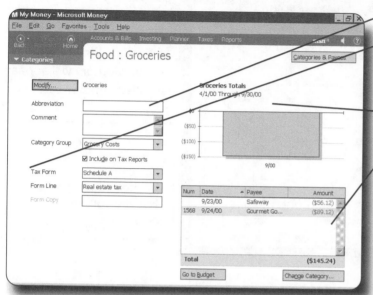

- Enter an abbreviation
- Specify tax information (such as assigning real-estate taxes to Schedule A)
- View a category or subcategory total
- Review recent transactions assigned to this category or subcategory

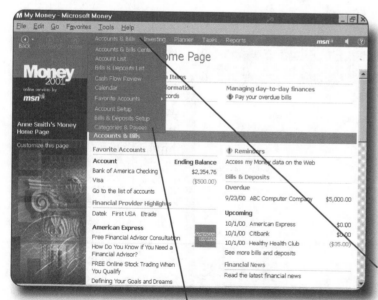

Adding a Classification

You can add up to two different classification types, each of which can include multiple classes and subclasses. Classifications enable you to organize transactions across multiple categories.

1. Click on **Accounts & Bills.** A submenu will appear.

2. Click on **Categories & Payees.** The Set up your categories page will appear.

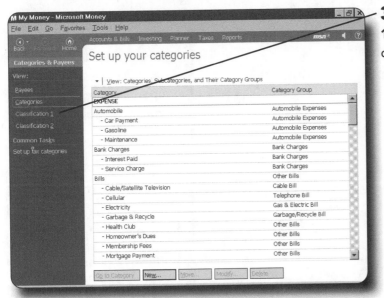

3. Click on **Classification 1.** The Add Classification dialog box will open.

4a. Click on a **type of classification**.

OR

4b. Enter your own **classification type** in the text box.

5. Click on **OK**. A setup page will appear.

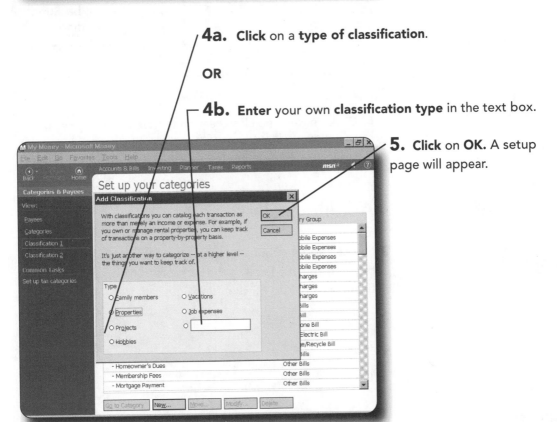

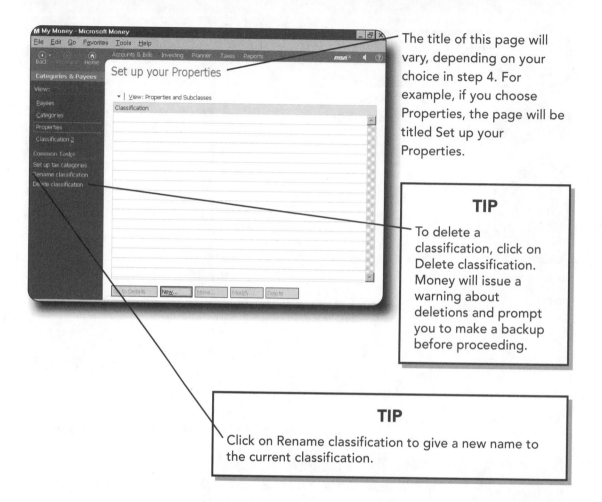

The title of this page will vary, depending on your choice in step 4. For example, if you choose Properties, the page will be titled Set up your Properties.

TIP

To delete a classification, click on Delete classification. Money will issue a warning about deletions and prompt you to make a backup before proceeding.

TIP

Click on Rename classification to give a new name to the current classification.

Adding a Class

You can add multiple classes to a classification, which makes tracking specific family members, properties, or other financial activities much easier.

1. Click on **New.** The New Class or Subclass dialog box will open.

2. Click on **New Class.** The option will be selected.

3. Enter the **name** for your class in the Name text box.

4. Click on **OK.** The class will display in your classification list.

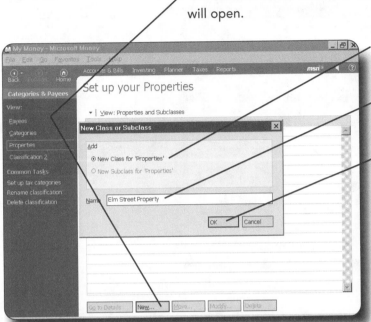

Adding a Subclass

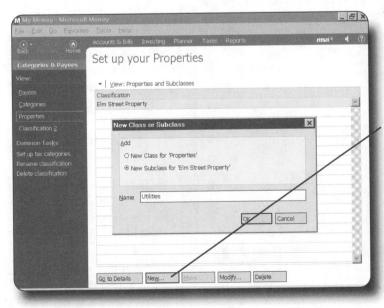

You can further refine classes by creating subclasses beneath them, similar to how you created subcategories of categories.

1. Click on **New.** The New Class or Subclass dialog box will open.

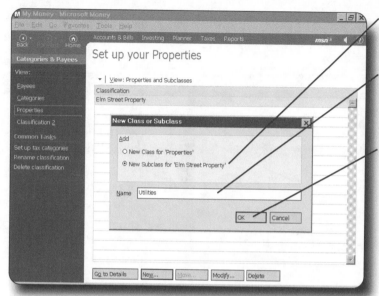

2. **Click** on **New Subclass.** Money will add a subclass.

3. **Enter** the **name** for your subclass in the Name text box.

4. **Click** on **OK.** The dialog box will close.

The subclass now displays in your classification list.

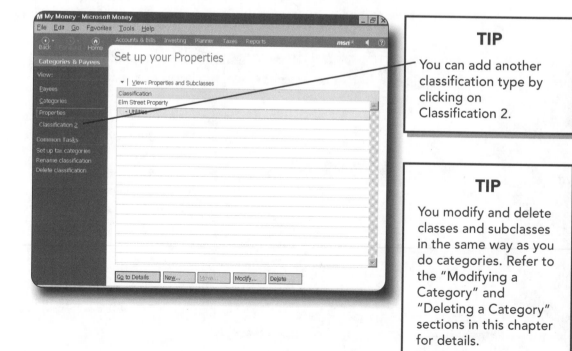

TIP

You can add another classification type by clicking on Classification 2.

TIP

You modify and delete classes and subclasses in the same way as you do categories. Refer to the "Modifying a Category" and "Deleting a Category" sections in this chapter for details.

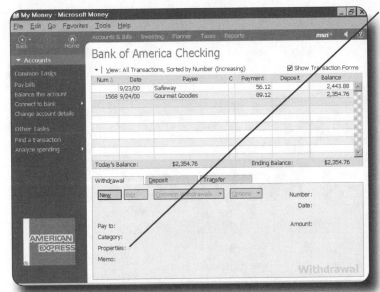

You can now assign your class or subclass to a transaction in any register. Chapter 23, "Recording Your Financial Activity," will show you how to enter transactions.

23

Recording Your Financial Activity

As soon as you set up your accounts and verify the categories and classifications you want to use, you're ready to start entering actual transactions into Money. In this chapter, you'll learn how to:

- Understand and use account registers
- Enter withdrawals, deposits, and transfers
- Create split transactions
- Modify and delete transactions

Using Account Registers

Every Money account you set up has its own account register where you can

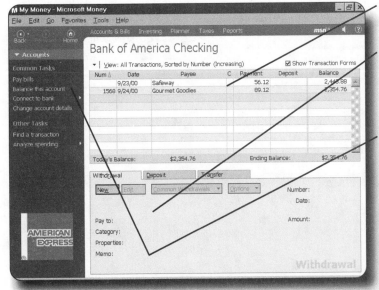

- View transactions for that account

- Enter account transactions such as withdrawals, charges, deposits, and transfers

- Balance (reconcile) your account

Account registers all have a similar look and feel, but vary slightly depending on the type of account—bank, credit card, investment, asset, or loan.

Entering Bank Account Transactions

You can enter bank withdrawals, deposits, and transfers in Money just as you would a paper checkbook register.

Entering a Withdrawal

Entering a bank withdrawal is an easy task with Money's transaction forms.

1a. **Click** on the **name of the bank account** on Your Money Home Page. If you specified this account as a favorite when you set up Money, it will appear under the Favorite Accounts list. Its register will open.

OR

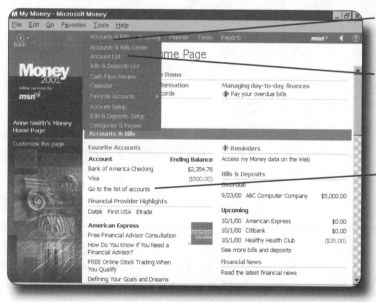

1b. **Click** on **Accounts & Bills.** A submenu will appear.

2. **Click** on **Account List.** The account list will display.

TIP

You can also click on Go to the list of accounts on Your Money Home Page.

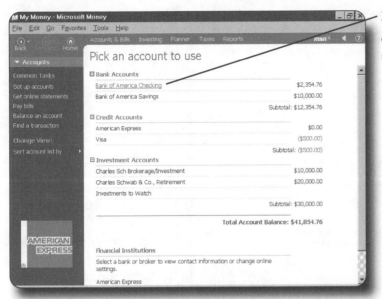

3. Click on the **bank account** you want to use. Its register will open.

4. Click on the **Withdrawal tab** on the transaction form. The tab will display.

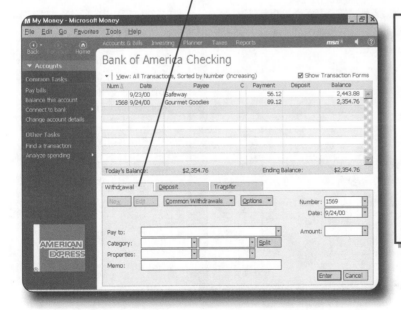

TIP

If you use Money's online banking features, you can download transaction information from your bank without having to enter anything. Chapter 25, "Tracking and Managing Your Money," tells you more about this feature.

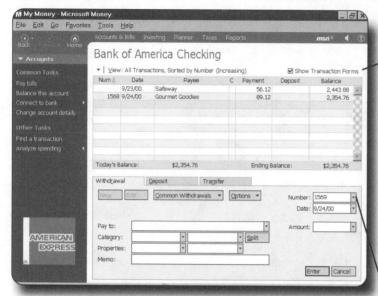

NOTE

You can bypass transaction forms and enter information directly in the register by removing the check in the Show Transaction Forms check box, but it's usually easier to use the forms—particularly if you're new to Money.

5. Enter the **check number** in the Number text box if this withdrawal was made by check. The next consecutive check number will display by default.

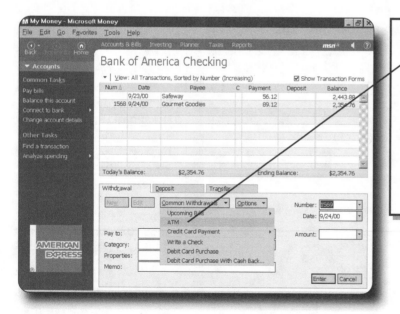

NOTE

If this is for an ATM withdrawal, click on the Common Withdrawals drop-down arrow and choose ATM. Money automatically sets up the form for you to enter an ATM transaction.

6. Click on the **Date drop-down arrow.** A monthly calendar will display.

7. Click on the **date of the withdrawal.** Today's date will display by default.

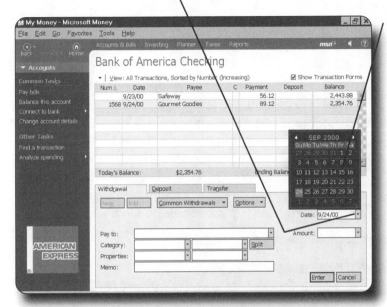

8. Enter the **payee** in the Pay to text box.

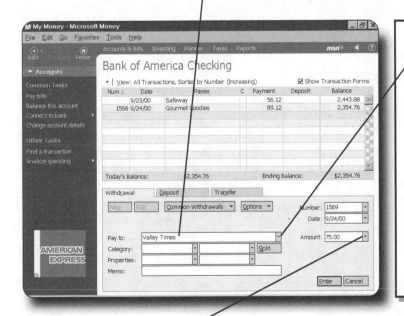

TIP

If you've made payments to this payee before, click on the drop-down arrow and choose the payee from the list. Money automatically enters the amount and category information from your previous payment to this payee, saving you entry time. Be sure to adjust the amount if it isn't the same.

9. Enter an **amount** in the Amount text box.

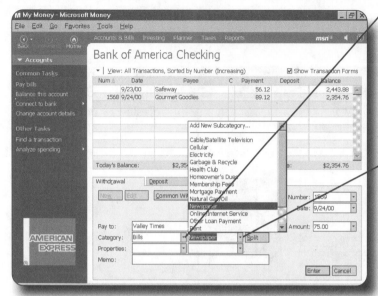

10. **Click** on a **category** to assign this transaction from the Category drop-down list. Chapter 22, "Categorizing Your Financial Activities," covers categories in more detail.

11. Optionally, **click** on a **subcategory** from the second category drop-down list. Only the subcategories related to the category you selected in the previous step will display in this list.

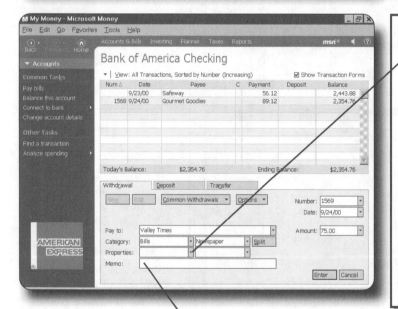

NOTE

If you created classifications, they display beneath the category information. The field titles will match the classification you created. You can then enter optional class and subclass information in the same way you entered category details. Chapter 22 shows you how to set up classifications.

12. Optionally, **enter** a **memo** in the Memo text box.

13. **Click** on **Enter.** The transaction will display in the upper part of the account register.

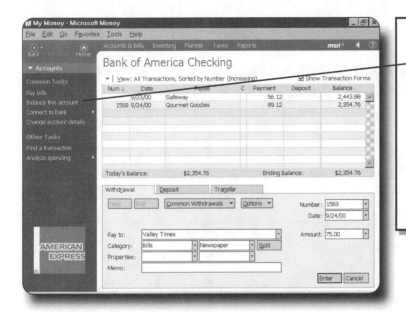

TIP

When you receive your bank statement and have entered all your transactions, you should balance your account. Click on Balance this account and let the wizard guide you through the process.

Entering a Deposit

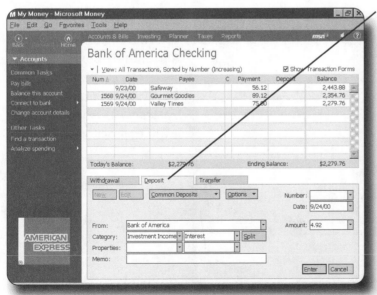

Entering a deposit transaction is nearly identical to entering a withdrawal, except that you click on the Deposit tab instead. From there, enter the person or company who paid you and complete the remaining information on the transaction form.

Entering a Transfer

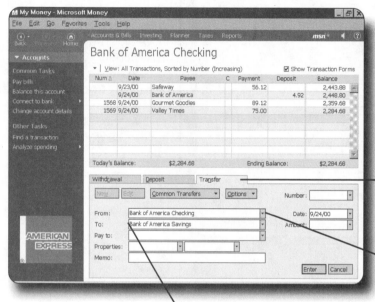

If you transfer funds from one account to another, you can easily record this information in the register.

1. **Follow steps 1–3** in the section "Entering a Withdrawal."

2. **Click** on the **Transfer tab.** The Transfer tab will display.

3. **Click** on the **account you're transferring from** in the From drop-down list.

4. **Click** on the **account you're transferring to** in the To drop-down list.

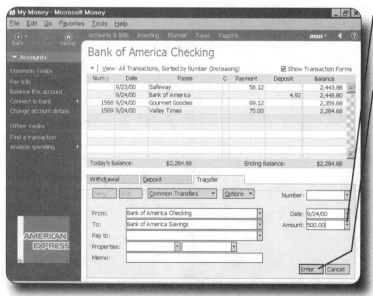

5. **Enter** the **amount you're transferring** in the Amount text box.

6. **Click** on **Enter.** The transfer will display in your list of transactions.

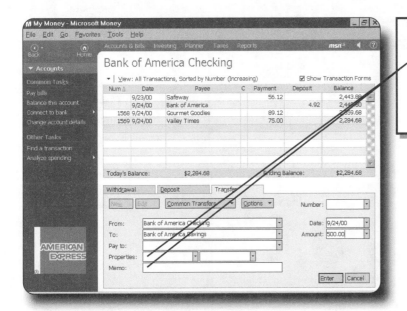

NOTE

If you wish, you can assign a class to this transfer or enter a memo describing it.

Modifying a Recorded Transaction

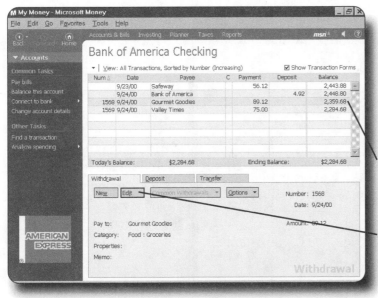

Sometimes you need to modify a transaction you've already entered. For example, you might discover a data entry error, or something about the transaction could change.

1. Click on the **recorded transaction** in the account register.

2. Click on **Edit.** The transaction form will become active.

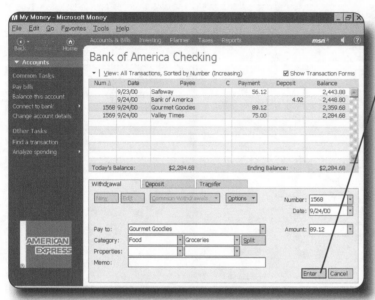

3. **Enter** any **desired changes** in the transaction form.

4. **Click** on **Enter.** Your changes will display in the transaction list.

Deleting a Transaction

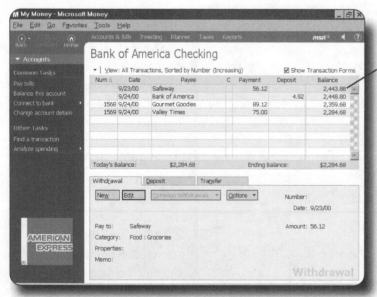

If you enter a transaction by mistake, you can delete it.

1. **Click** on the **recorded transaction** in the account register.

2. **Press** the **Delete key** on your keyboard. Money will open a warning dialog box asking if you're sure about the deletion.

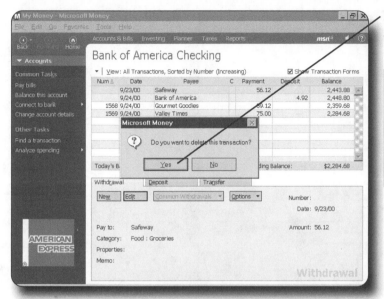

3. Click on **Yes.** The transaction will be deleted.

CAUTION

You can't undo a deletion; instead, you must re-enter a deleted transaction.

Entering Split Transactions

NOTE

In this example, we illustrate a split transaction for a withdrawal, but split transactions can also apply to a deposit.

Categories can greatly enhance your ability to analyze and track your finances, but some transactions apply to more than one category. For example, let's say you went shopping at a superstore and bought $150 worth of merchandise—snacks for the kids, dishes for the house, plants for the yard, sporting goods for your husband, dog food for Fido, and some personal items for yourself. This single transaction could apply to six categories, each of which you want to track. In this case, you can enter a single transaction and apply specified amounts to multiple categories. This is called a *split transaction*.

1. Follow steps 1–9 in the "Entering a Withdrawal" section of this chapter.

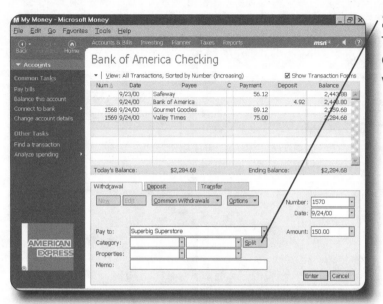

2. **Click** on **Split**. The Transaction with Multiple Categories dialog box will open.

3. **Click** on the **first category** to assign a portion of this transaction from the Category drop-down list.

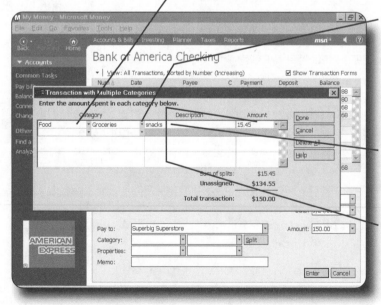

4. Optionally, **click** on a **subcategory** from the second category drop-down list. Only the subcategories related to the category you chose in step 3 will display.

5. Optionally, **enter** a **description** in the Description text box.

6. **Enter** the **amount** to apply to this category.

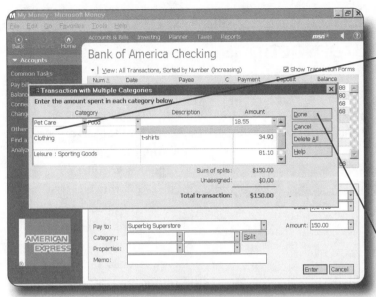

TIP

If you wish, you can assign a class or subclass to each portion on the second line.

7. **Continue** entering **categories and amounts** until you're finished.

8. **Click** on **Done.** The Transaction with Multiple Categories dialog box will close and the account register will display again.

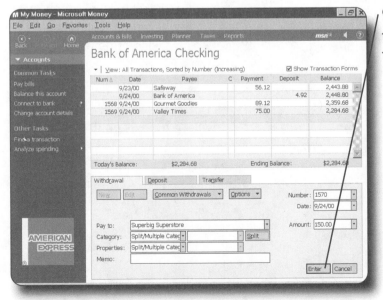

9. **Click** on **Enter.** The transaction will appear in the transaction list.

Entering Credit Card Transactions

You enter credit card transactions in much the same way you do bank account transactions. Money includes a register for each credit card account that looks very similar

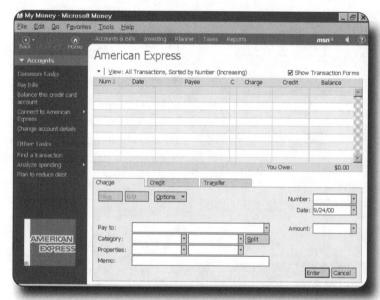

to the bank account registers you just saw. The main difference is that for credit card accounts, you'll enter transactions as charges rather than withdrawals and as credits rather than deposits. You can also download your credit card transactions directly from the Internet if your credit card company supports Microsoft Money. Chapter 25, "Tracking and Managing Your Money," tells you more about online banking options.

24

Working with Checks

Microsoft Money offers the added convenience of printing checks directly from your bank account register onto preformatted printer checks you can buy from Microsoft or other vendors. In this chapter, you'll learn how to:

- Understand checks in Microsoft Money
- Order checks
- Enter checks to print
- Print checks

Understanding Checks

Printing checks to your printer is an optional Money feature. You can also continue to use the checks your bank provides you to write checks by hand.

TIP

If you call 1-800-432-1285 to order Microsoft checks and mention code 20MSWEB, you can save 20% off your first order.

Ordering Checks

Before you can use Money's check-printing feature, you'll need to have checks you can insert in your printer. You can order printer checks directly from Microsoft, but they're also available from many other vendors. Printer checks come in many different styles, colors, and formats, including wallet, voucher, and standard. You can also choose from laser or continuous-feed checks.

1. Click on **Help.** The Help menu will appear.

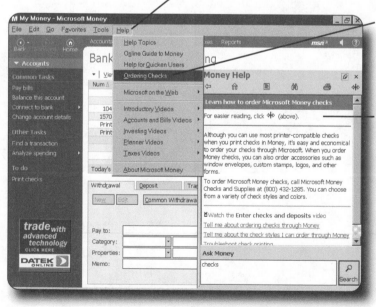

2. Click on **Ordering Checks.** The Help window will open, displaying information about ordering checks.

This window explains the check styles available in more detail, and provides contact information for check ordering.

Entering a Check to Print

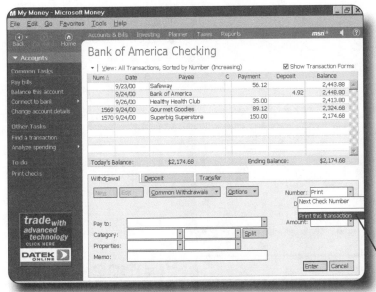

When you enter a transaction in your bank account register, you can specify that you want to print the check rather than write it by hand.

1. Follow steps 1–4 as outlined in "Entering a Withdrawal" in Chapter 23, "Recording Your Financial Activities."

2. Click on **Print this transaction** from the Number drop-down list.

3. Continue with **steps 6–13** as outlined in "Entering a Withdrawal" in Chapter 23.

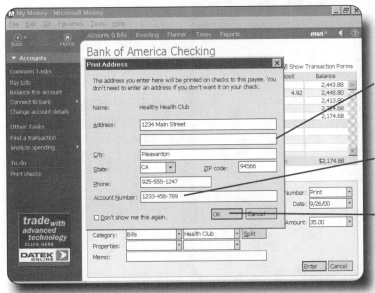

When you press Enter, the Print Address dialog box will open.

4. Enter the payee's **address information** in the appropriate text boxes.

5. Enter your **account number** with this payee.

6. Click on **OK.** The Print Address dialog box will close.

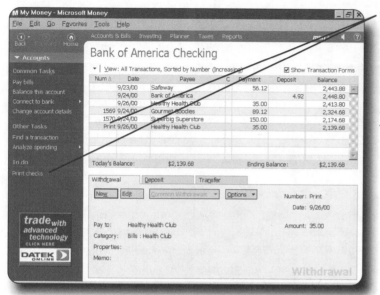

The word "Print" now appears in the Number column in the upper portion of the account register. In addition, the option to print checks displays in your To Do list.

TIP

Before continuing with the check-printing process, but sure that you understand the exact type of checks you have and how they work with your printer.

Printing Checks

After you've entered checks to print in the register, you can print them singly or in a group. There are numerous options for printing checks, but in this example, we'll use the defaults to print all available checks.

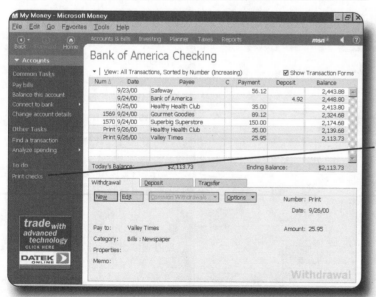

1. Click on **Print checks.** The Print Checks dialog box will open.

The dialog box indicates how many checks you have ready to print.

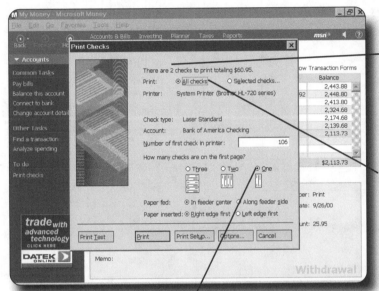

TIP

You can also open the Print Checks dialog box by choosing File, Print Checks from the main menu.

2. **Click** on **All Checks.** The check-printing process will prepare to print all checks.

3. **Enter** the **number** to display on the first check in the printer.

4. **Click** on the **number of checks** on the first page. This will vary depending on the type of printer checks you use.

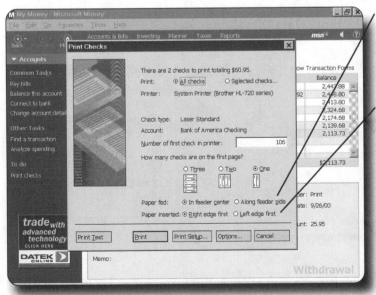

5. **Click** on a **paper-feed option**—either in the feeder center or along the feeder side.

6. **Click** on the **option** that matches how you insert paper in your printer—with either the right or left edge first.

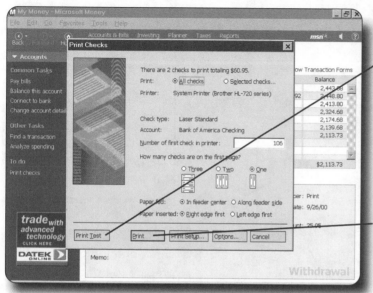

TIP

Click on Print Test to print a sample to the printer before inserting your actual checks. This will help you determine if your printer settings are correct without wasting checks.

7. Click on **Print.** The Print Checks dialog box will display a printer status message.

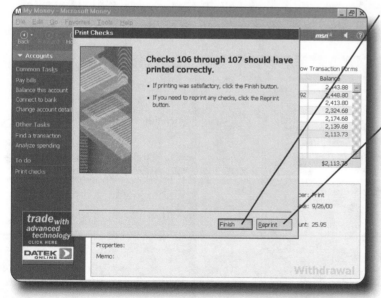

8. Click on **Finish.** The dialog box will close.

TIP

If the checks didn't print properly, click on Reprint to print them again. The Select Checks to Reprint dialog box opens and you can choose the checks you want to reprint.

Printing Selected Checks

Sometimes you might want to print only selected checks instead of all the checks available to print.

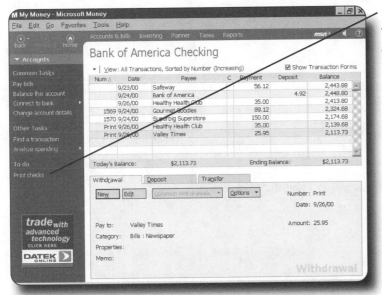

1. Click on **Print checks.** The Print Checks dialog box will open.

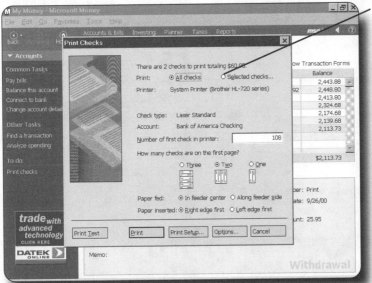

2. Click on **Selected checks**. The Select Checks dialog box will open.

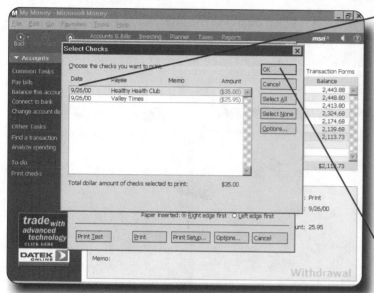

3. Click on the **specific checks** you want to print. They will be highlighted.

TIP

If you change your mind about a check you've selected, click on it again to deselect it.

4. Click on **OK**. The dialog box will close and you will return to the Print Checks dialog box.

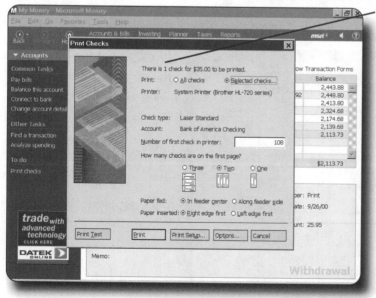

The total number of checks you've selected to print now appear in the Print Checks dialog box.

5. Continue with **steps 3–8** in the section "Printing Checks" earlier in this chapter.

Setting Up Print Options

If you want, you can change the default values for printing checks, such as printing to a different printer or changing the check style.

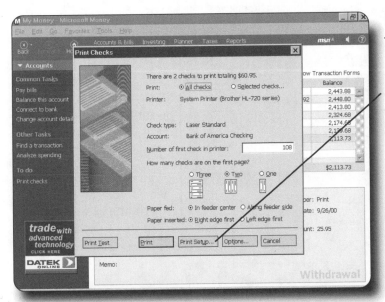

1. **Follow steps 1–6** in the previous section, "Printing Checks."

2. **Click** on **Print Setup**. The Check Setup dialog box will open.

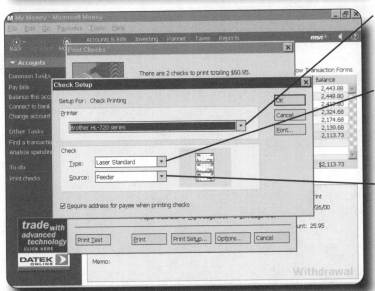

3. **Click** on the **printer** to which you want to print in the Printer drop-down list.

4. **Click** on the **type of checks**—standard, voucher, wallet, and so on—from the Type drop-down list.

5. **Click** on the **check source**—either feeder or manual—from the Source drop-down list.

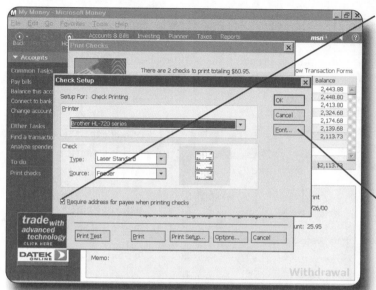

6. **Click** on the **Require address for payee when printing checks check box** to remove the check mark, entered by default, if you don't want to print payee addresses on your checks.

TIP

Click on Font if you want to change the font that displays on your printed checks. The Check Printing Font dialog box opens, where you can choose the font and size to print.

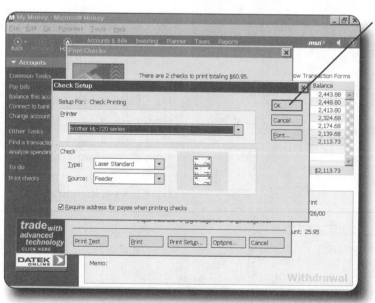

7. **Click** on **OK.** The Check Setup dialog box will close and you will return to the Print Checks dialog box.

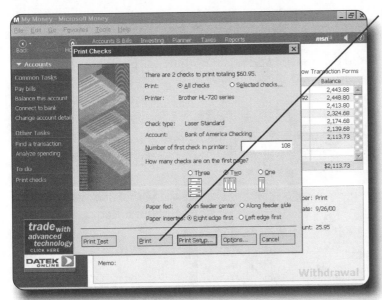

8. Click on **Print.** The Print Checks dialog box will display a printer status message.

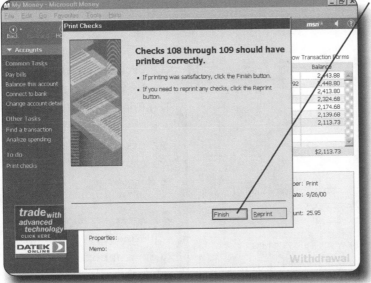

9. Click on **Finish.** The Print Checks dialog box will close.

Specifying Other Options

You can specify additional options, such as how your checks align.

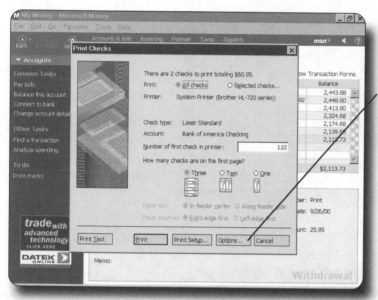

1. Follow steps 1–6 in the previous section, "Printing Checks."

2. Click on **Options.** The Options dialog box will open.

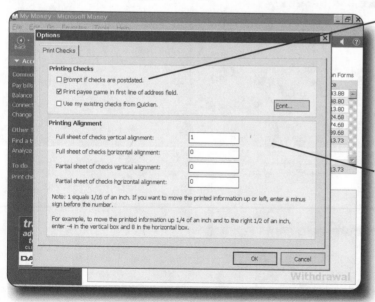

3. Click on any **check printing options** that apply. The Print payee name in first line of address field option is checked by default, but you can click on this option to deselect it.

4. Enter any **alignment adjustments** in the Printing Alignment box.

NOTE

The numeral 1 indicates $\frac{1}{16}$ of an inch. Positive numbers move to the right and down, whereas negative numbers move to the left and up. As an example, entering the number 2 would move right or down $\frac{1}{8}$ of an inch, whereas entering -2 would move left or up $\frac{1}{8}$ of an inch.

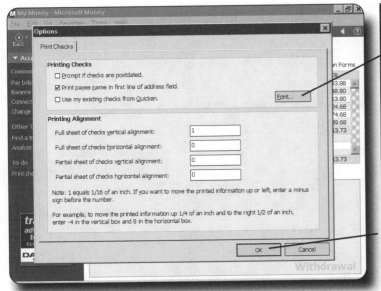

TIP

Click on Font if you want to change the font that displays on your printed checks. The Check Printing Font dialog box opens, where you can choose the font and size to print.

5. **Click** on **OK.** The Options dialog box will close and you will return to the Print Checks dialog box.

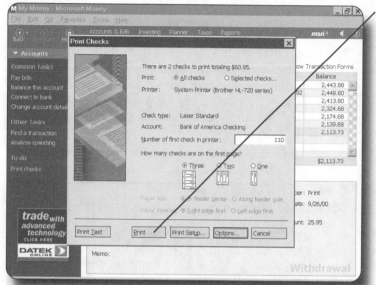

6. Click on **Print.** The Print Checks dialog box will display a printer status message.

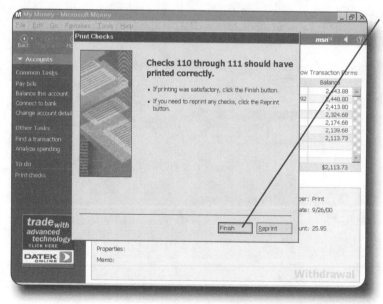

7. Click on **Finish.** The Print Checks dialog box will close.

25

Tracking and Managing Your Money

The previous four chapters covered the basics of using Microsoft Money—creating an account, setting up categories and classes, entering transactions, and printing checks. Now it's time to explore some of Money's many other useful features. In this chapter, you'll learn how to:

- View a financial calendar
- View charts and reports
- Get started with budgeting and reducing your debts
- Understand the basics of online banking and synchronization

Extending Your Knowledge of Microsoft Money

The previous four chapters just scratched the surface of what you can do with Microsoft Money. Creating accounts, entering transactions, and printing checks are just the beginning. From here you can create budgets, track and analyze your investments, reduce your debts, manage your 401(k), bank online, and do much more. Because detailed coverage of all Money's features are beyond the scope of a book on Works Suite, we'll just highlight a few areas you'll probably want to explore.

Viewing Your Financial Calendar

If you want to view all your financial activity for the current month—or the previous or future month—in one place, you'll want to refer to the financial calendar.

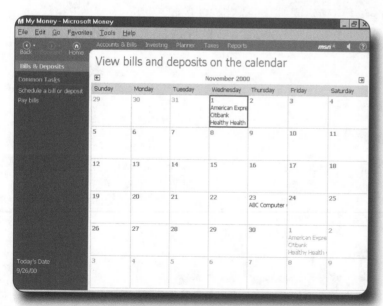

To view the calendar, click on Calendar from the Accounts & Bills menu.

From the calendar, you can view bills and deposits by day. Click on the arrows to move to the previous or next month.

Creating Budgets

One of the big advantages of using personal financial-management software is the ability to analyze and track your spending through the use of a budget.

To get started on the budgeting process, click on Budget Planner from the Planner menu. From here, you can learn more about budgeting and then create your own budget.

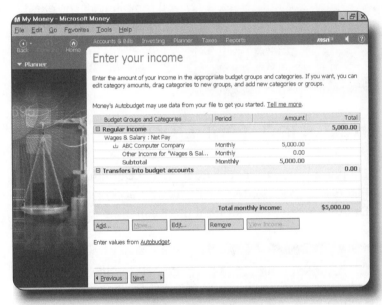

In Money, you can create your own budget from scratch (Money helps by suggesting categories to track) or use the Autobudget feature to create a sample budget from your existing transactions. Autobudget is great, but if you're a new user you won't have entered enough transactions to make it useful for a while.

Viewing Charts and Reports

Money's Reports Gallery enables you to view your financial information in a graphical or consolidated format. Click on Reports Gallery from the Reports menu to access the gallery.

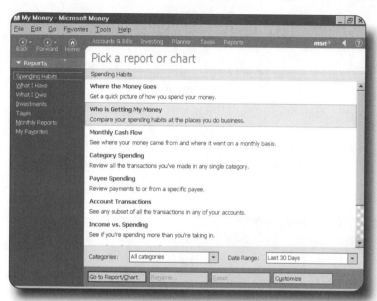

From the gallery, you can choose to see reports and graphs that tell you how much you have, how much you spend, what you owe, and how your investments are performing, among other things. All reports are customizable by date, category, and account so you can pinpoint the exact information you want to see.

Reducing Your Debt

Everyone wants to reduce debt, so the Debt Reduction Planner is a popular Money feature. To access it, click on Debt Reduction Planner from the Planner menu.

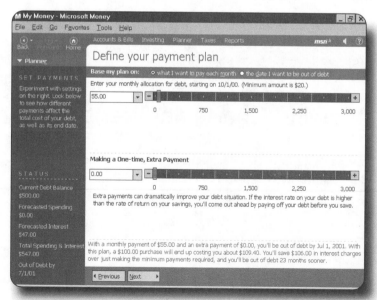

The planner walks you step-by-step through a series of questions designed to determine how much you owe and the fastest, most economical way to pay it off. The Debt Planner isn't just for people who have debt problems, but for everyone who owes money (mortgage, car loan, other loans, credit card accounts, and so on) and wants to minimize its effect.

Managing Your 401(k)

If you're like most people, your 401(k), or equivalent retirement account, is the most important investment account you'll ever have. So naturally, it makes sense to maximize your use of and return on such an investment. To open the 401(k) Manager, click on 401(k) Manager from the Investing menu.

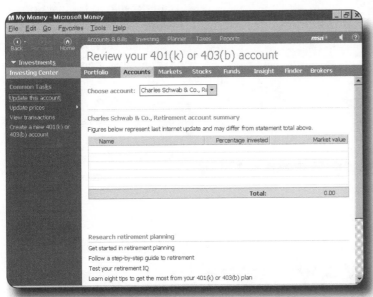

This tool not only helps you track the investments in your 401(k), but also provides tips and step-by-step guidelines for making the most of what it can offer. You can also download your 401(k) transactions from the Internet if your company is a supporting provider.

Banking Online

Complete Internet connectivity with your finances is one of the major reasons people want to use financial-management software like Money. To take advantage of it, you'll obviously need a connection to the Internet through an ISP (Internet service provider). You'll also need accounts at banks, credit card firms, and brokerages that support downloading to Money. Normally, you'll have to set up the connection to Money in addition to having a regular account with the firm. To get started with online banking, click on Account Setup from the Accounts & Bills menu.

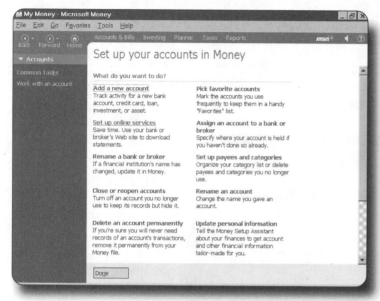

From this page, you can follow step-by-step guidance on connecting your accounts to Money.

Once you're connected, you can download transactions directly into your registers, pay bills, receive online statements, and transfer funds. The good news is that many firms now support Money, so there's a strong chance that you'll be able to access at least some, if not all, of your accounts online.

Synchronizing with MSN MoneyCentral

Another valuable Internet feature is the ability to synchronize with MSN MoneyCentral (http://www.moneycentral.msn.com). MoneyCentral is a useful financial Web site on its own, but for Money users it offers even more advantages. You can

• Enter transactions directly on the Web from any computer and then later download them into Money.

- Track your investment portfolios on the Web.

- Pay your bills.

- Check account balances.

- View financial alerts.

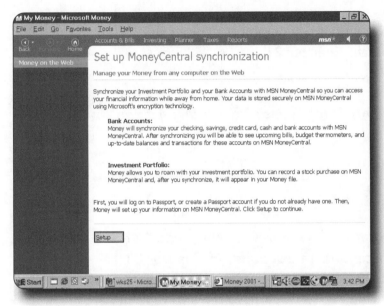

To get started with synchronization, click on **Access My Money Data on the Web** from the Tools menu and follow the step-by-step instructions.

Part V Review Questions

1. What's the easiest way to set up your finances in Microsoft Money? *See "Using the Money Setup Assistant" in Chapter 21*

2. Where can you view financial planning videos? *See "Getting Help with Money" in Chapter 21*

3. What's the difference between a category and a classification? *See "Understanding Categorization and Classification" in Chapter 22*

4. How many classifications can you create? *See "Adding a Classification" in Chapter 22*

5. Where do you enter bank withdrawals and deposits? *See "Entering Bank Account Transactions" in Chapter 23*

6. What do you do when a transaction applies to multiple categories? *See "Entering Split Transactions" in Chapter 23*

7. Where do you get printer checks that work with Money? *See "Ordering Checks" in Chapter 24*

8. How do you set up your printer to work with Money's check printing process? *See "Printing Checks" in Chapter 24*

9. How can money help you save money on your mortgage and other loans? *See "Reducing Your Debts" in Chapter 25*

10. How can you enter Money transactions directly from the Web? *See "Synchronizing with MSN MoneyCentral" in Chapter 25*

PART VI

Getting Creative with Picture It! Publishing

26

Getting Started with Picture It! Publishing

Imagine being able to touch up, repair, and enhance your photos, and publish exciting creations such as greeting cards, newsletters, or Web pages with one program. With Picture It! Publishing, you can do all that and more. In this chapter you'll learn how to:

- Open Picture It! Publishing
- Navigate the Picture It! Publishing window
- Use the Picture It! Publishing gallery
- Tour the program with the Picture It! Publishing demos

Looking at the Picture It! Publishing Environment

Picture It! Publishing works very similarly to a Web page. In the program, you'll find many options underlined like hyperlinks, ready for you to click and make selections.

Opening Picture It! Publishing

You can easily open the Picture It! Publishing application from the Works Task Launcher.

TIP

Optionally, open Picture It! Publishing by clicking on Start, Programs, Works, Picture It! Publishing.

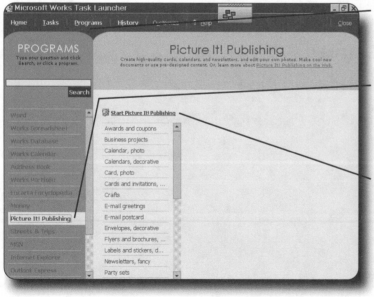

1. **Click** on **Programs**. A list of Works programs will appear.

2. **Click** on **Picture It! Publishing**. A list of Picture It! Publishing tasks will appear.

3. **Click** on **Start Picture It! Publishing**. The application will launch, displaying a list of different activities.

Navigating Picture It! Publishing

Picture It! Publishing begins by displaying the Home Page. The Home Page divides tasks into three main categories, each indicated by a tab at the top of the screen.

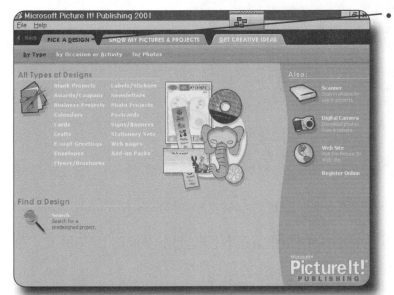

- **Pick a Design**. Choose this option to create new projects based on a variety of designs.

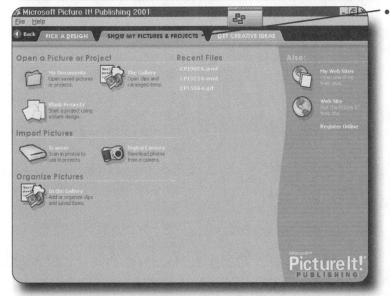

- **Show My Pictures & Projects**. Choose this option to open an existing photo or project.

- **Get Creative Ideas**. Choose this option to view demonstrations designed to assist you with Picture It! Publishing.

Exiting Picture It! Publishing

When you've completed a Picture It! Publishing session, close the Picture It! Publishing window.

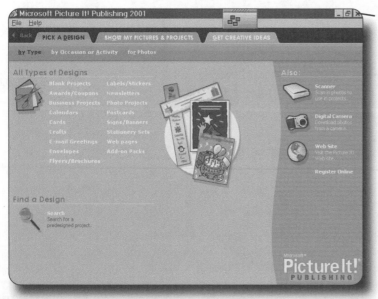

1. Click on the **Close button**. The Picture It! Publishing window will close.

If you have an unsaved project, you'll be prompted to save it. See "Saving, Publishing, and Printing Projects" later in this chapter.

The Microsoft Works Task Launcher reappears if you launched Picture It! Publishing from the Task Launcher.

Understanding Themes and Projects

To make it easy for you, Picture It! Publishing includes many predesigned themes and projects. All you need to do is change existing items to personalize the project.

1. **Click** on **Pick a Design**. The Pick a Design tab will appear in front.

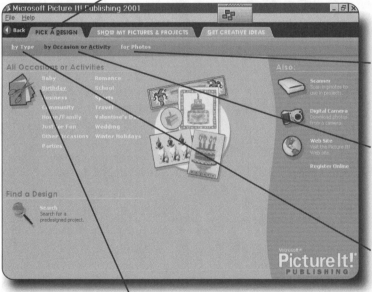

Three categories of projects appear:

- **For Photos**. This category organizes the different projects in which you can include photographs.

- **By Occasion or Activity**. This category organizes projects for occasions such as Valentines Day, birthdays, or weddings.

- **By Type**. This category organizes projects by type—for example, calendars, newsletters, or Web pages.

2. **Click** on a **Category**. The category you select will list available project types.

3. **Click** on a **project type**. A list of project subcategories will appear.

4. **Click** on a **subcategory**. A list of designs will appear.

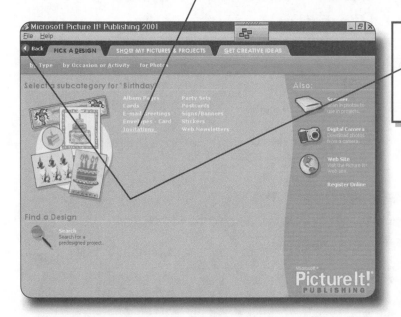

TIP

Click on the Back button to return to the previous screen.

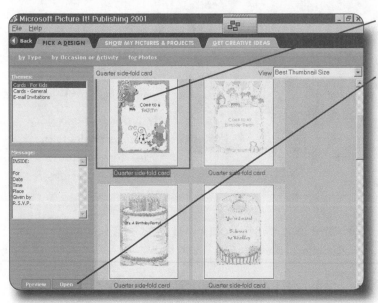

5. **Click** on a **design**. The item will be selected.

6. **Click** on **Open**. The project will appear ready for you to customize.

TIP

You might be prompted to insert a Works Suite CD. (Usually disk 3 or 4). Insert the requested CD, and then click Retry.

You'll learn how to modify the projects in Chapter 27, "Working with Photos and Images," and Chapter 28, "Creating Publications."

You can easily select another project.

7. Click on **Back to Home Page**. The Home Page will redisplay.

Using the Gallery

Picture It! Publishing includes a gallery where you can view the clip art provided by Picture It! Publishing and organize your photos, artwork, sound clips, and projects.

Browsing the Gallery

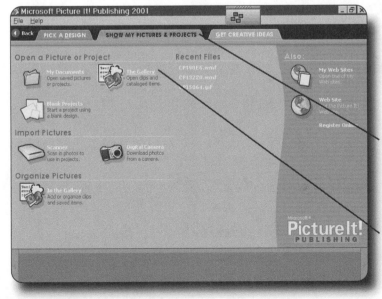

Picture It! Publishing organizes the many pieces of provided artwork into categories and displays thumbnail representations of the artwork.

1. Click on **Show My Pictures & Projects**. The Show My Pictures & Projects tab will come to the front.

2. Click on **The Gallery**. A list of collections will appear.

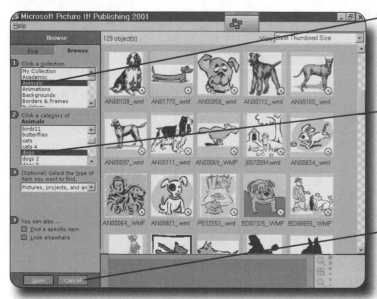

3. Click on a **collection**. Thumbnails (miniature replicas) of the first category in that collection will appear.

4. Click on a **category**. Thumbnails of the art in the selected category will appear.

TIP

Click on the Cancel button to return to the Picture It! Publishing Home Page.

5. Double-click on a **thumbnail image**. The image will open, ready for you to edit or add to a project.

TIP

Click on Back to Home Page to select another image or begin another project.

Creating a Collection

Use the Picture It! Publishing Gallery to organize your own photographs and projects—for example, your summer vacation photos or your family photographs.

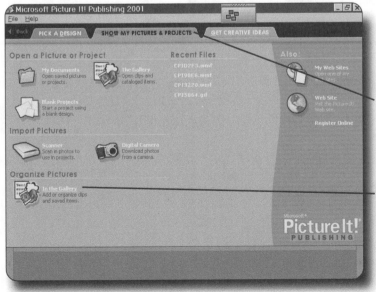

In Chapter 27, you'll learn how to download your photographs from your digital camera or scanner.

1. **Click** on **Show My Pictures & Projects**. The Show My Pictures & Projects tab will come to the front.

2. **Click** on **In The Gallery** under Organize Pictures. The Edit Gallery window will open.

Creating a Gallery Category

In order to organize your images, you'll want to create categories such as "Vacation 2000" or "Our First Christmas." You manage your categories from the Edit Gallery window. Go ahead...add as many categories as you wish.

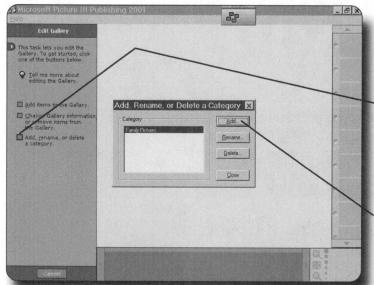

1. Click on **Add, rename, or delete a category**. The Add, Rename, or Delete a Category dialog box will open.

2. Click on **Add**. The Add Category dialog box will open.

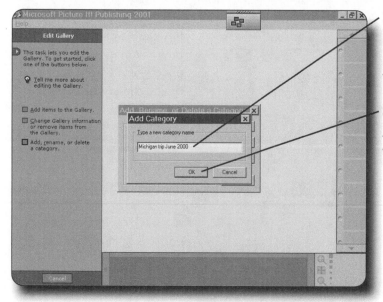

3. Type a **name** for your category. The name will appear in the displayed text box.

4. Click on **OK**. The Add Category dialog box will close.

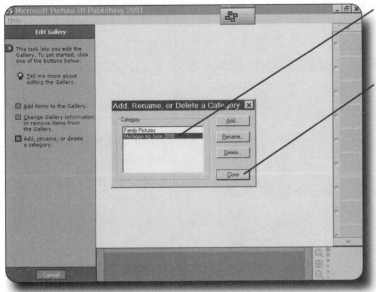

The new category will appear in the Category list box.

5. Click on **Close**. The Add, Rename, or Delete a Category dialog box will close.

Adding Images to a Collection

Images, sound clips, and video files can be added to the collections you create in the Gallery.

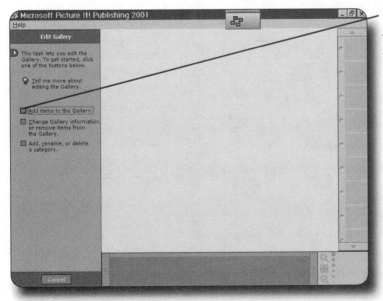

1. Click on **Add items to the Gallery**. The Edit Gallery window will display available images.

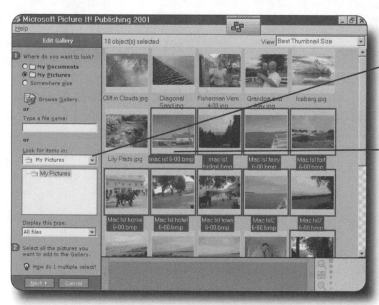

TIP

Click the Look for items in down arrow to change folders.

2. **Click** on a **picture** you want to add to a collection. The picture will be highlighted.

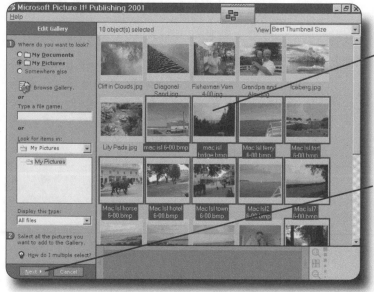

TIP

Optionally, press and hold the Ctrl key and click on additional images to select multiple images at the same time.

3. **Click** on **Next**. The selected images appear in the next window.

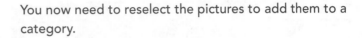

You now need to reselect the pictures to add them to a category.

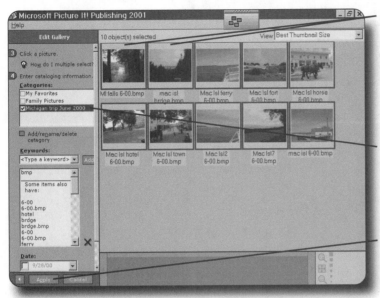

4. **Click** on the **first object** to add, **then press and hold the Ctrl key** and **select** any **additional items**. A highlighted border will surround the selected items.

5. **Click** on a **category name check box**. A check mark ✔ will appear in the selected check box.

6. **Click** on **Apply**. The objects will be added to the gallery category.

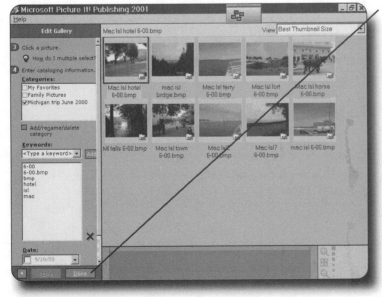

7. **Click** on **Done**. The Picture It! Publishing Home Page reappears.

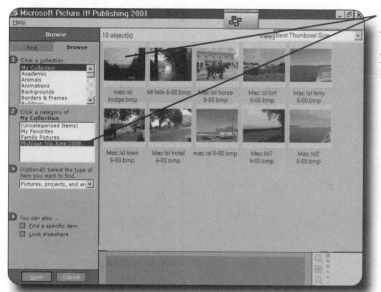

Now when you browse
The Gallery, you'll see
your category with your
images in it.

Saving, Publishing, and Printing Projects

Most applications require you to save your work to protect
against accidental loss. With Picture It! Publishing, you also
have the option of publishing the project to the Web, e-
mailing it to someone, or printing the project on paper.

Saving a Project

Most of the time, you'll want to save your project to your
disk drive for future reference or further modifications.

1. **Click** on **Save or send**. The Save or send submenu will appear.

2. **Click** on **Save**. The Save As window will open.

3. **Type** a **name** for the project in the Type a name text box.

4. Optionally, **double-click** on a **folder** in which to save the project.

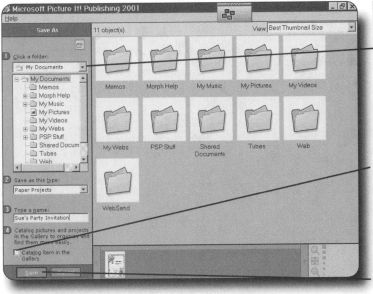

TIP

If you don't want to save in the My Documents folder, you can choose another from the drop-down list.

5. Unless you want this item in the Gallery, **click** on the **Catalog item in the Gallery check box** to remove the check mark.

6. **Click** on **Save**. The project is saved for future reference.

Publishing a Project

If you already have a Web site established, you can easily upload projects to your site.

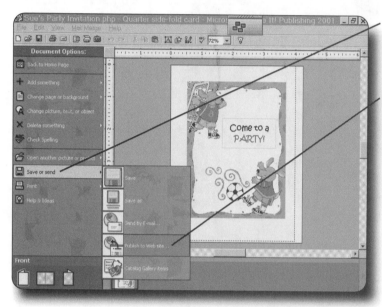

1. **Click** on **Save or send**. The Save or send submenu will appear.

2. **Click** on **Publish to Web site**. The Publish to Web dialog box will open.

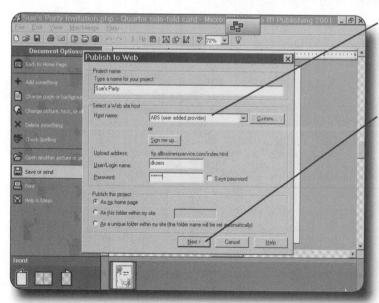

3. **Specify** the **host name** and **other requested information** in the Publish to Web dialog box.

4. **Click** on **Next**.

Picture It! Publishing creates an HTML version of your project and uploads it to your Web site.

E-mailing a Project

Use Picture It! Publishing to e-mail an image or project to someone.

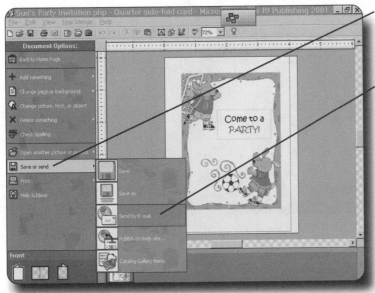

1. **Click** on **Save or send**. The Save or send submenu will appear.

2. **Click** on **Send by E-mail**. The Send by E-mail dialog box will open.

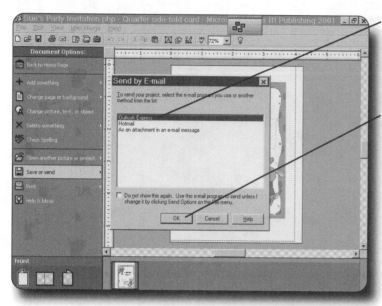

3. Click on the **e-mail program** you want to use to send the image. The program name will be selected.

4. Click on **OK**. Picture It! Publishing will convert the project to HTML format and open a new e-mail message with an attachment.

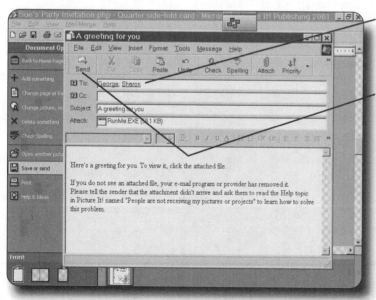

5. Enter the recipient's **e-mail address** in the To text box.

6. Click on **Send**. Your e-mail program will send the message with the attachment.

Printing a Project

Printing a Picture It! Publishing project is very similar to printing other Microsoft Works files.

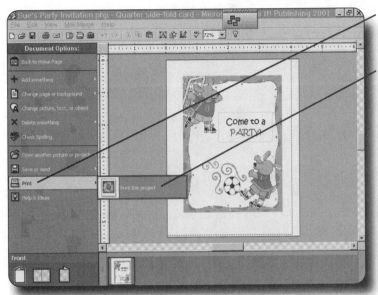

1. **Click** on **Print**. The Print submenu will appear.

2. **Click** on **Print this project**. The Print dialog box will open.

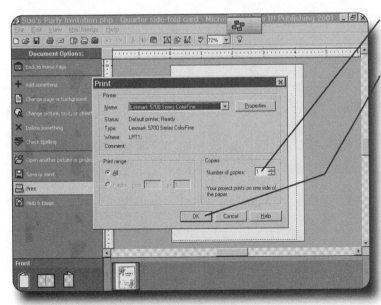

3. **Set** any desired **options** in the Print dialog box.

4. **Click** on **OK**. The project will print.

Getting Inspiration

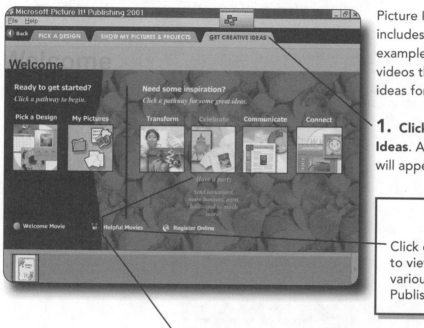

Picture It! Publishing includes several helpful examples, illustrations, and videos that provide cool ideas for different projects.

1. **Click** on **Get Creative Ideas**. A list of project types will appear.

TIP

Click on Helpful Movies to view short videos on various Picture It! Publishing projects.

2. **Click** on a **project type**. A list of topics will appear.

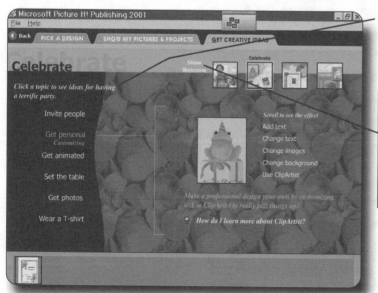

3. **Click** on a **topic**. Samples, ideas, or additional help options will appear.

TIP

Click on Show Welcome to return to the first Get Creative Ideas screen.

27

Working with Photos and Images

Picture It! Publishing enables you to manipulate your photographs and images by adding special effects, fancy edges, or other objects. Further, you might want to use the touchup tools to remove scratches, wrinkles, and red eye from your photos. In this chapter you'll learn how to:

- Import photos from scanners and digital cameras
- Enhance photos with touchups, effects, and borders
- Work with stamps
- Add and manage objects
- Use the tray

Importing Photos

Before you can edit a photo with Picture It! Publishing software, you must import the photograph into your computer. Photographs are imported through a scanner or digital camera.

Scanning Photos with a Scanner

Picture It! Publishing recognizes many scanners on the market today. Scan your image through your scanner and process it with Picture It! Publishing.

1. **Click** on the **Show My Pictures & Projects tab** or the **Pick a Design tab**. The selected tab will come to the front.

2. **Click** on **Scanner**. The Scan Picture window appears.

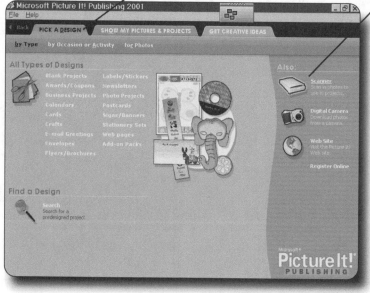

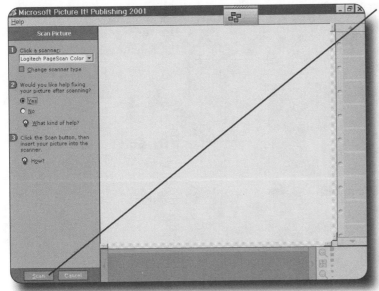

3. **Click** on **Scan**. Your scanning software launches and takes over the scanning process.

The scanning process varies with different scanners. When the scanning process is complete, your scanned image appears in the Picture It! Publishing window.

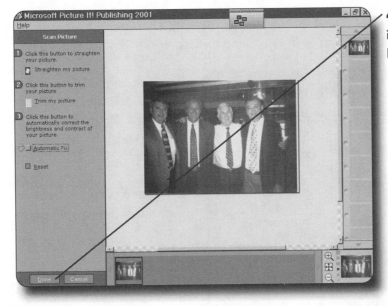

4. **Click** on **Done**. The image appears in the Picture It! Publishing editing window.

5a. **Click** on **Back to Home Page**. The Picture It! Publishing Home Page reappears.

OR

5b. **Edit** the **scanned image**. You'll learn how to edit images later in this chapter.

Downloading Photos from a Digital Camera

You can download images directly from your digital camera into Picture It! Publishing for further processing.

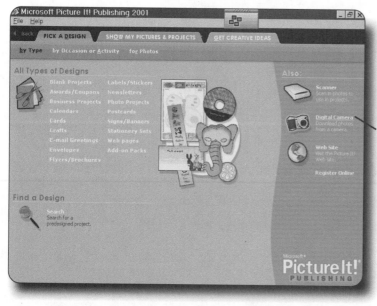

1. **Click** on the **Show My Pictures & Projects tab** or the **Pick a Design tab**. The selected tab will come to the front.

2. **Click** on **Digital Camera**. The Digital Camera window will appear.

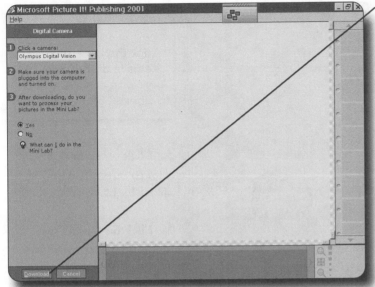

3. Click on **Download**. Your camera management software will launch and take over the downloading process.

The downloading process varies with different cameras. When it's complete, your images will appear in the Picture It! Publishing window.

Opening a Stored Image

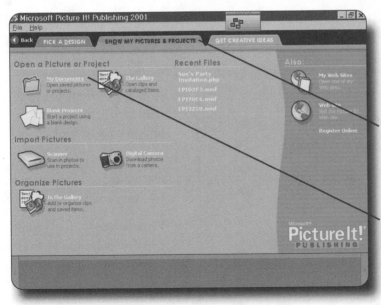

If you have already downloaded or scanned an image to your computer, you can open it using the Picture It! Publishing toolbar.

1. Click on the **Show My Pictures & Projects tab**. The Show My Pictures & Projects tab will come to the front.

2. Click on **My Documents**. The Open Pictures or Projects window will open, displaying items in either the My Documents or My Pictures folder.

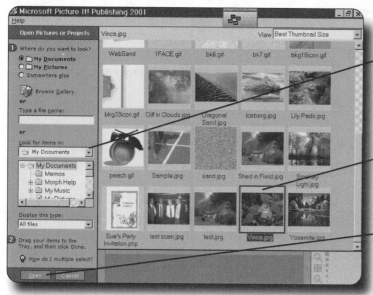

TIP

Click the Look for items in drop-down arrow to change folders.

3. Click on an **image** you want to open. The image will be highlighted.

4. Click on **Open**. The image opens in the image window.

Understanding the Image Window

Each area in the image window has a different purpose:

- **Toolbar**. The toolbar displays commonly used file-management and image-editing tools.

- **Task pane**. The Task pane lists all the available steps for the current project.

- **Picture pane**. The Picture pane displays the image-editing workspace.

- **Stack**. The stack displays each individual object in an image.

- **Tray**. The tray displays all the pictures and projects you currently have open.

- **Zoom tools**. This area displays tools that you can use to zoom in and out on specific areas of your image.

Enhancing Pictures

Clean up and enhance your photographs with special effects.

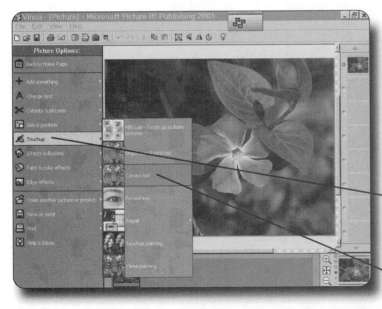

Touching Up a Photo

Use the photo retouch tools to remove red eye, scratches, wrinkles, and other blemishes from your photographs.

1. **Click** on **Touchup**. The Touchup submenu will appear.

2. **Click** on a **touchup tool**. The selected touchup tool options will appear.

The options will vary depending on which touchup tool you selected.

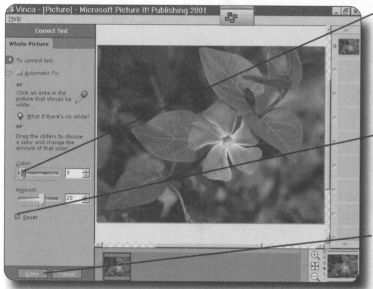

3. Adjust the **settings** until the photograph looks the way you'd like it to.

TIP

To start over, click on Reset to return the photo to its original state.

---

4. Click on **Done**. The Task pane will return to the Picture Options.

Adding Other Effects and Illusions

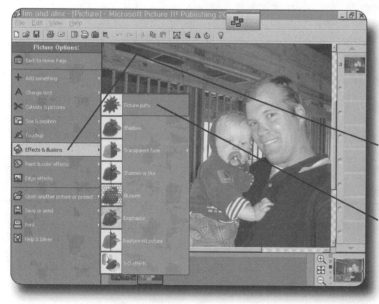

Have a little fun with your photos by adding special effects. It's impossible to show you each and every effect, so you should try them all.

1. Click on **Effects & Illusions**. The Effects & Illusions submenu will open.

2. Click on an **effect**. The options for the selected effect will appear.

The options will vary depending on which effect you selected.

3. Click an **option**. The option will be selected.

Some effect options lead to further options. The selections will vary according to the effect you select.

4. Continue selecting effect **options** until the effect is complete.

5. Click on **Done**. The image will be altered in the Picture Options window.

TIP

If you don't like the effect you applied, click on Edit, Undo to remove it.

Adding Edges and Borders

Add an edge or border to your photograph. Like the special effects, there are a number of different edge options, so keep trying them until you find the perfect border for your image.

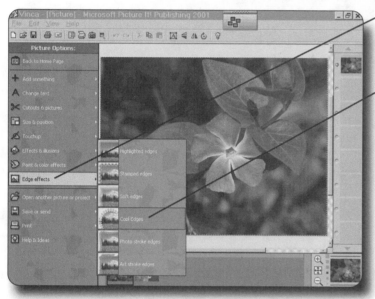

1. Click on **Edge effects**. The Edge effects submenu will appear.

2. Click on an **edge style**. The options for the selected edge style will appear.

3. Click an **option**. The option will be selected.

Some edge options lead to further options. The selections will vary according to the edge you select.

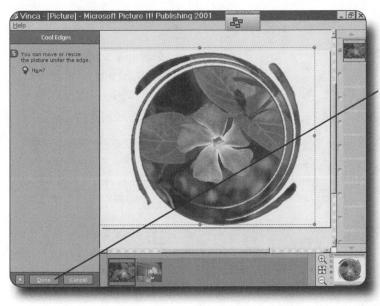

4. Continue selecting edge **options** until the edge is complete.

5. Click on **Done**. The image will be altered in the Picture Options window.

Adding Stamps

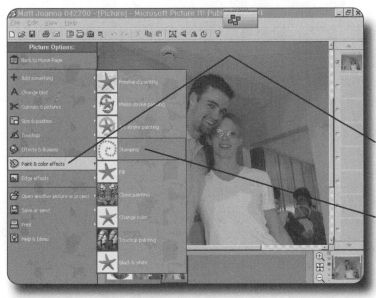

Stamps are predefined pictures you can add to an image, just like the rubber stamps you find in the school-supplies aisle at your local drug store.

1. Click on **Paint & color effects**. The Paint & color effects submenu will appear.

2. Click on **Stamping**. The Stamping options will appear.

3. Click on a **stamping style**. Four options are available:

- **Stamps**. Stamps are applied one at a time as you stamp them, or in a continuous row.

- **Overlap stamps**. These are the same as regular stamps, but if you stamp in a continuous row, the stamps are closer together and somewhat overlap each other.

- **Shapes**. Select this option to stamp a series of predefined shapes (different from the stamps collection).

- **Erase**. Erases a stamp or shape area without affecting the rest of the image.

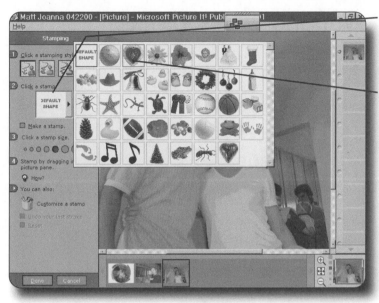

4. **Click** on the **Click a stamp box**. A selection of stamps will appear.

5. **Click** on a **stamp**. The selected stamp will appear in the Click a stamp box.

6. **Click** on a **stamp size**. The larger the circle, the larger the stamp will appear on the image.

7. **Click** in the **image window**. The stamp shape will appear on the image. Stamp as many times as you'd like!

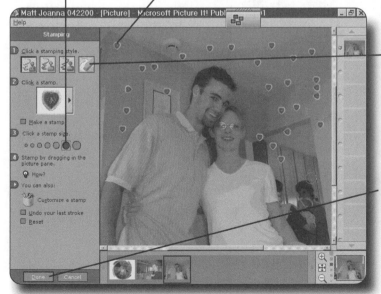

TIP

If you put a stamp where you don't want it, click the eraser style and drag the mouse over the area you stamped.

8. **Click** on **Done**. The Picture Options Task pane will reappear.

Working with Objects

Objects are individual components on an image. Examples of objects include photos, text, stars, or boxes. Individual objects can be manipulated, moved, modified, and deleted.

Adding Shapes

You don't have to be an artist to draw a perfect circle, Christmas tree, or puppy paw print. Picture It! Publishing includes lots of different shapes you can easily add to your image.

1. Click on **Add something**. The Add something submenu will appear.

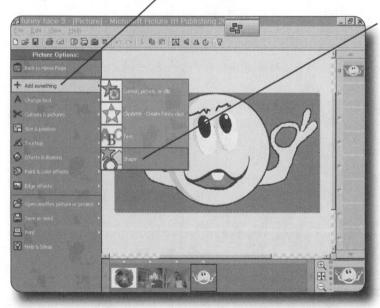

2. Click on **Shape**. The Add a Colored Shape options will appear; the default shape appears on your image with selection handles surrounding it.

3. Click on a **shape**. The shape you select will replace the existing shape on your image.

The left side of the color box displays available colors, while the right side of the color box displays the different hues for the currently selected color.

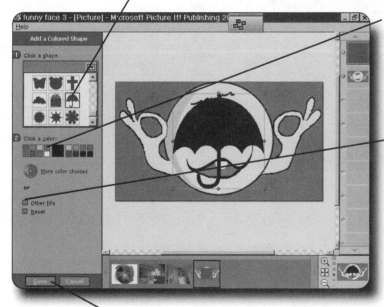

4. Click on a **color**. The shape will change to the currently selected color.

TIP

Click on Other fills to choose a gradient fill.

Later in this chapter, you'll discover how to move, resize, and edit the object.

5. Click on **Done**. The Picture Options Task pane reappears.

Adding Text

Say it with the right words using the text object feature. You can even make your text take special shapes!

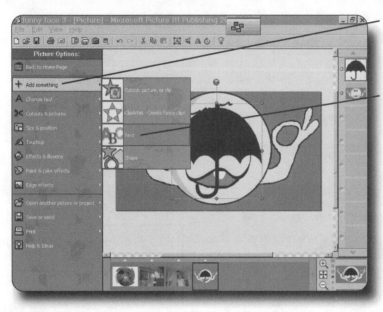

1. **Click** on **Add something**. The Add something submenu will appear.

2. **Click** on **Text**. The Add Text options will appear.

3. **Type** some **text**. The text appears in the Type your text area and as a selected object on the image.

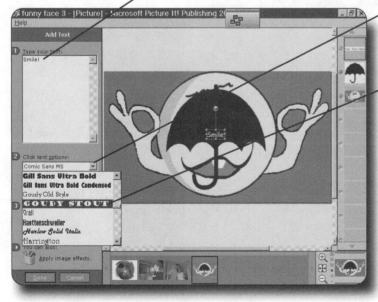

4. **Click** on the **font list**. A list of available fonts will appear.

5. **Click** on a **font name**. The font will be selected.

Your fonts might vary from the ones seen in this figure.

6. **Click** on a **font style** and **alignment**. The options will be selected.

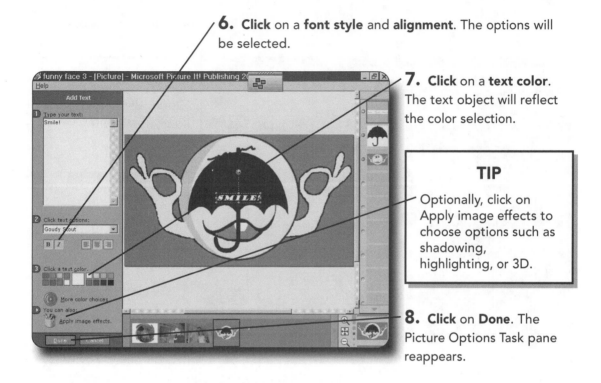

7. **Click** on a **text color**. The text object will reflect the color selection.

> ### TIP
>
> Optionally, click on Apply image effects to choose options such as shadowing, highlighting, or 3D.

8. **Click** on **Done**. The Picture Options Task pane reappears.

Managing Objects

Once you've created objects on your screen, you might want to move, resize, rearrange, or delete them.

Selecting Objects

In order to modify any object, the object must first be selected. Picture It! Publishing indicates selected objects with a border, eight handles, and a rotating knob.

1a. **Click** on an **object**. The object will be selected.

TIP

Optionally, hold down the Ctrl key and click on additional objects to select them.

OR

1b. **Click** on a **stack object**. The object will be selected.

If you have the wrong object selected, click anywhere outside of the image to deselect it and start again.

Moving Objects

Move any object to a different position on the page.

1. **Click** on an **object**. The object will be selected.

2. **Position** the **mouse pointer over** the selected **object**. The mouse pointer will turn into a hand with a small green object under it (it's supposed to be a suction cup).

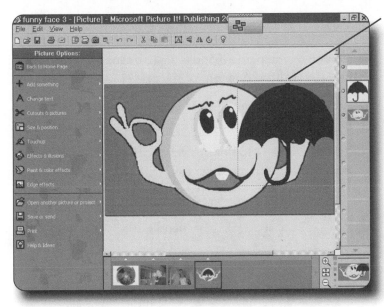

3. **Click** and **drag** the **mouse**. The object will move to a new position.

4. **Release** the **mouse button**. The object will stay in the new position.

Resizing Objects

Use the handles around a selected object to resize it if the object is too large or too small.

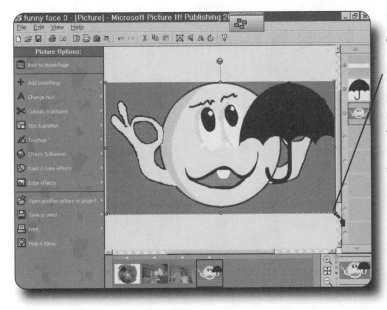

1. **Click** on an **object**. The object will be selected.

2. **Position** the **mouse pointer** over one of the eight handles surrounding the image (not the rotating knob). The mouse pointer turns into a hand with a small green object under it.

You can

- Position over a corner handle to simultaneously resize both the width and height of the object.

- Position over the left or right center handles to resize only the width of the object.

- Position over the top or bottom center handles to resize only the height of the object.

3. Click and drag the **handle**. The object will resize.

4. Release the **mouse button**. The object will remain the new size.

Rotating Objects

Rotate objects any direction you want—left, right, or anywhere in between.

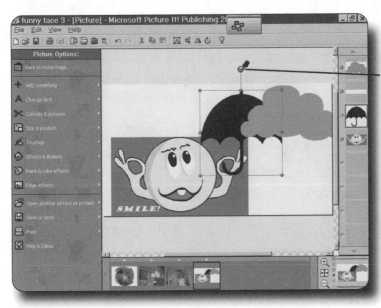

1. Click on an **object**. The object will be selected.

2. Position the **mouse pointer over** the **rotation knob**. The mouse pointer will turn into a small hand.

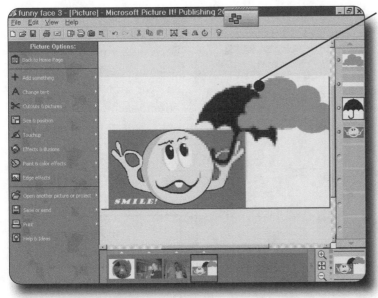

3. Click and **drag** the **rotation knob**. The object will rotate left or right, depending on where you drag the mouse.

4. Release the **mouse button**. The object will remain at the new angle.

Deleting Objects

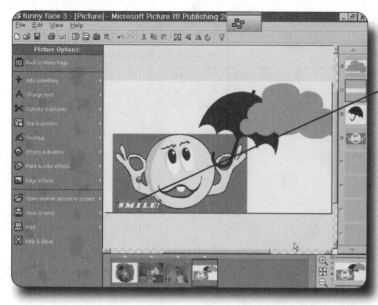

If you have an object you no longer want on your image, you can delete it.

1. **Click** on an **object**. The object will be selected.

2. **Press** the **Delete key** on your keyboard. The object will be deleted.

Working with the Stack

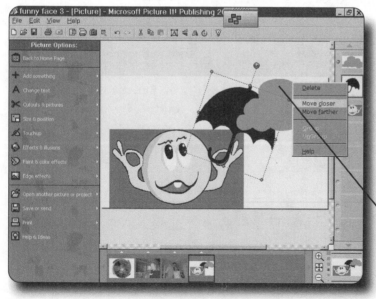

Each time you add an object to an image, the object gets its own spot in the stack. In effect, each object is on its own layer of the image. By changing the stack order, you rearrange the order of the objects.

NOTE

Notice that the cloud is on top of the umbrella.

The objects at the top of the stack are on the upper layers of the image.

1. Right-click on the **stack object** you want to restack. The object will be selected, and a shortcut menu will appear.

2a. Click on **Move closer** to move the object closer to the top of the stack. The object moves up in the stack.

OR

2b. Click on **Move farther** to move the object farther down the stack. The object moves down in the stack.

NOTE

Because the umbrella was moved farther up the stack, it is now on top of the cloud.

Managing the Tray

Each time you open or create a different image, Picture It! Publishing places a thumbnail of the image at the bottom of your screen in an area called the tray.

Switching to a Different Tray Object

Make a different object in the tray the current object.

1. Click on a **thumbnail image** in the tray. The image will become the current active image.

The tray indicates the current image by placing a highlighted border around it.

Closing a Tray Object

If you have objects in your tray you no longer need for the current project, close them to free up computer resources.

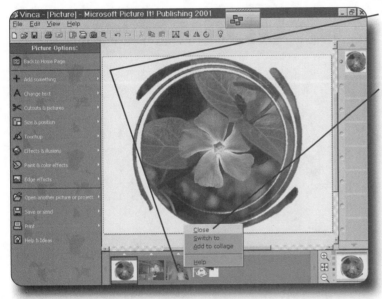

1. **Right-click** on the **image** you want to close. A shortcut menu will appear.

2. **Click** on **Close**. If the image hasn't been saved, Picture It! Publishing will prompt you to save it.

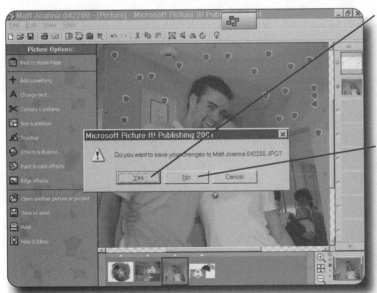

3a. **Click** on **Yes** to save the current image. You might be prompted for a file name.

OR

3b. **Click** on **No**. Changes to the image will be discarded.

28

Creating Publications with Picture It! Publishing

Picture It! Publishing includes lots of great templates to use when creating publications. Choose from cards, calendars, brochures, newsletters, invitations, and even Web pages. In this chapter you'll learn how to:

- Create a greeting card
- Design a simple Web page
- Work with photo projects

Create a Greeting Card

These cards might not say Hallmark on the back, but even so, you can let others know how you feel by creating a personalized card!

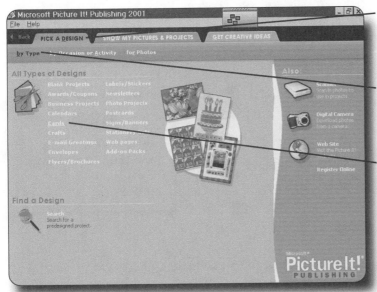

1. Click on **Pick a Design**. The Pick a Design tab will come to the front.

2. Click on **by Type**. A list of types of designs will appear.

3. Click on **Cards**. A listing of card subcategories will appear.

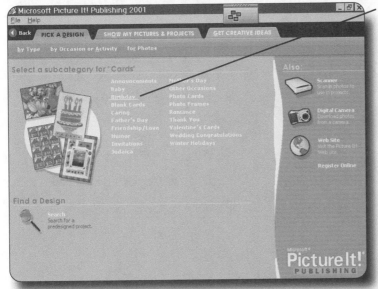

4. Click on the **card type** you want to create. A list of themes will appear.

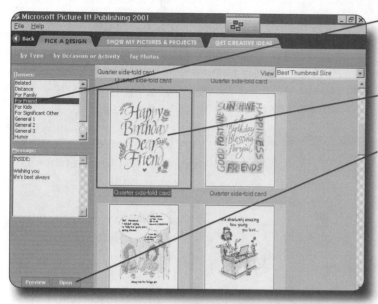

5. **Click** on a **theme**. Sample cards representing the selected theme will appear.

6. **Click** on a **card**. The card will become selected.

7. **Click** on **Open**. The card will open in the image-editing window.

NOTE

You might be prompted to insert one of the Works Suite 2001 CDs.

Editing a Card Message

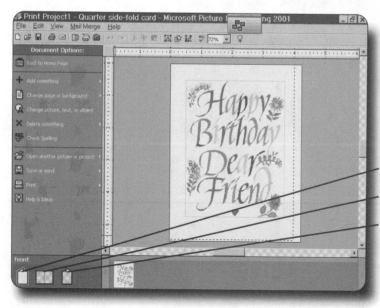

You can add your signature, or modify the card message.

1. **Click** on the **card area** you want to modify. The selected card area will appear.

- Card front

- Card inside spread

- Card back

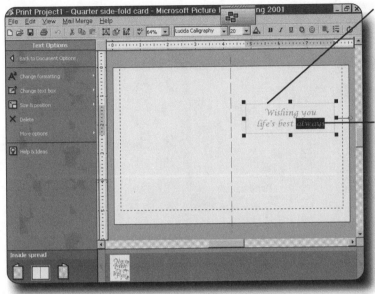

2. Click on any **existing text object**. The text object will become selected and a blinking insertion point will appear.

3. Drag the **mouse across** the existing **text**. The existing text will become highlighted.

4. Type some **text**. The text you type will replace the highlighted text.

Adding Items

If you want to add text or other objects to the card, use the Document Options pane on the left.

Adding Clip Art

The Picture It! Publishing software includes thousands of pieces of clip art you can easily add to any project.

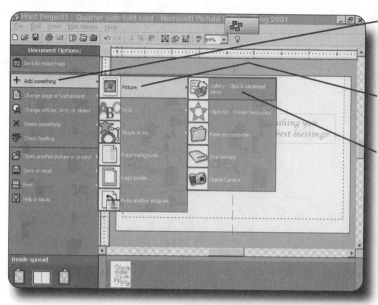

1. Click on **Add something**. The Add something submenu will appear.

2. Click on **Picture**. The Picture submenu will appear.

3. Click on **Gallery**. The clip-art gallery will open.

4. Click on a **collection**. A collection will be highlighted and the categories associated with the collection will appear.

5. Click on a **category**. The images associated with the category will appear.

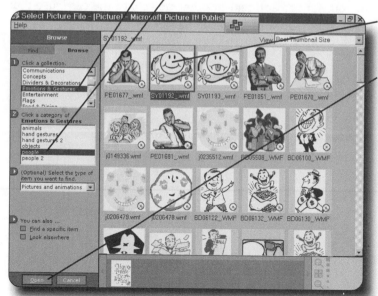

6. Click on an **image**. The image will be highlighted.

7. Click on **Open**. The image will appear on your card.

TIP

Similar to the way you learned in Chapter 27, "Working with Photos and Images," the objects on the card can be selected, moved, resized, deleted, or rotated.

Adding Shaped Text

In "Working with Objects" in Chapter 27, you learned how to add text to an image. Taking that one step farther, Picture It! Publishing lets you create text in any of 30 different shapes.

1. Click on **Add something**. The Add something submenu will appear.

2. Click on **Text**. The Text submenu will appear.

3. Click on **Shaped text**. A menu of special shapes will appear.

4. Click on a **shape**. The Edit Shaped Text dialog box will open with highlighted sample text.

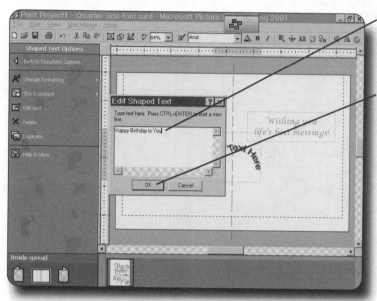

5. Type some **text**. The text you type will replace the highlighted sample text.

6. Click on **OK**. The Edit Shaped Text dialog box will close.

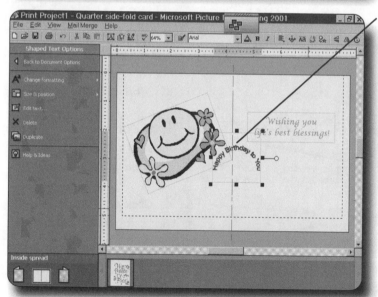

Your shaped text appears on the card.

TIP

Edit shaped text in the same manner as any other type of object.

Working with Grouped Objects

The backs of the pre-defined greeting cards feature a logo and message that you can customize. The card back has only a single object on it, but that object consists of several different objects combined together to make one completed object. The process of combining objects is called *grouping*.

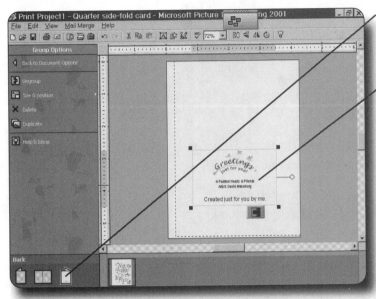

1. **Click** on the **card back area**. The card back area will appear.

2. **Click** on the **object** on the back of the card. The object will become selected, and an icon that looks like pieces of a picture puzzle will appear.

The picture puzzle icon represents a group. In order to modify any element of a grouped object, you must first ungroup it.

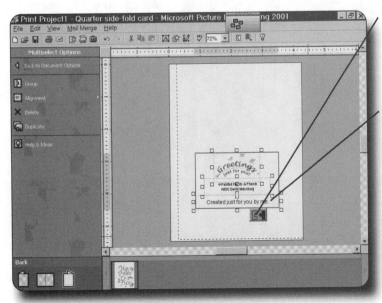

3. **Click** on the **puzzle icon**. The back of the card will display several selected objects.

4. **Click** on the **object** you want to modify. Only that object will be selected.

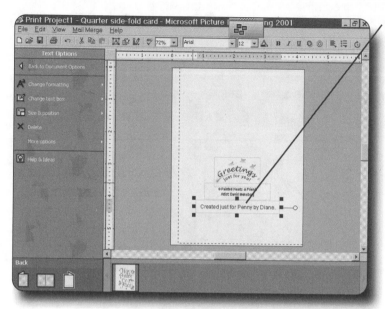

5. Modify the **object** as desired. The object will reflect your changes.

Now you should regroup the objects so they stay together.

6. Click on **Edit**. The Edit menu will appear.

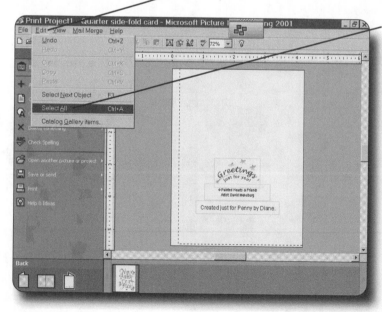

7. Click on **Select All**. All objects on the back page will be selected.

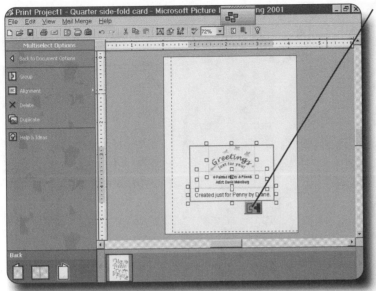

8. Click on the **puzzle icon**. The objects will regroup into a single object.

Creating a Web Page

When the Internet first became popular, creating Web pages was difficult— mainly because doing so involved using a special computer language called HTML. Now creating Web pages is simple, thanks to applications like Picture It! Publishing, which automatically translates your ideas into HTML for you.

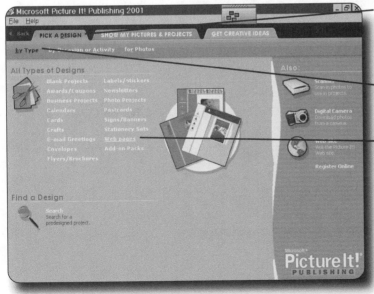

1. Click on **Pick a Design**. The Pick a Design tab will come to the front.

2. Click on **by Type**. A list of types of designs will appear.

3. Click on **Web pages**. A listing of subcategories will appear.

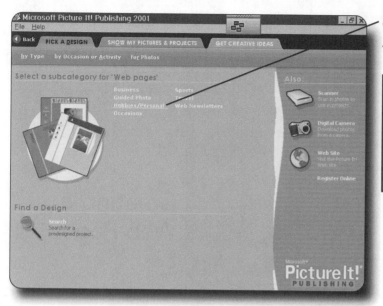

4. **Click** on a **subcategory**. A list of themes will appear.

NOTE

You might be prompted to insert one of the Works Suite 2001 CDs.

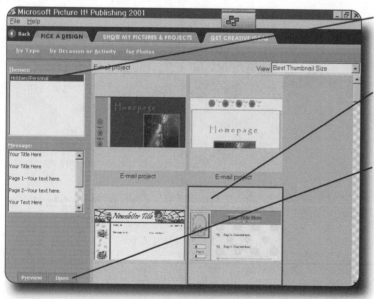

5. **Click** on a **theme**. Thumbnails of the selected theme will appear.

6. **Click** on the **style** you want for your Web page. The thumbnail will be selected.

7. **Click** on **Open**. The first page of the Web page will open in the image-editing window.

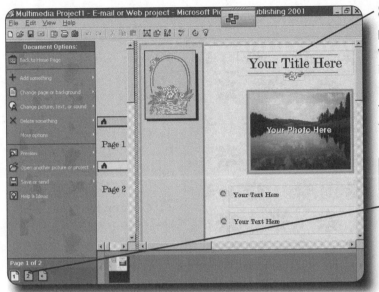

8. Click on a **text** or **image placeholder** and **replace** it with your own text or image. You learned in "Adding Items" earlier in this chapter how to replace text and images.

TIP

Most Picture It! Publishing Web page templates contain multiple pages. Click on a different page to activate and edit it. You can add or delete pages as needed by using the Add something or Delete something menu selections.

See "Publishing a Project" in Chapter 26, "Getting Started with Picture It! Publishing," to upload the Web page you created to the Internet.

Working with Photo Projects

Picture It! Publishing includes several creative projects you can use to show off your favorite photographs.

Magazine Covers

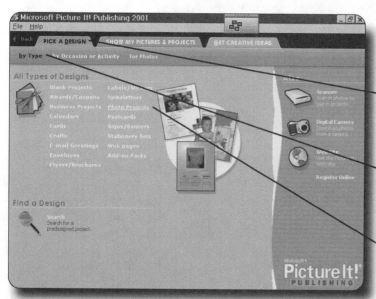

Discover instant fame! Use your photo to create magazine covers.

1. Click on **Pick a Design**. The Pick a Design tab will come to the front.

2. Click on **by Type**. A list of types of designs will appear.

3. Click on **Photo Projects**. A listing of subcategories will appear.

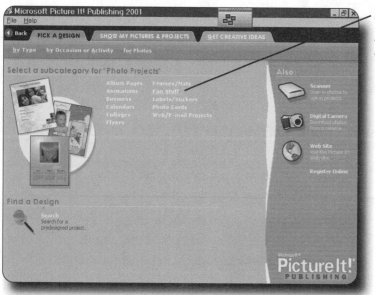

4. Click on **Fun Stuff**. A selection of themes will appear.

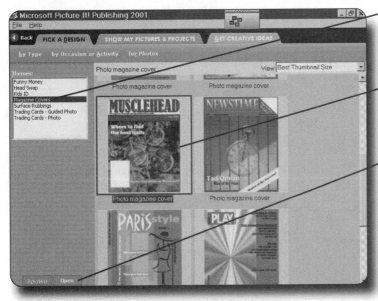

5. **Click** on **Magazine Covers**. A selection of magazine covers will appear.

6. **Click** on a **magazine cover**. The magazine cover will be selected.

7. **Click** on **Open**. The magazine cover will open, ready for you to insert your photograph.

> **NOTE**
>
> You might be prompted to insert a Works CD.

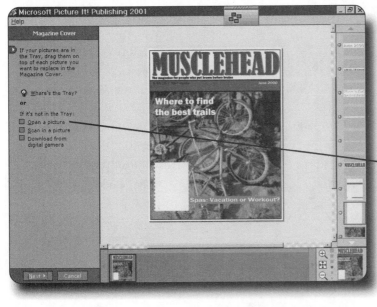

Adding an Unopened Photo

If you have not already opened the photo you want to place in your magazine cover, you can open it now.

1. **Click** on **Open a picture**. The Open Pictures or Projects pane will open.

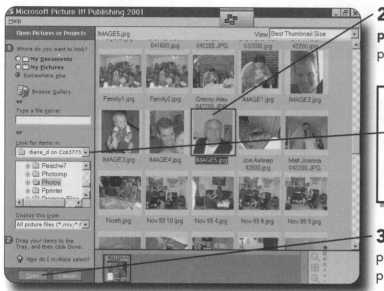

2. **Locate** and **click** on the **photo** you want to add. The photo will be selected.

> **TIP**
>
> Click on the Look for items in drop-down arrow to locate the photo.

3. **Click** on **Open**. The photo will open and be placed in the tray.

Adding an Image from the Tray

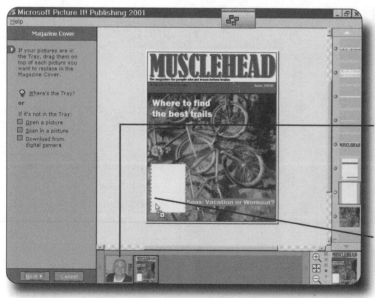

If you already have the photo open and sitting in the Picture It! Publishing tray, you can quickly add it to your magazine cover.

1. **Click** and **drag** the **photo** to the picture frame. The mouse pointer will change to a white arrow with a plus sign under it.

2. **Release** the **mouse button**. The picture will be inserted into the frame.

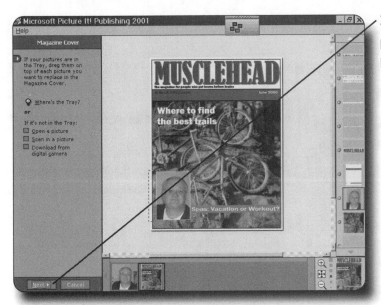

3. Click on **Next**. The next page of the Magazine Cover pane will open.

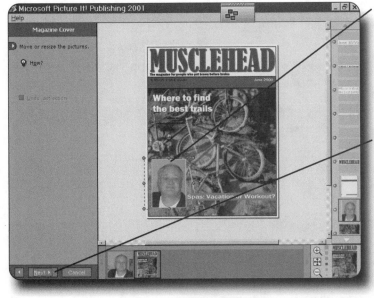

4. If needed, **click** on the **image** and **resize** or **move** it. (Refer to "Managing Objects" in Chapter 27.) The image will be resized or moved to a new position.

5. Click on **Next**. The next page of the Magazine Cover pane will open.

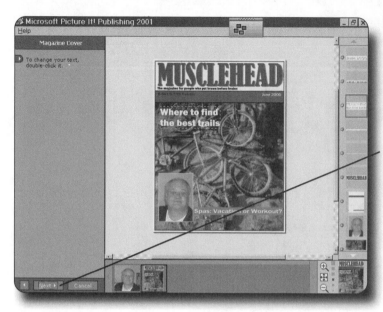

TIP

Optionally, double-click on any text object to edit the text.

6. Click on **Next**. The final page of the Magazine Cover pane will open.

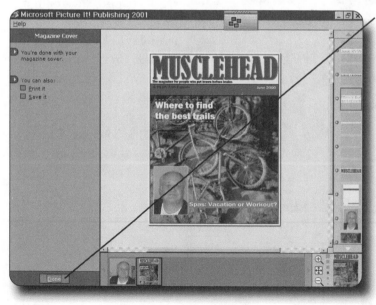

7. Click on **Done**. The Picture Options pane will appear.

Adding Picture Frames

Add a cool picture frame around your favorite photo.

1. **Click** on **Pick a Design**. The Pick a Design tab will come to the front.

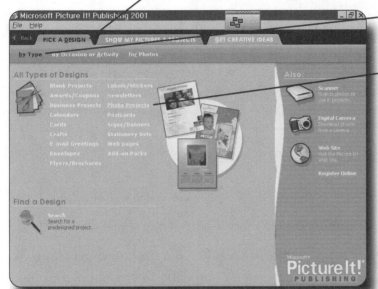

2. **Click** on **by Type**. A list of types of designs will appear.

3. **Click** on **Photo Projects**. A listing of subcategories will appear.

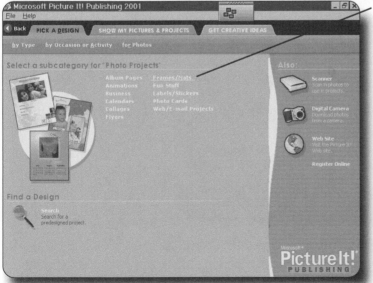

4. **Click** on **Frames/Mats**. A selection of frames will appear.

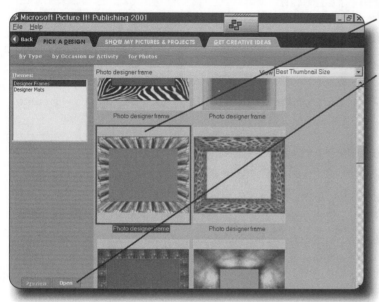

5. **Click** on a **frame**. The frame will be selected.

6. **Click** on **Open**. The Designer Frame pane will open.

NOTE

You might be prompted to insert a Works CD.

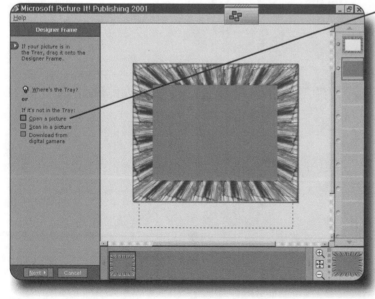

7. **Click** on **Open a picture**. The Open Pictures or Projects pane will open.

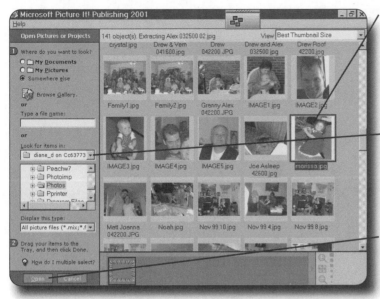

8. Locate and **click** on the **photo** you want to add. The photo will be selected.

TIP

Click on the Look for items in drop-down arrow to locate the photo.

9. Click on **Open**. The photo will open and be placed in the picture frame.

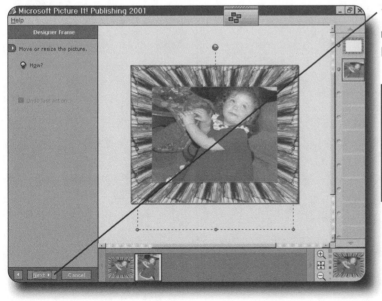

10. Click on **Next**. The next page of the Designer Frame pane will open.

TIP

Optionally, to move the photo, click on the image and drag it to a new location.

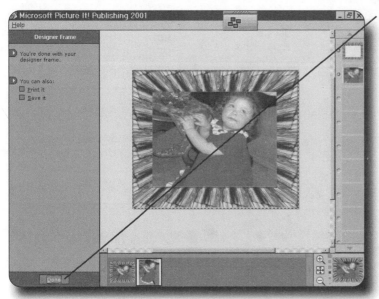

11. **Click** on **Done**. The Picture Options window will reappear.

Part VI Review Questions

1. How many categories of tasks are displayed on the Picture It! Publishing Home Page? *See "Navigating Picture It! Publishing" in Chapter 26*

2. Using what feature provided by Picture It! Publishing can you view clip art and organize images and projects? *See Using the Gallery" in "Chapter 26*

3. Besides printing a project, what other options do you have to relay the project to others? *See "Saving, Publishing and Printing Projects" in Chapter 26*

4. What format does Picture It! Publishing convert a project to before you send it in an e-mail? *See "E-mailing a Project" in Chapter 26*

5. How are photos imported into your computer? *See "Importing Photos" in Chapter 27*

6. What can you do to a photo with the photo retouch tool? *See "Touching Up a Photo" in Chapter 27*

7. What are Picture It! Publishing stamps? *See "Adding Stamps" in Chapter 27*

8. What are four examples of objects? *See "Working with Objects" in Chapter 27*

9. What is the name of the area where Picture It! Publishing places thumbnails of open images? *See "Managing the Tray" in Chapter 27*

10. What does Picture It! Publishing include lots of to use when creating publications? *See "Creating Publications with Picture It! Publishing" in Chapter 28*

PART VII

Enhancing Productivity with Works

29

Tracking People with the Address Book

Works contains an address book that you can use to maintain a variety of information about business and personal contacts. You can use the address book to print a phone or an address list, telephone a contact, or send e-mail to a contact. In this chapter, you'll learn how to:

- Add an Address Book entry
- Delete a contact
- Print a contact list

Opening the Address Book

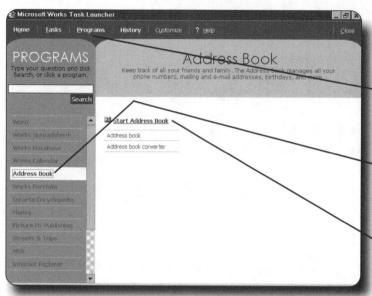

Access the Works Address Book through the Works Task Launcher.

1. Click on **Programs**. A list of Works Suite components will appear.

2. Click on **Address Book**. A list of Address Book tasks will appear.

3. Click on **Start Address Book**. The Address Book will open.

Adding an Address

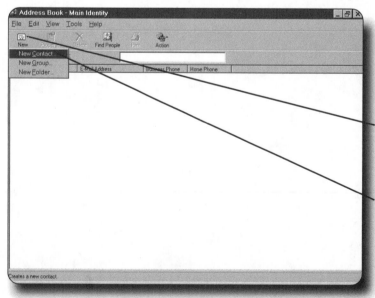

It's easy to add entries to the address book in Works. As you add contacts, they will be listed in alphabetical order by last name.

1. Click on the **New button**. A drop-down list will appear.

2. Click on **New Contact**. The Properties dialog box will open.

The Name tab appears first. This is where you'll store a contact's name and e-mail address.

3. Type the contact's **first name** in the First text box.

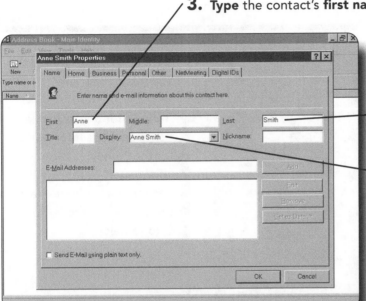

4. Press the **Tab key twice.** The insertion point will move to the Last text box.

5. Type the contact's **last name** in the Last text box.

As you enter the name, Works automatically fills in the Display text box.

6. Press the **Tab key** four times. The blinking insertion point will be in the E-Mail Addresses text box.

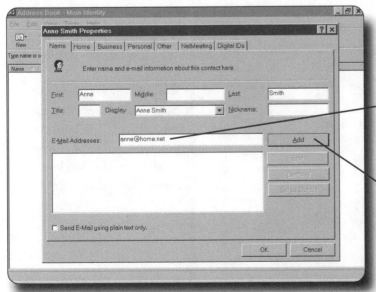

7. Type the contact's **e-mail address** in the E-Mail Addresses text box.

8. Click on **Add**. The e-mail address will be added.

TIP

Repeat steps 7 and 8 to add as many e-mail addresses as you want for this contact.

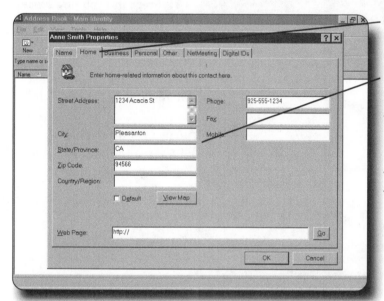

9. Click on the **Home tab**. The tab will display.

10. Enter any available **home address information** for the contact. The information you type will appear in each field. Press the Tab key to move from field to field.

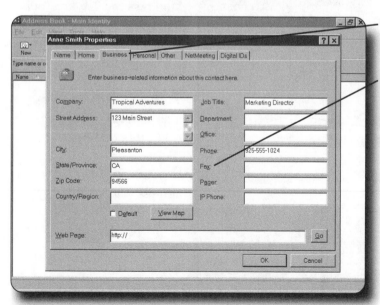

11. Click on the **Business tab**. The tab will display.

12. Enter any available **business information** for the contact. The information you type will appear in each field. Press the Tab key to move from field to field.

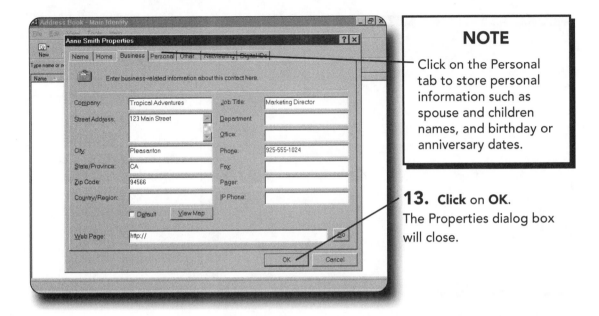

NOTE

Click on the Personal tab to store personal information such as spouse and children names, and birthday or anniversary dates.

13. **Click** on **OK**. The Properties dialog box will close.

Displaying Contact Information

Only the name, e-mail address, and two phone numbers appear in the Address Book. You'll need to open the record to see the entire contact information.

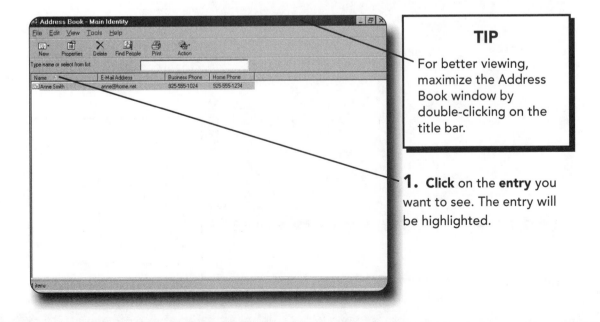

TIP

For better viewing, maximize the Address Book window by double-clicking on the title bar.

1. **Click** on the **entry** you want to see. The entry will be highlighted.

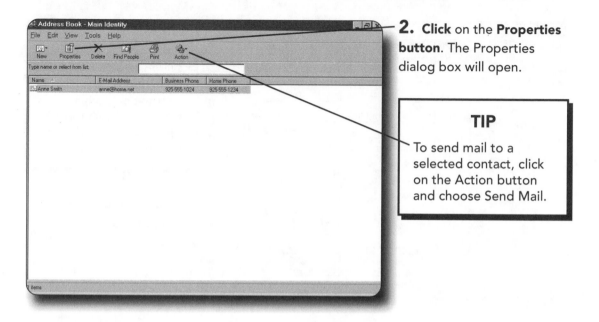

2. Click on the **Properties button**. The Properties dialog box will open.

TIP

To send mail to a selected contact, click on the Action button and choose Send Mail.

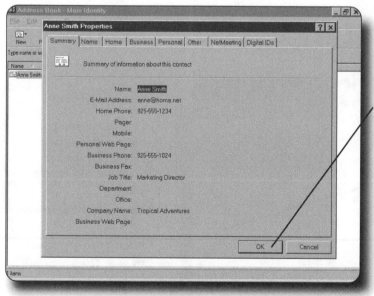

3. Click on the **tab** you want to see. The information on the selected contact will appear.

4. Click on **OK**. The Properties dialog box will close.

TIP

You can also edit information in the Properties dialog box if your contact's phone number, e-mail, address, or any other information changes.

Deleting an Address

If you no longer want a contact listed in your Address Book, you can easily delete it.

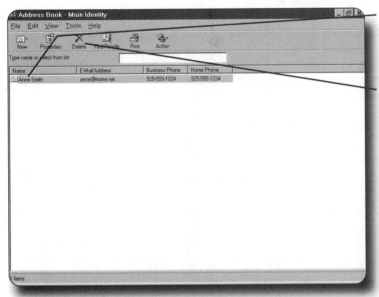

1. Click on the **contact name** to be deleted. The name will be selected.

2. Click on the **Delete button**. A confirmation box will appear.

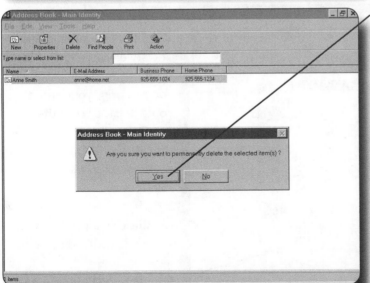

3. Click on **Yes**. The contact and all its information will be deleted.

CAUTION

You can't undo the delete action.

Printing a Phone List

You can print the information you store about your contacts in a variety of formats: Memo Style, Business Card Style, and Phone List Style.

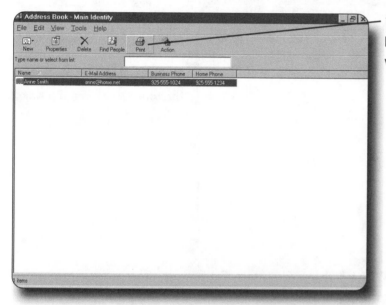

1. Click on the **Print button**. The Print dialog box will open.

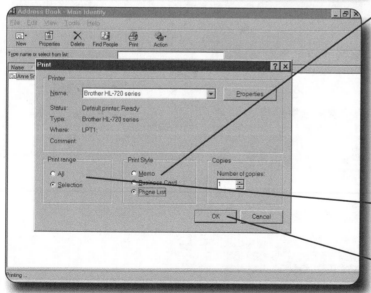

2. Click on a **print style**. The style will be highlighted.

You can print your entire contact list, or only the currently selected record— the one highlighted before you clicked on the Print button.

3. Click on a **print range**. The option will be selected.

4. Click on **OK**. The Address Book content will print.

Exiting the Address Book

Works automatically saves the information in the Address Book. When you are finished with the Address Book, close it like any other Works application.

1. **Click** on **File**. The File menu will appear.

2. **Click** on **Exit**. The Address Book will close, and the Works Task Launcher will appear.

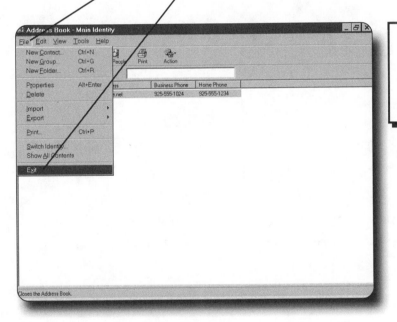

> **TIP**
>
> Optionally, click on the Address Book Close button.

30

Managing Your Schedule with the Calendar

Do you lose track of time or forget appointments? Works Calendar can help you manage and control all the things you need to do during the day. In Works Calendar, an *appointment* is anything that requires your time during a specific period. Items such as meetings, calls to clients, or interviews are considered appointments. In this chapter, you'll learn how to:

- View a calendar
- Add and delete appointments
- Assign reminders to appointments
- Find appointments
- Print a calendar

Starting the Works Calendar

Like other Works components, you open the calendar from the Task Launcher.

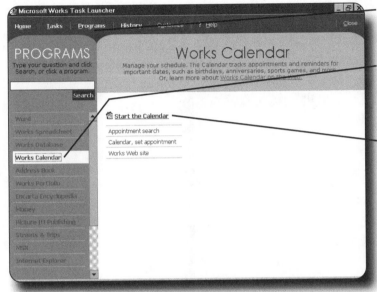

1. **Click** on **Programs**. The Programs menu will appear.

2. **Click** on **Works Calendar**. A list of calendar tasks will appear.

3. **Click** on **Start the Calendar**. The calendar will open.

NOTE

The first time you open Works Calendar, a message might display, asking if you would like to make Works your default calendar. Click on Yes. The message box will close.

Viewing the Calendar

Although the calendar opens in Day view—allowing you to see the appointments for the current day—you can also view it in Month or Week view.

Viewing by Week

To see your appointments for seven consecutive days, switch to Week view.

1. **Click** on **View**. The View menu will open.

2. **Click** on **Week**. A list of your weekly appointments will appear.

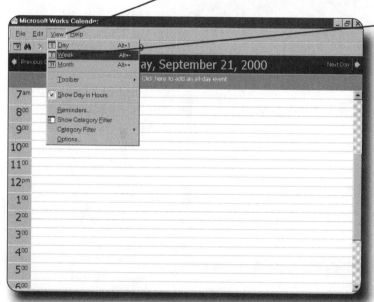

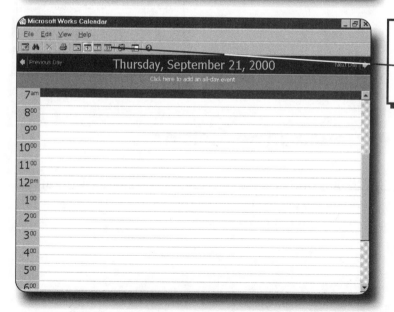

TIP

Optionally, click on the View Week button.

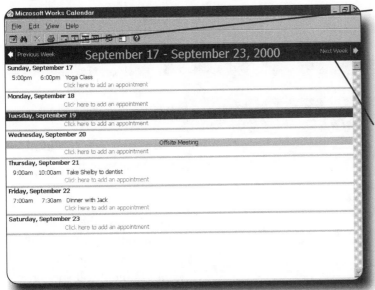

3a. **Click** on **Previous Week**. The prior week's appointments will appear.

OR

3b. **Click** on **Next Week**. The next week's appointments will appear.

Viewing by Month

View your appointments for an entire month.

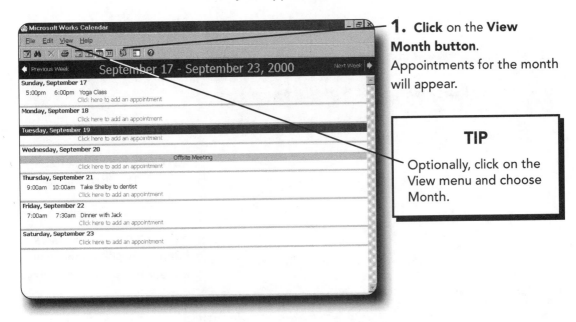

1. **Click** on the **View Month button**. Appointments for the month will appear.

TIP

Optionally, click on the View menu and choose Month.

2. Click on **Previous Month**. The appointments for the previous month will appear.

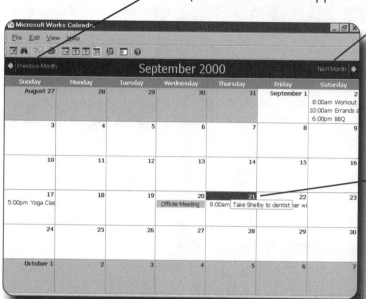

3. Click on **Next Month**. The appointments for the next month will appear.

Many appointments are abbreviated in the monthly view.

4. Position the **mouse** over any appointment. The full description of an appointment will appear.

Viewing by Day

Returning to Day view is only a mouse click away.

1. Click on the **day** to be viewed. The date will be highlighted.

2. Click on the **View Day button**. Appointments will appear for the selected day.

3. Click on **Previous Day**. The previous day's appointments will appear.

4. Click on **Next Day**. The next day's appointments will appear.

5. Click on **Go To Today**. Today's appointments will appear.

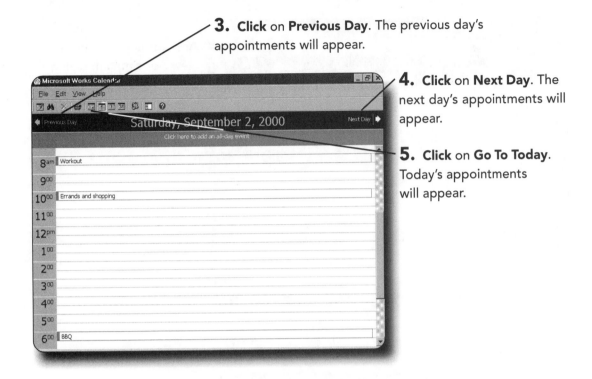

Creating a New Appointment

You can create appointments with a specified starting and ending time, such as an all-day event, or as a recurring event, such as a birthday or weekly meeting.

Adding a Timed Appointment

When creating an appointment, you can specify a beginning and/or ending time for the appointment.

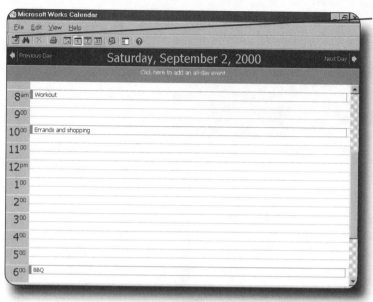

1. **Click** on the **New Appointment button**. The New Appointment dialog box will open.

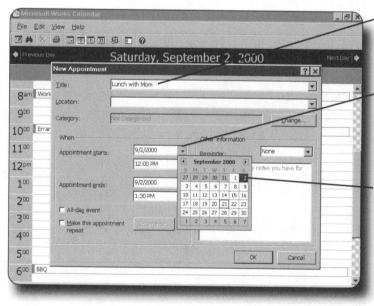

2. **Type** a **description** of the appointment in the Title text box.

3. **Click** on the **Appointment starts drop-down arrow**. A monthly calendar will appear.

4. **Click** on the **starting date** for the appointment. The date will appear in the Appointment starts text box.

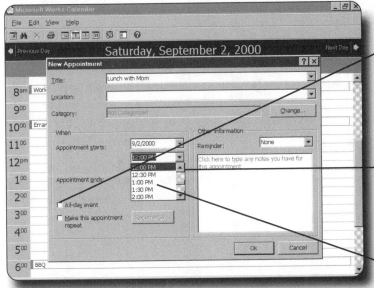

TIP

If your event will last all day, click on the All-day event check box. Note that the starting and ending times disappear.

5. **Click** on the **drop-down arrow** in the box below the Appointment starts text box. A list of times will appear.

6. **Click** on the **starting time** for the appointment. The time will appear in the text box.

Works assumes that the appointment will end half an hour after it begins. You can, however, set an appointment ending time.

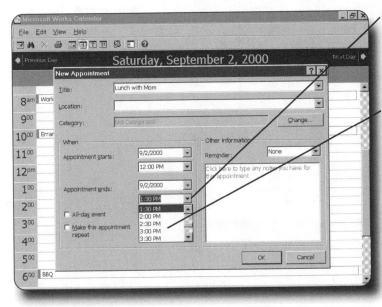

7. **Click** on the **drop-down arrow** in the box below the Appointment ends text box. A list of times will appear.

8. **Click** on the **ending time** for the appointment. The time will appear in the text box.

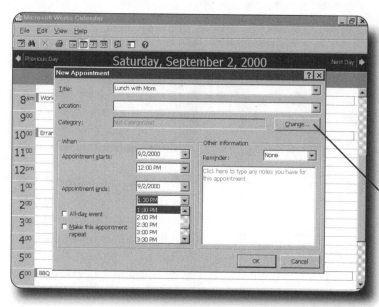

The Works Calendar includes 12 predefined categories for you to optionally assign your appointments. Applying a category allows you to search for or display items by category.

9. Click on **Change**. The Choose Categories dialog box will open.

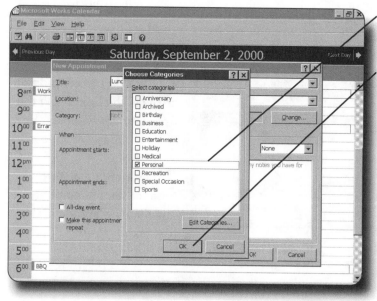

10. Click on a **category**. The option will be selected.

11. Click on **OK**. The Choose Categories dialog box will close.

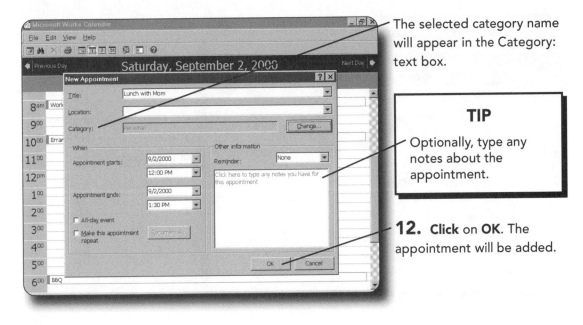

The selected category name will appear in the Category: text box.

TIP

Optionally, type any notes about the appointment.

12. **Click** on **OK**. The appointment will be added.

Adding a Recurring Appointment

A *recurring appointment* is one that you schedule for the same time every day, week, month, and so on, such as a class you attend regularly or a weekly sales meeting. By specifying these types of appointments as recurring, you avoid having to enter them repeatedly.

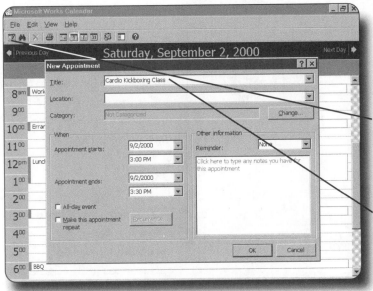

1. **Click** on the **New Appointment button**. The New Appointment dialog box will open.

2. **Type** a **description** of the appointment in the Title text box.

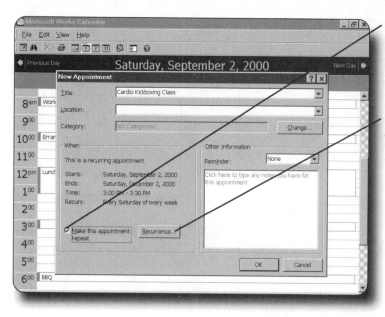

3. **Click** on **Make this appointment repeat**. A check mark ✔ will be placed in the box.

4. **Click** on **Recurrence**. The Recurrence Options dialog box will open.

5. **Click** on a **recurrence frequency.** The options displayed will vary with the frequency selected.

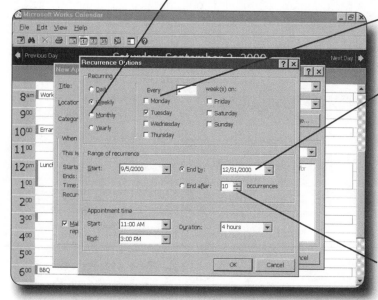

6. **Choose** the appropriate **day of the week.** The day will be selected.

7a. **Choose** an **ending date** using the drop-down arrow in the End by text box under the Range of recurrence options**.** The date will display.

OR

7b. **Click** on the **up/down arrows** to select the maximum number of occurrences in the End after text box.

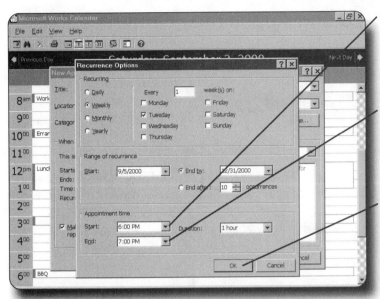

8. Choose a **start time** using the drop-down arrow in the Start text box. The time will display.

9. Choose an **end time** using the drop-down arrow in the End text box. The time will display.

10. Click on **OK**. The Recurrence Options dialog box will close.

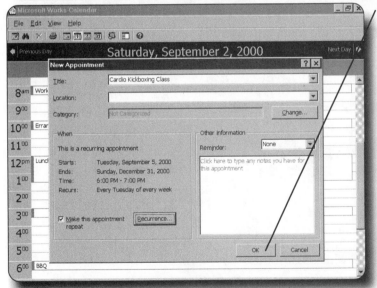

11. Click on **OK**. The New Appointment dialog box will close, and the appointment will be repeated in the Calendar at the specified intervals.

Editing Appointments

It's a fact of life—plans change. Fortunately, it's simple to update an event in your Works Calendar.

Editing Appointment Information

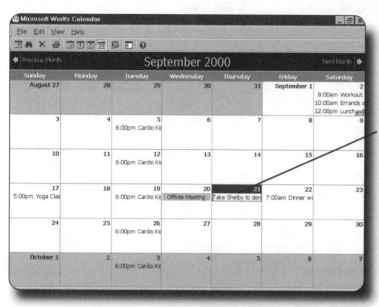

If you need to change the text or reminder information of an appointment, you'll use the Edit Appointment dialog box.

1. Double-click on the **appointment** to be edited. The Edit Appointment dialog box will open.

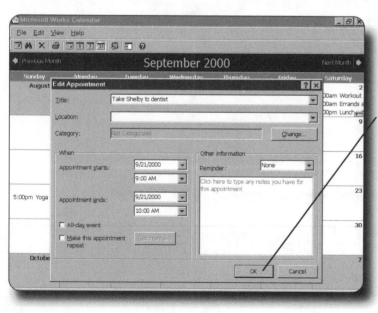

2. Make any **changes** to the appointment. The changes will appear in the dialog box.

3. Click on **OK**. The Edit Appointment dialog box will close.

Rescheduling Events

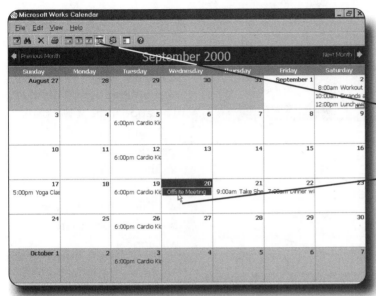

If your company picnic has been postponed to the next weekend, move it by using the Month view.

1. **Click** on the **View Month button**. The calendar will display for the month.

2. **Press** and **hold** the **mouse** over the **event** to be moved. The event will be highlighted.

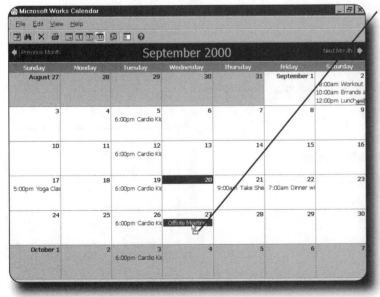

3. **Drag** the **event** to the new date. Both the new and old dates will be highlighted.

4. **Release** the **mouse button**. The event will be rescheduled.

TIP

If you're moving your appointment to a different time on the same day, do so in the Day view.

Deleting Appointments

If an appointment has been canceled, delete it from your calendar. It doesn't matter which view you are using.

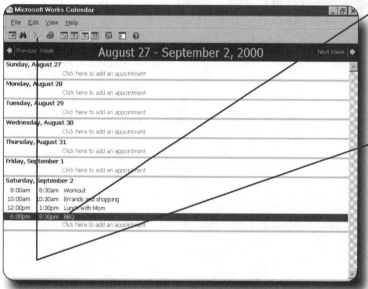

1. Click on the **appointment** to be deleted. The appointment will be highlighted, or a blinking insertion point will appear on the appointment.

2. Click on the **Delete button**. A confirmation box will appear.

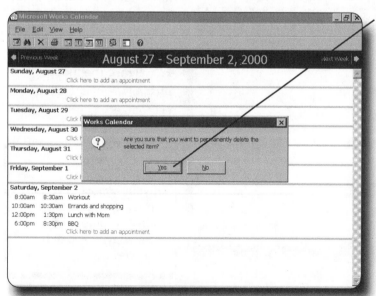

3. Click on **Yes**. The appointment will be permanently deleted.

CAUTION

The Windows Undo command does not work with deleted appointments.

Finding Appointments

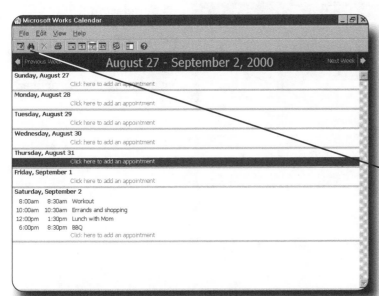

Can't remember when a particular appointment is scheduled? Let Works Calendar locate the appointment for you. The Find command locates appointments from any view.

1. Click on the **Find button**. The Find dialog box will open.

TIP

Optionally, click on the Edit menu and then choose Find.

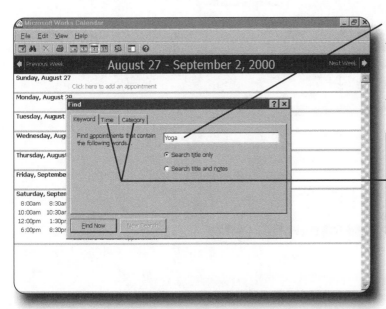

2. In the Keyword tab, **type** the **search text**. The text will appear in the Find appointments that contain the following words text box.

NOTE

You can also search for appointments by time or category.

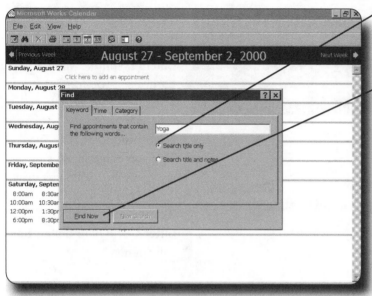

3. **Click** on a **search location option**. The option will be selected.

4. **Click** on **Find Now**. A list of all appointments that match the criteria will appear.

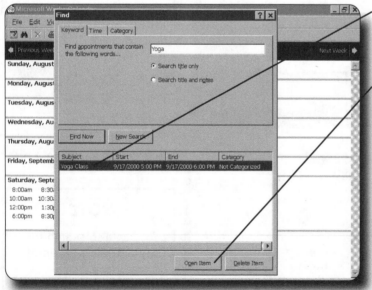

5. **Click** on the **item to be viewed**. The appointment will be highlighted.

6. **Click** on **Open Item**. The Edit Appointment dialog box will open.

You can then review or edit the appointment.

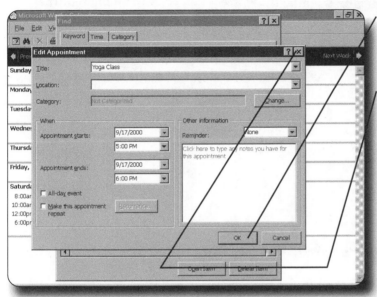

7. Click on **OK**. The Edit Appointment dialog box will close.

8. Click on the Find dialog box **Close button**. The Find dialog box will close.

Printing a Calendar

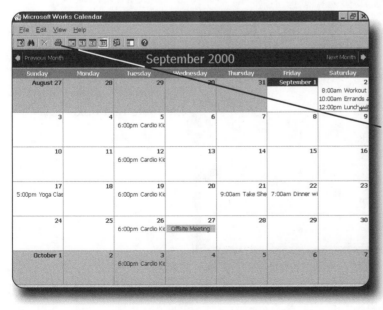

If you need a paper copy of your calendar, you can print it by the day, week, month, or even hour of the appointments.

1. Click on the **Print button**. The Print dialog box will open.

TIP

Optionally, click on the File menu and choose Print.

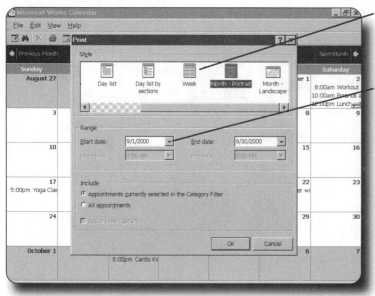

2. **Click** on the **calendar style** to be printed. The style will be highlighted.

3. **Click** on a **starting date** from the Start date drop-down list.

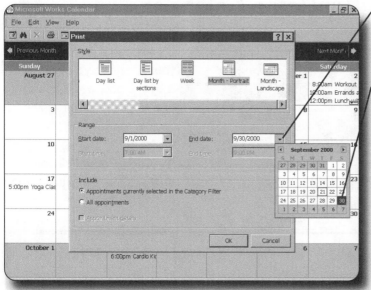

4. **Click** on the **End date drop-down arrow**. A monthly calendar will appear.

5. **Click** on the **ending date** that you want to print. The date will appear in the End date text box.

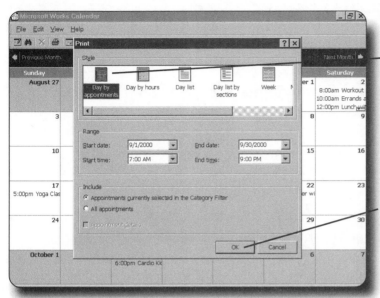

NOTE

If you select Day by appointments or Day by hours for the style to be printed, you'll also need to select the starting and ending time to be printed.

6. Click on **OK**. The calendar will print with the options that you specified.

Exiting the Works Calendar

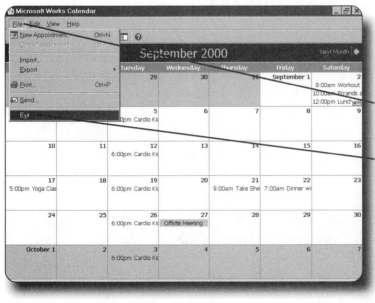

There is no Save command necessary for the Works Calendar. It automatically saves each time you exit.

1. Click on **File**. The File menu will appear.

2. Click on **Exit**. The Works Calendar will close, and the Task Launcher will appear.

TIP

Optionally, click on the Calendar Close button.

Part VII Review Questions

1. As you add contacts to the Address Book, how do they display? *See "Adding an Address" in Chapter 29*

2. Where can you add personal information about your contacts? *See "Adding an Address" in Chapter 29*

3. How do you edit information in the Address Book? *See "Displaying Contact Information" in Chapter 29*

4. How do you delete a contact? *See "Deleting an Address" in Chapter 29*

5. What types of lists can you print from the Address Book? *See "Printing a Phone List" in Chapter 29*

6. What views does the Works Calendar provide? *See "Viewing the Calendar" in Chapter 30*

7. What is a recurring appointment? *See "Adding a Recurring Appointment" in Chapter 30*

8. What feature does the Calendar provide to help you locate a scheduled appointment? *See "Finding Appointments" in Chapter 30*

9. Do you need to use the Save command with the Calendar? *See "Exiting the Works Calendar" in Chapter 30*

10. How do you print your calendar by the week? *See "Printing a Calendar" in Chapter 30*

PART VIII

Collaborating and Connecting with Works Suite

31

Sharing Data Among Programs

One reason the Microsoft Works Suite 2001 is such a popular program is its capability to share information among its individual applications. For example, using Works, you can document a piece of information in one area, such as the word processor, then quickly combine it with information in a spreadsheet, or your calendar. In this chapter you'll learn how to:

- Use the Portfolio
- Work with collections
- Use Mail Merge to create form letters

Using Works Portfolio

New to Works Suite 2001 is the Portfolio. The Microsoft Works Portfolio is a feature used to gather and organize information into a collection. You can copy, store, and organize pictures, text, and entire files from documents you create or scan, download or copy from the Internet or from e-mail attachments. For example, you might create a photo journal of your recent vacation, a collection of tips on a particular hobby, or a collection of research materials including written documents, Internet sites, and images.

Understanding Works Portfolio

You access the Portfolio via the little icon that's been hanging around on your Windows desktop since you installed Works Suite.

Viewing the Portfolio

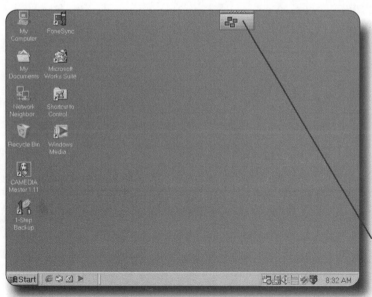

Works provides three different ways to view the Portfolio, each with its own unique icon. The different views are designed to help you work efficiently. When first installed, the Portfolio is minimized in Compact view. Compact view is the default view, and the smallest of the three views.

1. Click on the **Portfolio icon**. The Portfolio will open in Compact view, displaying view icons and tasks.

TIP

Click on the Portfolio again to close the Compact view.

2. Click on the **Docked View button.** The Portfolio will open on the side of your screen, and display thumbnail representations of items in the collections.

TIP

Click on the Compact View button to close the Docked view and return to the minimized Compact view.

3. Click on the **Gallery View button.** The Portfolio will display a large window containing items in the collections along with comments. This view is best used while working with collections.

TIP

Click on the Close button or the Compact View button to close the Gallery view and return to the minimized Compact view.

Making Menu Selections

The Portfolio contains several menus from which you can choose.

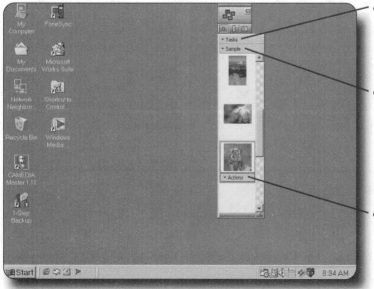

- **The Tasks menu**. This menu displays options for creating and managing collections.

- **The Collections menu**. This menu displays options for viewing different collections, and displays the name of the active collection.

- **The Actions menu**. This menu contains tasks you can engage in when using and creating collections.

Keeping a Collection Open

While using the Portfolio in Compact view, you can keep the Portfolio collection open for frequent use.

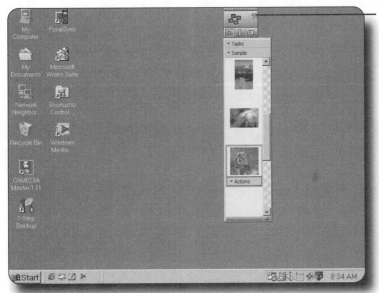

1. **Click** on the **Lock push-pin button**. The collection will remain open.

2. **Click** on the **Lock push-pin button** again. The collection will close.

Moving the Portfolio

You can place the Works Portfolio along any edge of your computer's screen.

1. **Position** the **mouse** over the Portfolio icon.

2. **Click** and **drag** the **Portfolio** to a new location. An outline shape will appear to represent the new position.

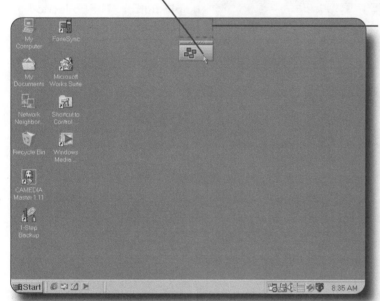

NOTE

If you move the Portfolio to any corner, Works automatically switches to Docked view.

3. **Release** the **mouse button**. The Portfolio will move to the new position.

Working with Collections

The information you gather is stored in a *collection*. Each piece of information you add to a collection is called an *item*.

Creating a New Collection

Organize your own projects into their own collections. Create as many different collections as you need.

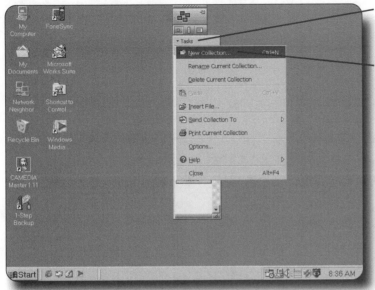

1. **Click** on **Tasks**. The Tasks menu will appear.

2. **Click** on **New Collection**. The New Collection dialog box will open.

Naming collections helps you organize different collections and identify the contents of each. Collection names can be up to 100 characters in length.

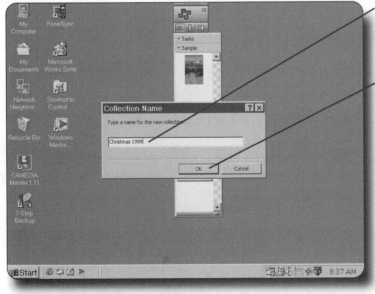

3. **Type** a **name** for the collection. The name will appear in the text box.

4. **Click** on **OK**. The new empty collection will appear.

Selecting and Displaying a Collection

Before you can view, use, add to, rename, delete, or otherwise modify a collection, you need to select it.

1. **Click** on the **Collections menu**. The Collections menu will appear.

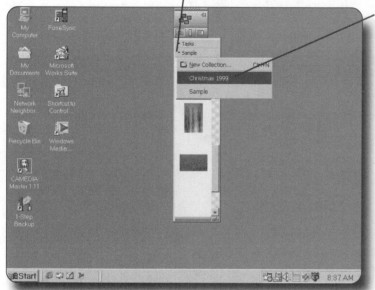

2. **Click** on the **name of the collection** you want to activate. The collection name will appear in the Collections menu, and the items stored in the collection will appear below it.

Renaming a Collection

If the contents of a collection change so that the name no longer describes the contents, you can easily rename the collection.

1. **Display** the **collection** you want to rename. The current collection name will appear in the Collections menu.

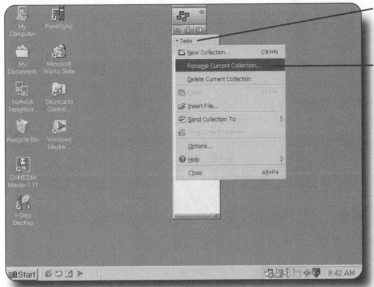

2. **Click** on **Tasks**. The Tasks menu will appear.

3. **Click** on **Rename Current Collection**. The Rename a Collection dialog box will open.

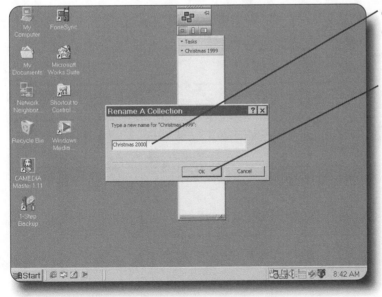

4. **Type** a **new name** for the collection. The new name will appear in the text box.

5. **Click** on **OK**. The collection will display with a new name.

Deleting a Collection

Deleting a collection does not actually delete files, only the thumbnail references to files. Works always maintains at least one collection, so if you delete all your collections, Works creates one empty collection for you to work with.

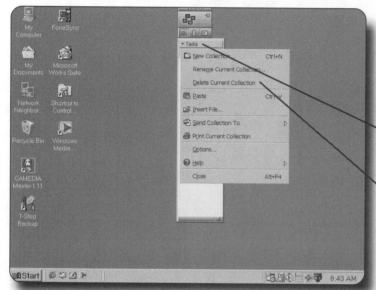

1. Display the **collection** you want to delete. The current collection name will appear in the Collections menu.

2. Click on **Tasks**. The Tasks menu will appear.

3. Click on **Delete Current Collection**. A confirmation dialog box will open.

NOTE

If a collection is empty, no confirmation dialog box will appear.

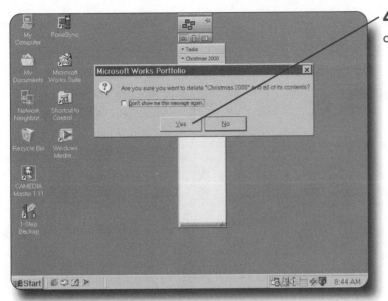

4. **Click** on **Yes**. The collection will be deleted.

Adding Items

Depending on the type of item you want to add to a collection, Works provides several methods for adding items.

NOTE

Some pictures and text on the Web are copyrighted. Be sure to observe all copyright laws before using copyrighted images and text.

Dragging and Dropping

Switch to the Compact or Docked view when you want to quickly drag and drop items into a collection while maximizing the screen area.

Although not limited to use with images saved in their own files or with complete documents, the drag-and-drop function works best with these types of items.

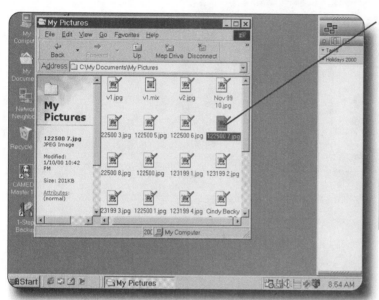

1. Locate and **click** on the file you want to copy to the collection. The file icon will be highlighted.

TIP

Hold down the Ctrl key and click to select multiple files at the same time.

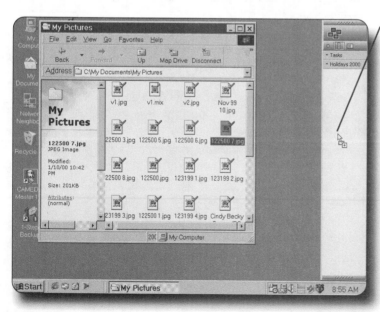

2. Press and **hold** the **mouse button** over the selected icon and **drag** the icon to the Portfolio. A vertical bar will appear representing the location of the new item.

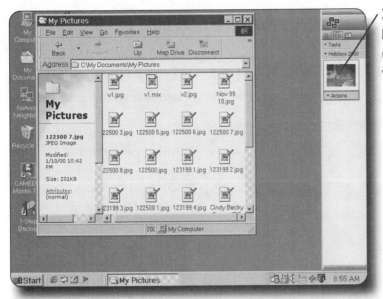

3. Release the **mouse button**. A sample representation of the item will appear in the collection.

Copying and Pasting

In some instances, you'll find dragging and dropping items just doesn't seem to work. In those situations, you'll want to use the Copy and Paste commands.

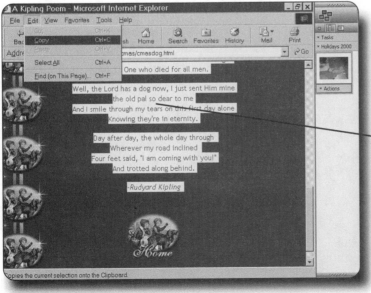

To select text, drag the mouse across the desired text. To select a picture, click on the picture.

1. Highlight the **information** you want to copy into a Portfolio collection. The text or picture will be selected.

NOTE

When selecting information on a Web page, select only the information you want to copy to the collection.

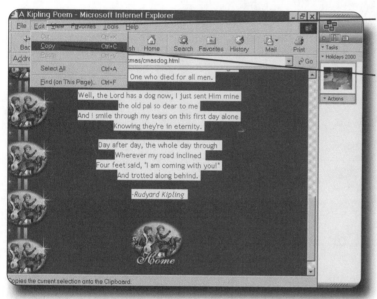

2. Click on **Edit**. The Edit menu will appear.

3. Click on **Copy**. The selection will be copied to the Windows clipboard.

Now you're ready to place the information in your Portfolio collection.

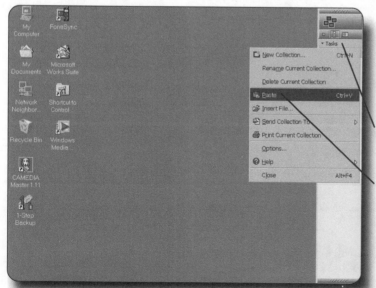

4. In the Portfolio, **click** on the **Collection** you want to add to. The selected collection will become the current active collection.

5. Click on **Tasks**. The Tasks menu will appear.

6. Click on **Paste**. Works will place a copy of the text or picture at the end of the current collection.

TIP

Easily rearrange items in a collection by dragging an item to a new location in the collection.

Selecting Items

In order to manage the items in a collection, you'll need to first select them. Selected items appear with a gray box surrounding them.

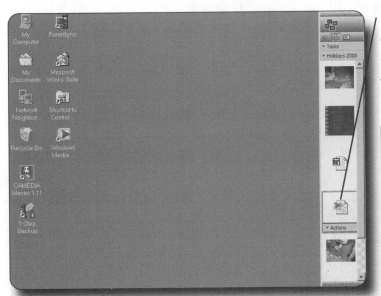

1. Click on an **item** in a collection. The item will appear selected, and the Actions menu will appear under the selected item.

TIP

You can also select multiple items by pressing and holding the Ctrl key and clicking on additional items.

Adding Comments to an Item

You can add comments to an item to explain why you copied the item, how you plan to use it, and so on.

Adding Comments in Compact or Docked View

If you are using Compact or Docked view, follow these steps:

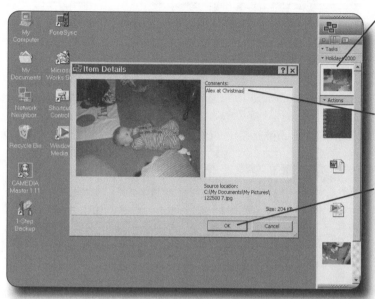

1. **Double-click** on the **item** to which you want to add a comment. The Item Details dialog box will open.

2. **Type** the **comment**. The text will appear in the Comments text box.

3. **Click** on **OK**. The Item Details dialog box will close.

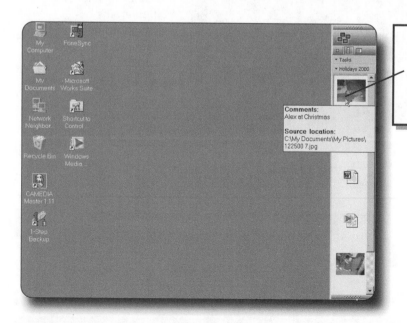

TIP

Position the mouse over the image to view the comment.

Adding Comments in Gallery View

If you are using Gallery view, follow these steps to add a comment:

1. **Click** on the **image** to which you want to add a comment. The image will be displayed.

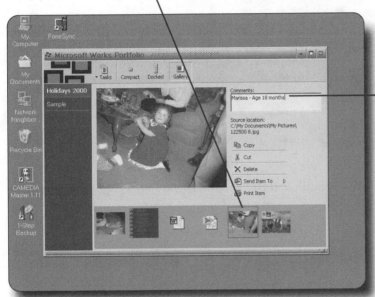

2. **Click** in the **Comments text box**. A blinking insertion point will appear.

3. **Type** the **comment**. The text will appear in the Comments text box.

Deleting Items from a Collection

Deleting items is a good way to keep collections at a manageable size and make them easy to browse. As with deleting entire collections, deleting items doesn't delete the item from your hard drive, only from the collection.

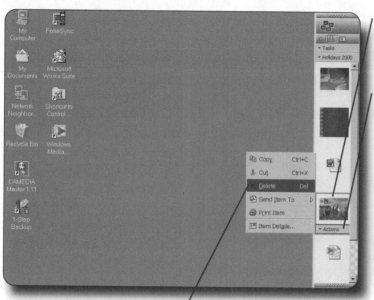

1. **Click** on the **item** you want to delete. The item will be selected.

2. **Click** on **Actions**. The Actions menu will appear.

TIP

Optionally, click on the item you want to delete and press the Delete key.

3. **Click** on **Delete**. A confirmation message will appear.

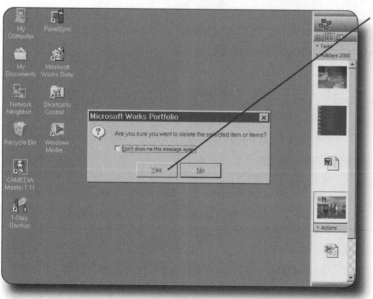

4. **Click** on **Yes**. The item will be deleted from the collection.

Using Collected Items in Another Document

Once you've added items to a collection, you can quickly insert one, several, or all items in a collection into other documents or an e-mail message.

Microsoft provides several different methods to insert Portfolio collection items into other documents or e-mail messages, but I have found the drag-and-drop method the fastest and easiest.

1. **Open** the **document or e-mail message** to which you want to add items. The document or message will appear onscreen.

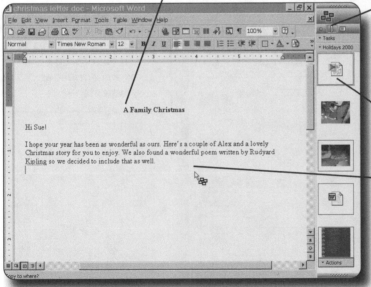

2. **Open** the **Portfolio** to **Docked view**. The Portfolio will appear along the edge of your computer screen.

3. **Select** the **item** you want to copy. The item will be selected.

4. **Press** and **hold** the **mouse button** and **drag** the **items** to the document or e-mail message.

5. **Release** the mouse **button**. If you drag the items to a document, the following will occur, depending on the type of item:

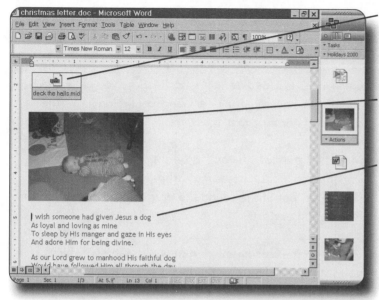

- **Sound file**. An icon representing the sound file will appear in the document.

- **Picture file**. The image will open in the document.

- **Document**. The text will appear in the document.

- **Web page**. An image of the Web page will appear in the document.

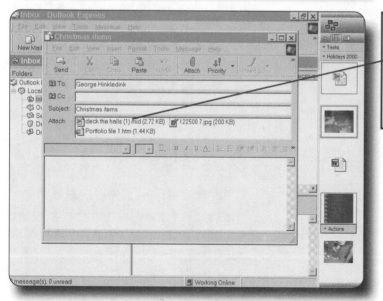

NOTE

If you drag the items to an e-mail message, the items will appear as attachments.

Understanding Mail Merge

Form letters are multiple printed copies of the same document, with different information such as names and addresses printed on each copy automatically.

We've all received such letters—like the ones telling us, "You may already be a winner." If creating a form letter seems intimidating, you can relax. In Part II, "Creating Documents with Word," you learned how to create a document using the Microsoft Word word-processing component of Works Suite, and in Part IV, "Working with Databases," you learned how to create and work with a database. By merging a word-processing document and a database, you can create form letters for mass mailings.

Designing a Form Letter

Create and save your database before designing the form letter. Refer to Chapter 16, "Creating a Database," for a refresher on creating a database.

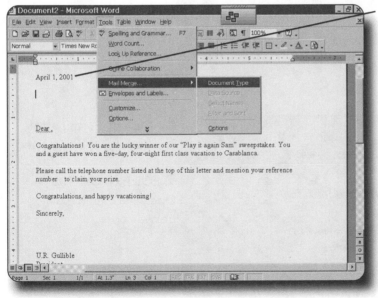

1. Using Microsoft Word, open or create the letter with the common information. Common information includes the standardized text you want to appear on each letter. The document will appear on your computer screen.

NOTE

When preparing a document for merging, leave the space blank where the variable information, such as name and address, will appear.

2. Click the **mouse** where you want the first data field to appear. The blinking insertion point will appear.

3. Click on **Tools**. The Tools menu will appear.

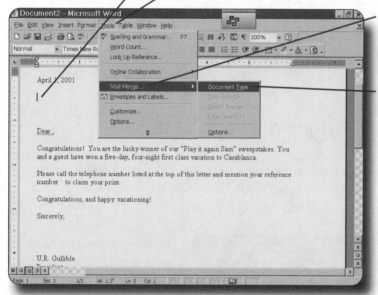

4. Click on **Mail Merge**. The Mail Merge submenu will appear.

5. Click on **Document Type**. The Document type dialog box will open.

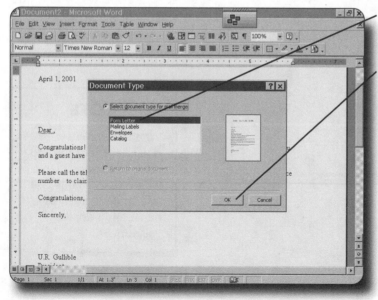

6. Click on **Form Letter**. The option will be selected.

7. Click on **OK**. The first Open Data Source dialog box will open.

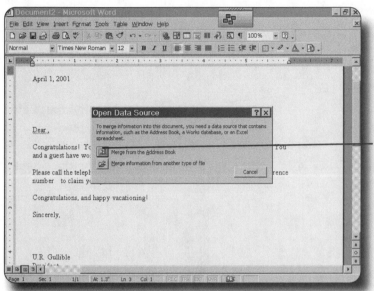

You'll need to specify whether the data will come from the Works address book or from another source such as a Works database or Excel spreadsheet.

8. **Click** on the **Merge information from another type of file button**. The second Open Data Source dialog box will open.

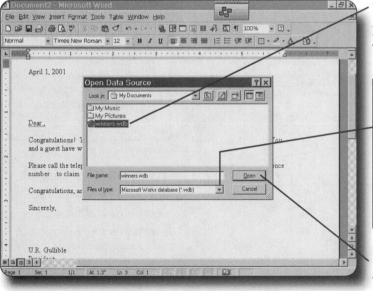

9. **Click** on the **data file** you want to merge. The filename will be highlighted.

TIP

If the data file is not a Works database, click on the Files of type drop-down arrow to choose a different file type.

10. **Click** on **Open**. The Mail Merge toolbar will appear in the document window.

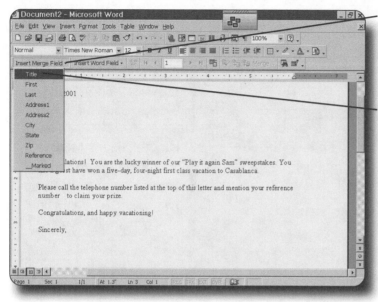

11. **Click** on **Insert Merge Field**. A list of field names from the selected database will appear.

12. **Click** on the **first field** to be added in the form letter. The field will be inserted into the document.

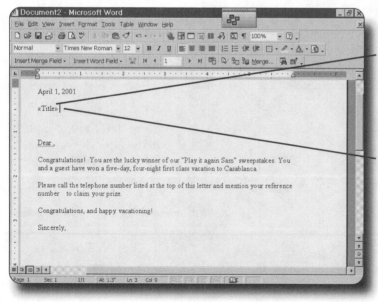

NOTE

Field name placeholders appear as <<field name>> in a form letter.

13. **Click** the **mouse** where you want to place the next field. The blinking insertion point will appear.

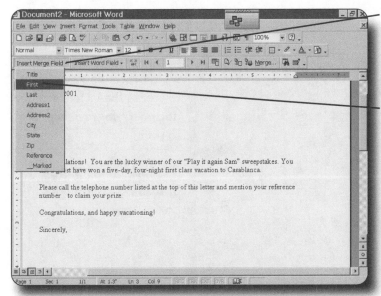

14. **Click** on **Insert Merge Field**. A list of field names from the selected database will appear.

15. **Click** on the **next field** to be added to the form letter. The field name will be inserted into the document.

NOTE

Not all fields have to be used in the document, and any field can be used more than once.

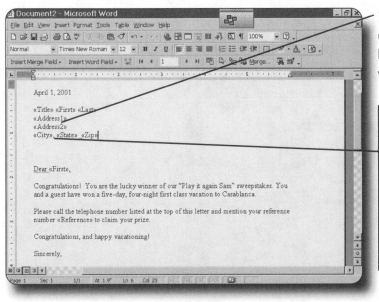

16. **Repeat steps 13–15** until all the fields you want have been added. The fields will appear in the document.

TIP

Place any necessary spaces or punctuation between the fields. The spaces or punctuation marks should not be between the << and >> field markers.

Previewing a Merge

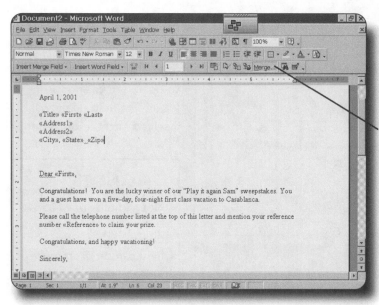

Combine the data into the word-processing document to create the letters in a new document for review prior to printing.

1. Click on the **Merge button**. The Merge dialog box will open.

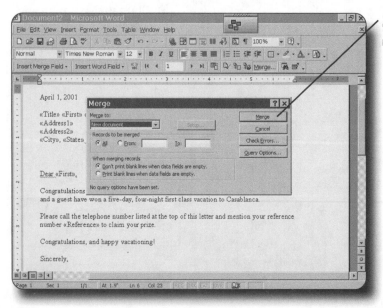

2. Click on **Merge**. The first merged letter will appear.

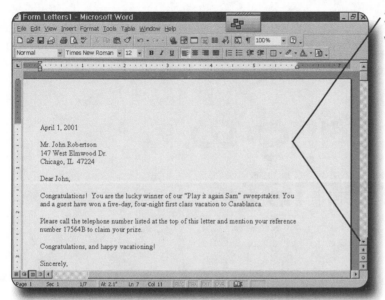

3. Click on the **scroll bar** to view other merged letters.

NOTE

Notice that data from the database has replaced the field placeholders.

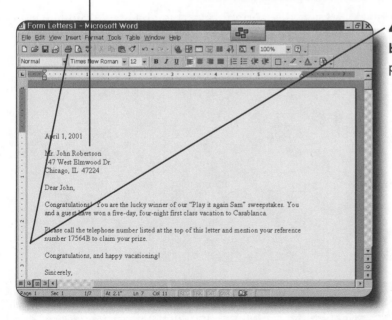

4. Click on the **Print button**. The form letters will print to your default printer.

32

Connecting to the Internet

In this book, you've explored the basic applications of Microsoft Works Suite 2001. You've also learned how to integrate these applications. Works Suite also includes three additional programs that enable you to access and make the most of the Internet: Internet Explorer, Outlook Express, and the MSN Network. These programs aren't technically part of Works Suite, but are included on the CDs and are available through the Works Task Launcher. In this chapter, you'll learn how to:

- Connect to the Internet
- Use Internet Explorer
- Access the MSN Web portal
- Use Outlook Express

Getting Started

Before you can connect Works Suite to the Internet, you'll need a way to access the Internet. In many cases, you may already have access and can just get started exploring the new tools Works Suite provides. But if you aren't connected to the Internet, you'll need to sign up with an Internet service provider to do so (assuming you have a computer with a modem). Works Suite can help you get connected to the Internet by guiding you through the process of setting up your computer as well as choosing an ISP. You do this in the Task Launcher.

1. **Click** on **Tasks.** A list of tasks will appear.

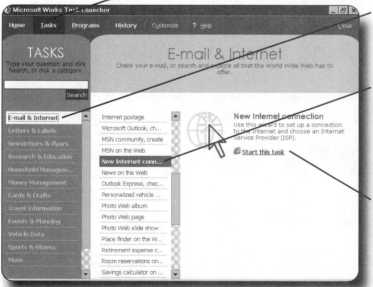

2. **Click** on **E-mail & Internet.** A selection of related tasks will appear.

3. **Click** on **New Internet connection.** Information about setting up a new Internet connection will appear.

4. **Click** on **Start this task.** The Internet Connection Wizard will open.

5. Follow the **step-by-step instructions** the wizard provides. Steps will vary depending on your choices.

When you're finished with the wizard, you should be ready to connect to and explore the Internet.

Using Internet Explorer

Internet Explorer is a popular Web browser used to access the Internet. With Internet Explorer, you can visit Web sites, mark them as favorites so you can easily return to them, or track your Web usage with the History button.

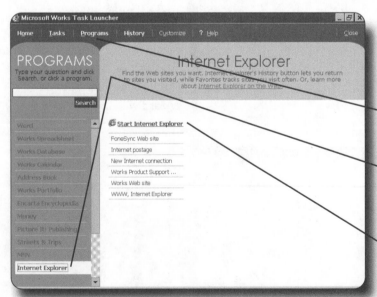

1. Click on **Programs.** A list of programs will appear.

2. Click on **Internet Explorer.** A list of Internet Explorer tasks will appear.

3. Click on **Start Internet Explorer.**

Internet Explorer will open, displaying the MSN Web portal.

Using MSN

Works Suite provides numerous links to common areas of MSN directly through the Microsoft Works Task Launcher.

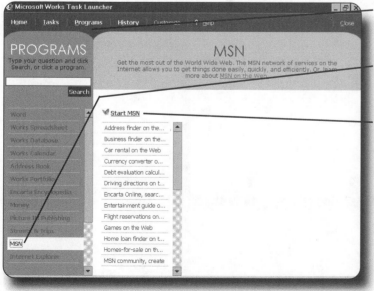

1. **Click** on **Programs.** A list of programs will appear.

2. **Click** on **MSN.** A list of MSN tasks will appear.

3. **Click** on **Start MSN.** MSN will open using Internet Explorer.

From here, you can explore the varied content of this site as well as follow links to other sites.

Using Outlook Express

Outlook Express is a full-featured e-mail and news-reading program that comes with Microsoft Works Suite 2001. With Outlook Express, you can send and receive e-mail or transfer files to others.

Starting Outlook Express

To send or receive e-mail, you must have a modem hooked up to your computer, and you must have Internet access through an ISP. You can start Outlook Express from the Works Task Launcher.

1. **Click** on **Programs**. A listing of Works Suite programs will appear.

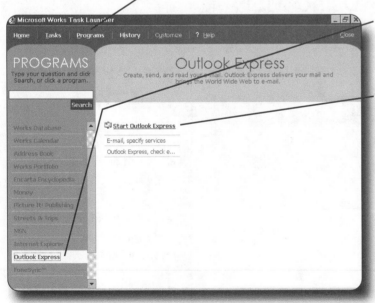

2. **Click** on **Outlook Express**. A listing of Outlook Express tasks will appear.

3. **Click** on **Start Outlook Express**. The Outlook Express program will start.

Setting Up Outlook Express

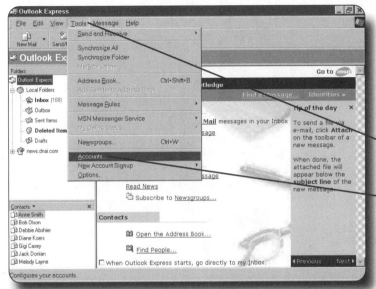

If you are new to Outlook Express, Works Suite uses the Internet Connection Wizard to quickly lead you through the process of setting up a new e-mail account.

1. **Click** on **Tools**. The Tools menu will appear.

2. **Click** on **Accounts**. The Internet Accounts dialog box will open.

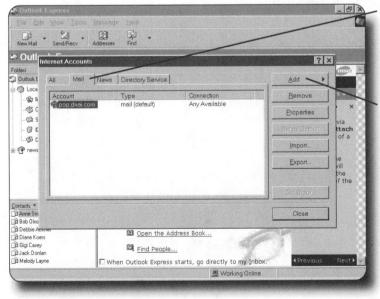

3. **Click** on the **Mail tab**. This tab will come to the front with a listing of current e-mail accounts.

4. **Click** on **Add**. The Add menu will appear.

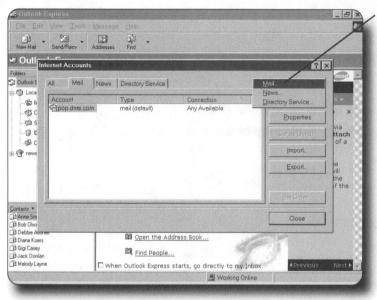

5. Click on **Mail**. The Internet Connection Wizard will open to assist you through the e-mail account setup process.

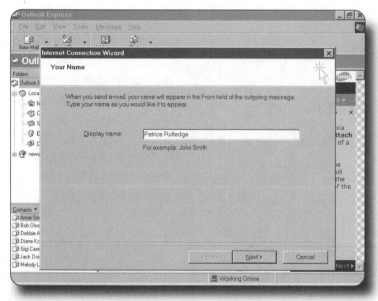

6. Continue through the steps of the Internet Connection Wizard to complete setup.

The steps may vary depending upon which ISP you use. Most ISPs provide information on setting up e-mail accounts, and some even provide specific details for Microsoft Outlook or Outlook Express.

Working with Outlook Express

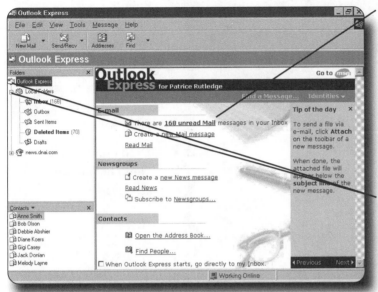

When you first open Outlook Express, you'll see a start page with a variety of links as well as panes for folders and contacts. When you read e-mail, the start page is replaced with a list of e-mails and a viewing window.

Click on the top folder, Outlook Express, any time you want to display the start page again. Beneath that folder are local folders where you store your e-mail.

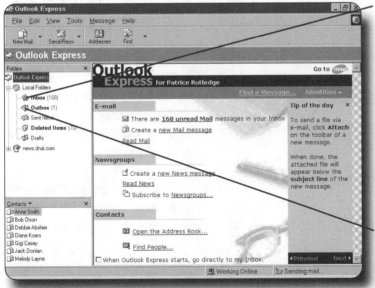

When you connect to your ISP, Outlook Express places incoming mail in the Inbox folder. A number (in parentheses) on the right side of the Inbox folder indicates how many new messages you have. Click on the Inbox folder to display your e-mail on the right side of the screen.

When you create e-mail messages, you have the option to send them immediately or send them later. Any messages waiting to be sent are indicated in the Outbox folder.

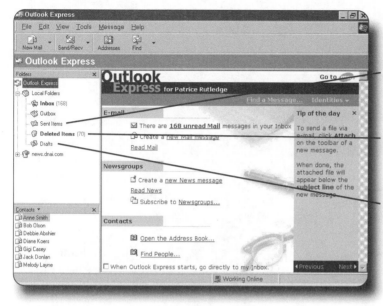

Other folders created with Outlook Express include

- A Sent Items folder to keep copies of any e-mail you send

- A Deleted Items folder to store e-mail you've thrown away

- A Drafts folder in which to keep unfinished messages

Creating an E-mail Message

In Outlook Express, you can read, create, send, and manage all your e-mail messages.

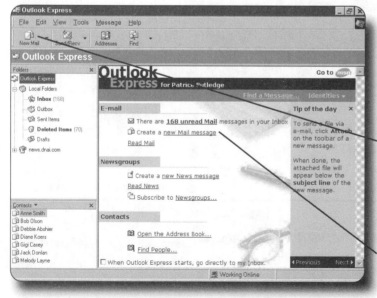

The start page displayed on the right side of the screen can be your entry point to Outlook Express. It lets you quickly jump to the task you need to do.

1a. Click on the **New Mail button**. The New Message dialog box will open.

OR

1b. Click on **Create a new Mail message** on the start page. The New Message dialog box will open.

NOTE

You may be prompted to choose Outlook as your default mail program. If you will use Outlook for most of your e-mail, click on Yes.

2. **Type** the **e-mail address** of the person to whom you want to send the message. The name will appear in the To line.

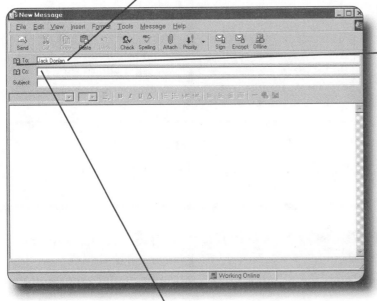

TIP

Optionally, click on the To icon to locate an e-mail address in your Address Book. See chapter 29, "Tracking People with the Address Book," to learn more about this feature.

3. **Press** the **Tab key**. The insertion point will move to the Cc line.

4. **Type** an **e-mail address** of anyone to whom you want to send a carbon copy (CC) of the message, if desired.

NOTE

If you have more than one person to list on any of the address lines, separate the e-mail name of each recipient by a comma or semicolon.

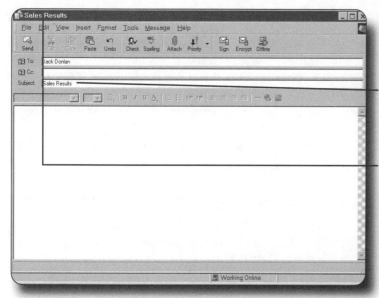

5. **Press** the **Tab key**. The insertion point will move to the Subject line.

6. **Type** a **subject** for the message. The text will appear in the Subject line.

The Subject line isn't required, but is recommended. If you try to send a message without a subject, Outlook Express will ask if you're sure you want to send it that way.

NOTE

When you type a subject, the New Message title bar reflects the subject.

7. **Press** the **Tab key**. The insertion point will move to the body of the message.

8. **Type** your **message** in the message box. The typed text will appear in the lower half of the window.

TIP

Don't type in ALL CAPS. That's considered SHOUTING!

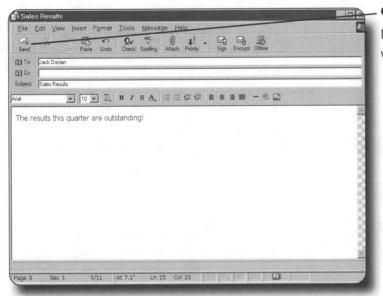

9. Click on **Send**. The New Message dialog box will close.

Your message will be placed in the Outbox folder.

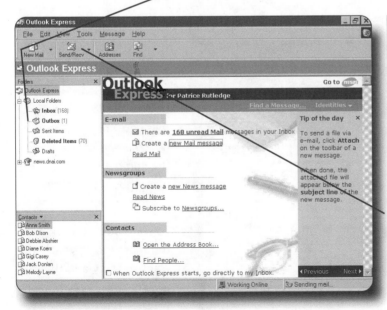

NOTE

If you're connected to the Internet at the time you create your message, it will be sent automatically as soon as you place it in the Outbox.

10. Click on the **Send/Recv button**. Outlook Express will connect to the Internet and send your message.

CAUTION

If you aren't connected to the Internet, you'll be prompted to do so.

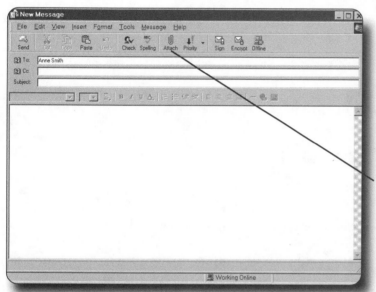

Handling Other Common E-mail Tasks

It's easy to handle other common e-mail tasks in Outlook Express:

- To attach a file to an e-mail you're sending, click on the Attach button.

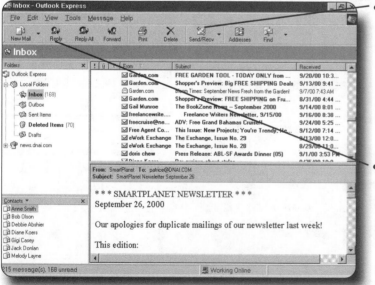

- To receive incoming e-mail, click on the Send/Recv button. Outlook Express tells you when you have new messages by putting the number of new messages in parentheses next to the Inbox.

- To send a reply, click on the message to which you want to reply and then click on the Reply button.

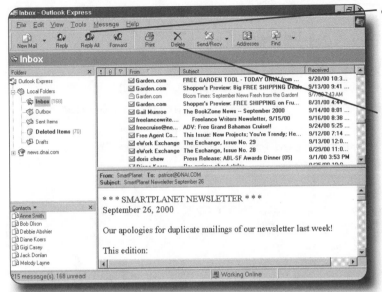

- To forward a message, click on the message you want to forward and then click on the Forward button.

- To delete a message, click on the message you want to delete and then click on the Delete button. Deleted messages are moved to the Deleted Items folder.

NOTE

For more detailed information on using Internet Explorer and Outlook Express, you might want to take a look at another book Prima publishes called *Internet Explorer 5 Fast & Easy* by Coletta Witherspoon.

Part VIII Review Questions

1. What new Works Suite 2001 feature helps you to gather and organize information? *See "Using Works Portfolio" in Chapter 31*

2. What three views are provided for the Portfolio? *See "Viewing the Portfolio" in Chapter 31*

3. What are the pieces of information in a collection called? *See "Working with Collections" in Chapter 31*

4. What two types of documents merge together to create a form letter? *See "Understanding Mail Merge" in Chapter 31*

5. What toolbar appears after you specify a database for a mail merge? *See "Designing a Form Letter" in Chapter 31*

6. How can I find an ISP to connect to the Internet? *See "Using MSN" in Chapter 32*

7. Which version of Internet Explorer comes with Works Suite? *See "Using Internet Explorer" in Chapter 32*

8. How do I set up a new e-mail address in Outlook Express? *See "Setting Up Outlook Express" in Chapter 32*

9. How can I send e-mail? *See "Using Outlook Express" in Chapter 32*

10. How can I receive incoming e-mail? *See "Handling Other Common E-mail Tasks" in Chapter 32*

PART IX

Appendixes

Installing Microsoft Works Suite

Installing Microsoft Works Suite 2001 is a painless process. In this chapter, you'll learn how to:

- Determine hardware requirements
- Install Microsoft Works Suite 2001
- Uninstall Microsoft Works Suite 2001

Discovering System Requirements

Works Suite 2001 has minimum requirements to run properly. The following table lists these specifications:

Component	Requirement
Processor	Pentium 166 MHz or higher
Operating system	Win 95, 98, 2000, or Millennium Edition (ME)
Memory	32MB RAM required for 95 and 98 (64MB recommended); 64MB required for 2000 and ME
Disk space	850MB disk
CD	4X or higher CD-ROM or DVD drive
Monitor	Super VGA 256-color
Mouse	Microsoft mouse or compatible

Installing Works Suite 2001

TIP

Before installing Microsoft Works Suite 2001, be sure to temporarily disable any anti-virus software running on your system and close any open applications.

Microsoft Works 2001 comes on six CDs. The Works setup CD starts the setup process and includes the Works 6.0 and Word 2000 components.

1. Place the **Microsoft Works Suite 2001 Setup CD** (Disc 1) in your CD-ROM drive. If your computer has the autoplay feature, the setup program will automatically begin.

If the setup program appears, skip to step 6. If the setup program doesn't begin, you'll have to start it manually.

2. Click on **Start**. The Start menu will appear.

3. Click on **Run**. The Run dialog box will open.

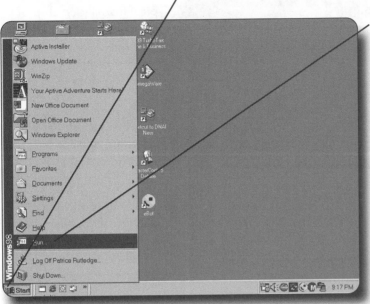

4. Type G:\setup.exe in the Open text box, substituting for D: the drive letter for your CD-ROM drive.

5. Click on **OK**. The Microsoft Works Suite 2001 Setup welcome screen will appear.

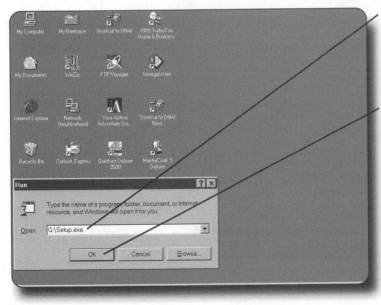

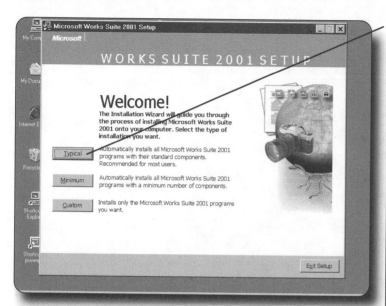

6. **Click** on **Typical**. The Typical Installation step of the setup wizard will appear.

TIP

Although it's recommended that you use the typical installation, you can also click on Minimum if you have disk-space constraints, or click on Custom if you want to customize your installation.

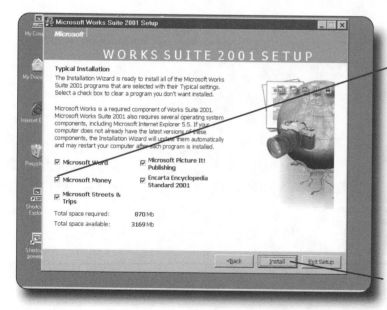

TIP

Click on any applications you don't want to install, and they'll be deselected. The default is to select all applications. Note that Microsoft Works itself is a required component of Works Suite, so you can't choose to deselect it.

7. **Click** on **Install**. The installation process will begin.

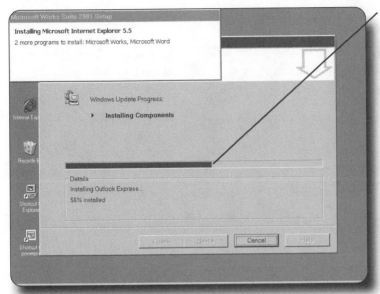

A progress indicator will appear. Depending upon your choices, Works Suite might prompt you to restart your computer when installation is complete.

Uninstalling Works Suite 2001

If you no longer want Microsoft Works Suite on your system, you can easily uninstall it.

1. Place the **Microsoft Works Suite 2001 Setup CD (Disc 1)** in your CD-ROM drive. If you have autoplay, the setup program will automatically begin. If the setup program appears, skip to step 6. If the setup program doesn't begin, you'll have to start it manually.

2. Click on **Start**. The Start menu will appear.

3. Click on **Run**. The Run dialog box will open.

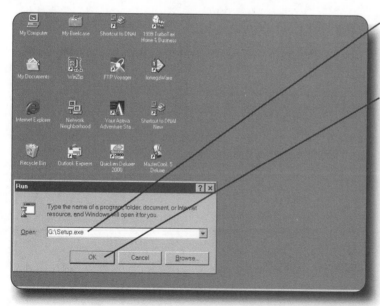

4. Type G:\setup.exe. Substitute for D: the drive letter to your CD-ROM drive.

5. Click on **OK**. The Microsoft Works Suite 2001 Setup wizard will begin, with a Welcome Back message.

CAUTION

Be sure to close all open applications before trying to uninstall Works Suite components.

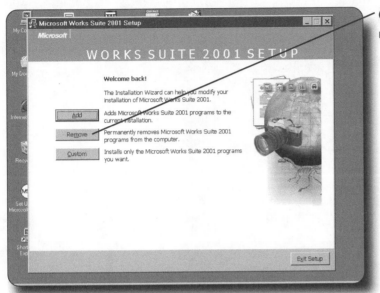

6. Click on **Remove**. The next screen will appear.

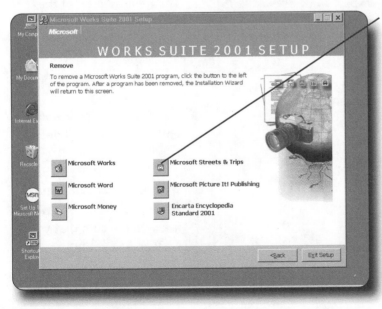

7. Click on **the application you want to remove.** A warning dialog box will ask if you're sure that you want to remove the application.

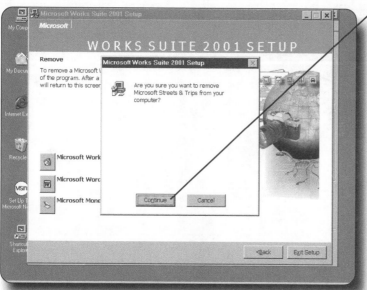

8. **Click** on **Continue.** The application you selected will be removed.

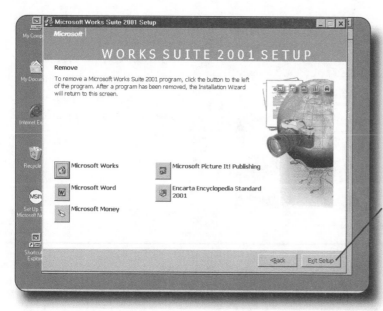

The Remove step of the setup wizard appears again, without an icon for the application you just removed.

9. **Repeat steps 7 and 8** until you remove all desired applications.

10. **Click** on **Exit Setup.** A warning dialog box will ask if you're sure that you want to exit setup.

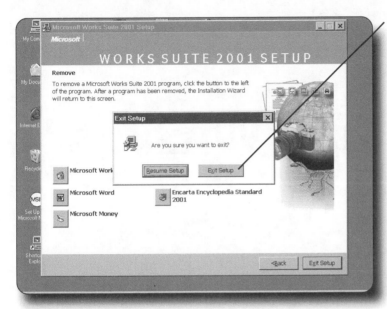

11. **Click** on **Exit Setup.**
Setup will close.

B

Using Task Wizards

Microsoft Works Suite includes numerous task wizards that you can use for home, business, employment, education, volunteer, and civic activities. A task wizard is a shortcut for creating a Works Suite document or file. You make a few choices, and the task wizard sets everything up for you. You can then edit the document as usual. Works Suite includes numerous task wizards that enable you to perform a variety of common tasks. In this appendix, you'll learn how to use two sample task wizards to:

- Create a loan analysis spreadsheet
- Create a garage sale flyer

Starting a Task Wizard

Task wizards are predesigned documents that you can use
and modify. All you do is replace the sample data with your
own information. Some task wizards use Word or PictureIt!
Publishing, whereas others use Works' spreadsheet or
database components. You access task wizards from the
Works Task Launcher.

Creating a Loan Analysis Spreadsheet

With Works, you can discover how much the payments
would be on that new house or car you've been thinking
about buying.

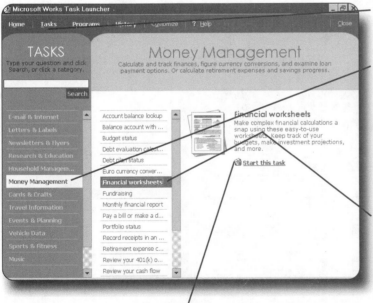

1. **Click** on **Tasks**. A list of
task categories will appear.

2. **Choose** the **category** of
your project (in this case,
choose **Money
Management**). A selection
of projects will appear. A
description of each wizard
will appear as you click on it.

3. **Click** on a **project**. For
the loan worksheet, choose
Financial worksheets.
Additional information will
appear on the right side of
the screen.

4. **Click** on **Start this task**. The Works Financial
Worksheets Wizard will display a variety of financial
worksheets.

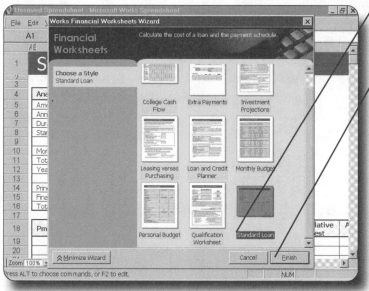

5. **Click** on **Standard Loan**. A green box will appear around the selection.

6. **Click** on **Finish**. A loan schedule using a Works spreadsheet will be created for you.

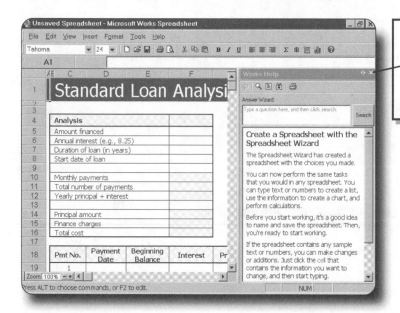

TIP

To see more of the spreadsheet, close the Works Help window.

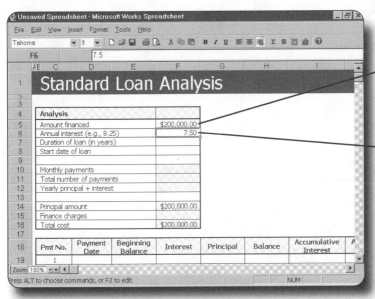

7. **Click** cell **F5**. The cell will be selected.

8. **Enter** the **amount of loan** to be financed. The value will display.

9. **Enter** the annual **interest rate** in cell F6. The value will display.

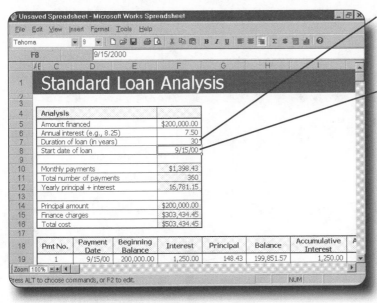

10. In cell F7, **enter** the **duration** of the loan (in years). The value will display.

11. **Enter** the **starting date** of the loan in cell F8. The value will display.

12. **Press Enter**. The loan amounts and an amortization table will be calculated.

NOTE

Do not enter data in any cells other than F5 through F8. Doing so can alter the structure of the spreadsheet.

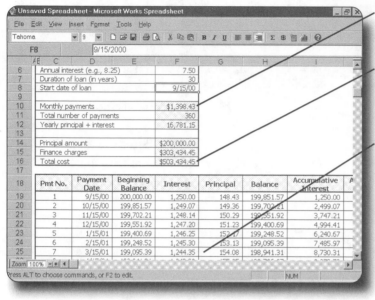

Your monthly payment amount displays in cell F10.

Your total cost of the purchase—including interest—displays in cell F16.

The amortization of payments displays below the calculations.

Creating a Garage Sale Flyer

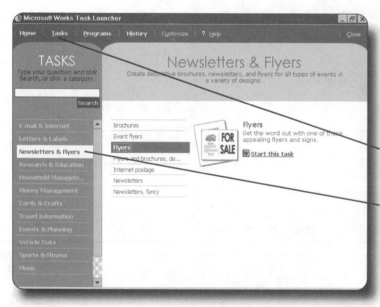

Having a garage sale? There's a lot to do, so save yourself some time by using the Works predefined template to create a flyer you can distribute.

1. Click on **Tasks**. A list of task categories will appear.

2. Choose the **category** of your project (in this case, choose **Newsletters & Flyers**). A selection of projects will appear.

3. **Click** on a **project**. For the garage sale flyer, choose **Flyers**. Additional information will appear on the right side of the screen.

4. **Click** on **Start this task**. The Works Flyer Wizard will display a variety of flyers.

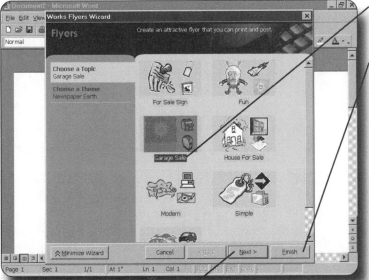

5. **Click** on **Garage Sale**. The item will be selected.

6. **Click** on **Finish**. A new Word document will be created with sample information supplied.

TIP

Click on Next if you want to adjust the fonts and colors in your flyer.

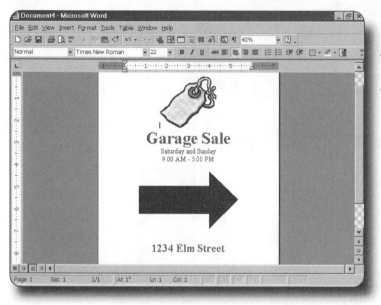

Edit the flyer to display your information. You can change the formatting, graphics, or layout as you would in any Word document.

C

Researching with Works Suite

Included with Microsoft Works Suite 2001 are tools bursting with information; tools that answer the old questions, who, what, when, where, and how. In this chapter you'll learn how to:

- Search for information with Encarta
- Plan a trip with Streets & Trips

Researching with Encarta Encyclopedia

As you might expect, Encarta Encyclopedia features articles on a variety of topics. Unlike a regular encyclopedia, however, Encarta Encyclopedia also includes animations, video clips, charts and tables, maps, pictures, sounds, quick facts, interactive multimedia, and 360-degree views on thousands of topics.

Starting Encarta Encyclopedia

Open the Encarta Encyclopedia application from the Works Task Launcher.

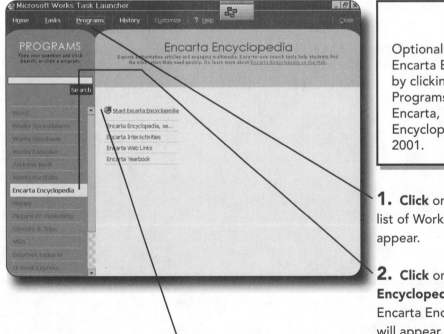

TIP

Optionally, open Encarta Encyclopedia by clicking on Start, Programs, Microsoft Encarta, Encarta Encyclopedia Standard 2001.

1. Click on **Programs.** A list of Works programs will appear.

2. Click on **Encarta Encyclopedia**. A list of Encarta Encyclopedia tasks will appear.

3. Click on **Start Encarta Encyclopedia**. The Encarta Encyclopedia application will launch.

> **NOTE**
>
> You might be prompted to insert the Encarta Encyclopedia CD.

Viewing the Encarta Encyclopedia Home Window

The Encarta Encyclopedia Home window is a very busy place! From the Home window you can access the

- **Find box**. Type the topic you want to research in this box.

- **Navigation buttons**. Use these buttons to move back and forth to the previous or next pages.

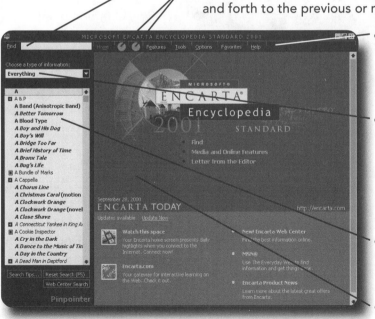

- **Menu bar**. Make selections to set preferences and other choices from the menu bar.

- **Information type drop-down list**. From here, you can select the type of information you want, ranging from articles to sounds to maps to videos.

- **Topic list**. A list of all available topics display here.

- **Viewing window**. Information about the topic you select displays here.

Finding a Topic

When searching for a topic, Encarta Encyclopedia displays topics directly relating to your search as well as any article containing the words you type in the search.

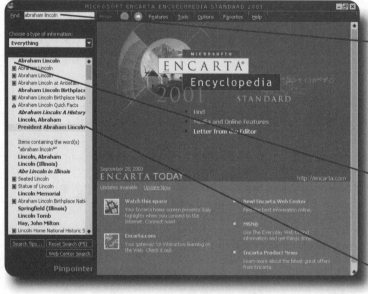

1. **Type** the **topic** you want to research. A list of items on the topic will appear in the topic list.

TIP

Icons on the left of the topic items indicate the type of information.

---

2. **Click** on the **item** you want to see. The item will display in the viewing window and the topic list will close.

After viewing the information, you might want to find other articles.

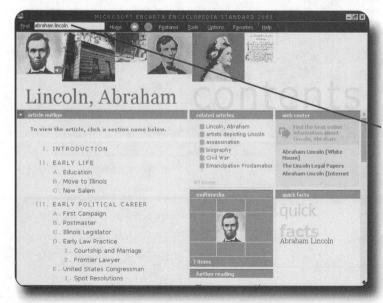

3. **Click** in the **Find box**. The topic list will redisplay with the current list of topic items.

TIP

Click the Close box when you are finished with Encarta Encyclopedia.

Finding Your Way with Streets & Trips

Planning a trip? Need to visit a new client but don't know how to get there? Microsoft Streets & Trips can route your stops for you, and even calculate the time it will take and how much you can expect to spend in fuel costs.

Starting Streets & Trips

Open the Streets & Trips application from the Works Task Launcher.

1. Click on **Programs**. A list of Works programs will appear.

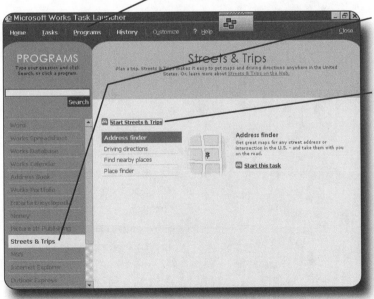

2. Click on **Streets & Trips**. A list of Streets & Trips tasks will appear.

3. Click on **Start Streets & Trips**. The Streets & Trips application will launch.

NOTE

You might be prompted to insert the Streets & Trips CD.

Finding an Address

Use the Find an address feature to locate a particular location or landmark.

1. Click on **Edit**. The Edit menu will appear.

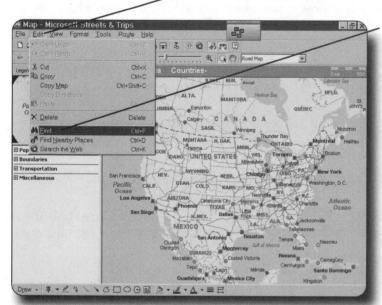

2. Click on **Find**. The Find dialog box will open.

TIP

Optionally, press Ctrl+F to open the Find dialog box.

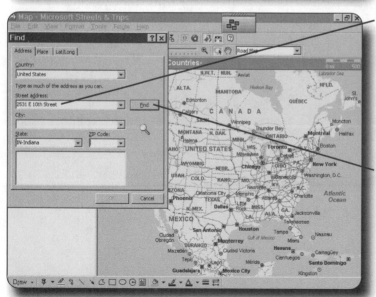

3. In the text boxes provided, **type** as much of the **address** as you have. If you don't have a complete address, don't worry; Streets & Maps is pretty good at approximating a location.

4. Click on **Find**. A selection of addresses that closely match your criteria will appear.

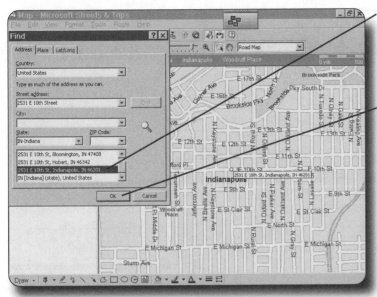

5. Click on the **address** you seek. A map of the area where the requested address is located will display.

6. Click on **OK**. The Find dialog box will close.

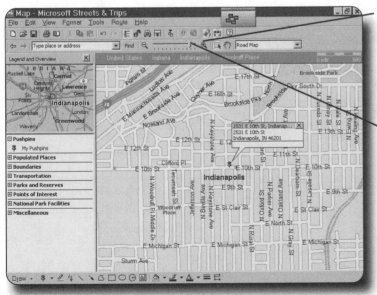

7. Click on the **Zoom in button** for a closer look. The map will enlarge.

TIP

Optionally, drag the view slider to zoom in or zoom out.

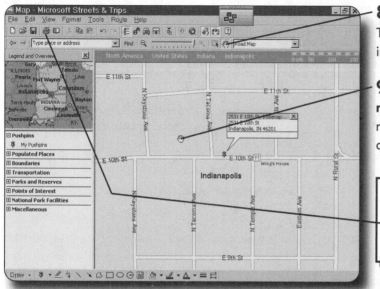

8. **Click** on the **Pan button**. The mouse pointer turns into a small hand.

9. **Click** and **drag** the **mouse pointer** across the map. The map moves in different directions.

TIP

Click on Print to print a copy of the map.

Routing a Trip

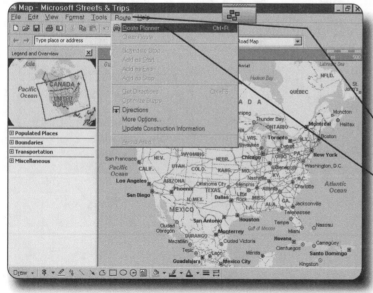

Are you one of those people who doesn't like to stop and ask for directions? You won't need to if you let Streets & Trips route your trip for you!

1. **Click** on **Route**. The Route menu will appear.

2. **Click** on **Route Planner**. The Route Planner window will open.

3. **Type** a start **location**. The text will appear in the Type a place or address box.

4. **Click** on **Add to Route**. The Find dialog box will open.

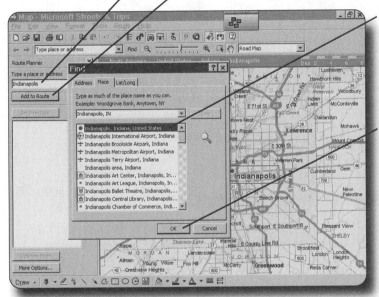

5. **Click** on the **location** that most closely matches your starting location. The location name will be highlighted.

6. **Click** on **OK**. The beginning location will appear in the Route Planner pane.

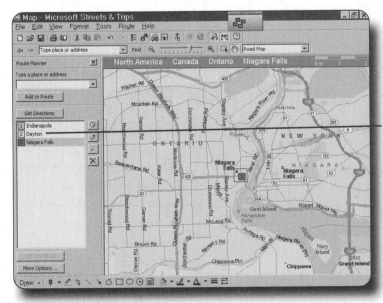

Next you need to tell Streets & Trips the intermediate stops you plan on making, as well as the ending destination.

7. **Repeat steps 3–6** for each stop on your trip, including your final destination. Each stop will appear in the Route Planner pane.

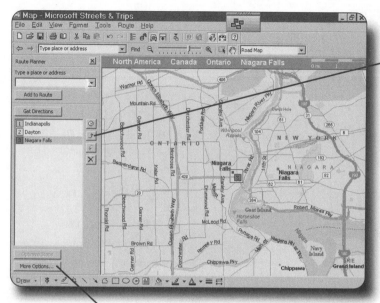

TIP

The numbers to the left of the stops represent the order of the stops. If you need to reorder the stops, click on the stop you want to move, and then click on the Move up button or the Move down button.

When a trip is routed, Streets & Trips also calculates the time and cost of the trip. The More Options dialog box allows you to customize the routing based on your driving preferences. If you prefer not to customize your trip, skip to step 16.

8. Click on **More Options**. The More Route Options dialog box opens.

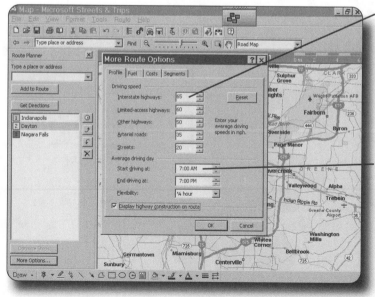

9. In the Driving speed section, **enter** the **average speeds** you expect to drive. Different boxes exist for different types of roads you might encounter. Enter your speeds in miles per hour.

10. In the Average driving day section, **enter** an **estimated start** and **end time** for your driving day. For example, if you're an early riser and like to be on the road by 6 AM, enter 6:00 AM in the Start driving by box.

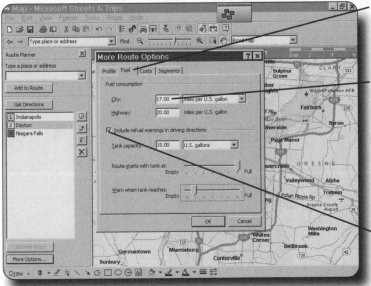

11. **Click** on the **Fuel tab**. The Fuel tab will come to the front.

12. **Enter** the **average miles per gallon** you get for the vehicle you'll be driving, for both city and highway driving.

TIP

Optionally, click on Include refuel warnings in driving directions to include recommended fuel stops.

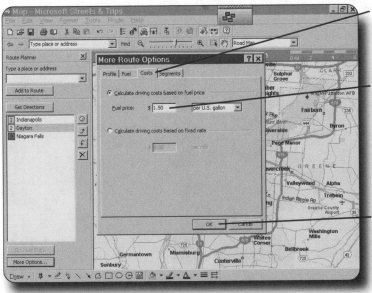

13. **Click** on the **Costs tab**. The Costs tab comes to the front.

14. **Enter** the **current cost of a gallon of gasoline**. (These days, the price might change every couple of hours, but take a shot and enter an average!)

15. **Click** on **OK**. The More Route Options dialog box will close.

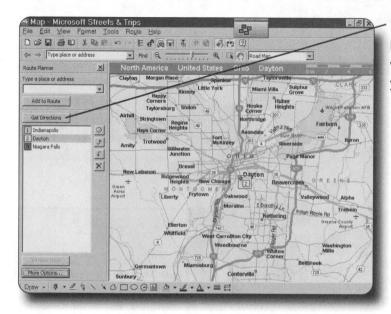

16. **Click** on **Get Directions**. Streets & Trips will route your trip based on your input.

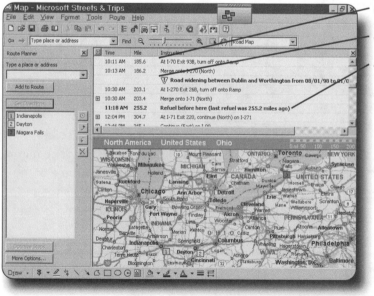

- Driving directions

- Construction warnings

- Refuel warnings

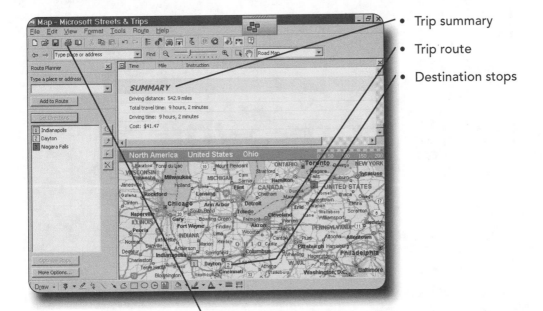

- Trip summary
- Trip route
- Destination stops

TIP

Click on the Print button to print your driving directions.

D

Using FoneSync

Works Suite 2001 includes a software package called FoneSync that works with your cellular phone. You can download names and phone numbers from a FoneSync address book to your telephone and from your telephone to the address book, thereby giving you access to the names and numbers you need when you need them—wherever you are.

- Synchronize your cell phone to Works
- Change FoneSync options
- Edit a FoneSync FoneList entry

Synchronizing FoneSync and Your Cell Phone

Works Suite 2001 includes a product called FoneSync, which synchronizes most cellular phones to a FoneSync address book.

Purchasing a Connectivity Kit

If you don't already have a connectivity kit, you'll need to purchase one. The connectivity pack includes a cable that attaches to the serial port of your computer, then to your cellular phone. To purchase a connectivity kit, contact Paragon Software at 1-888-777-6820 or http://www.paragonsoftware.com.

Using FoneSync

Access FoneSync from the Works Task Launcher.

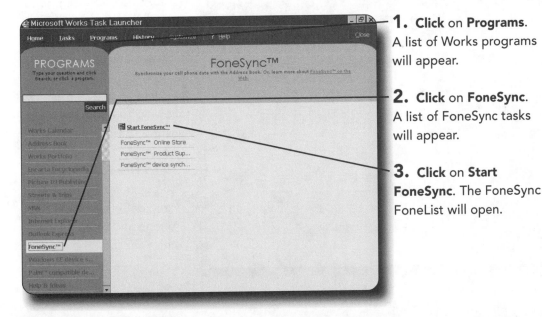

1. Click on **Programs**. A list of Works programs will appear.

2. Click on **FoneSync**. A list of FoneSync tasks will appear.

3. Click on **Start FoneSync**. The FoneSync FoneList will open.

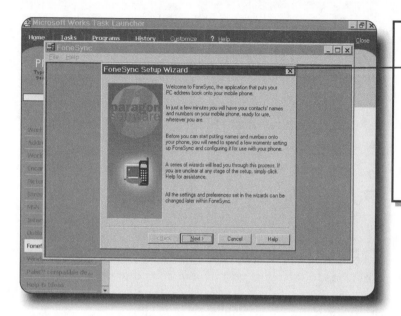

NOTE

The first time you use the FoneSync software, you'll need to run through the FoneSync Setup Wizard to configure FoneSync with your particular cell phone.

Items needing synchronization are indicated by a blank area in the Synchronized column.

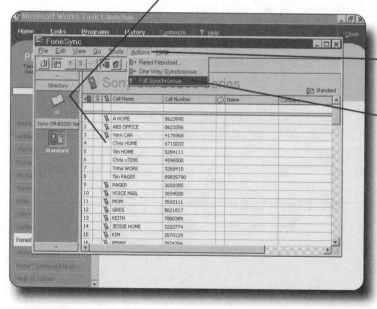

4. Turn on your **cell phone**.

5. Click on **Actions**. The Actions menu will appear.

6. Click on one of the following to begin the synchronization process:

• **Read Handset**. Select this to command FoneSync to read data from the cell phone and place it into the FoneList.

- **One Way Synchronise**. Select this to command FoneSync to read data from the FoneList and place it into the cell phone.

- **Full Synchronise**. Select this to command FoneSync to read data from both the FoneList and the cell phone, and place data from each into the other. (See the next section, "Setting FoneSync Options," for more information about full synchronization.)

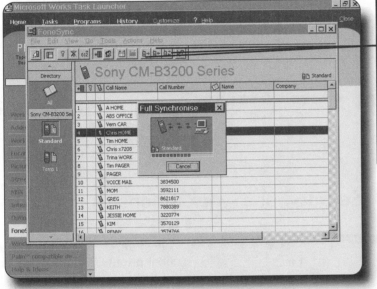

TIP

Optionally, click on the Read Handset, One Way Synchronise, or Full Synchronise button to launch the synchronization process.

When the synchronization process is complete, a message box might open.

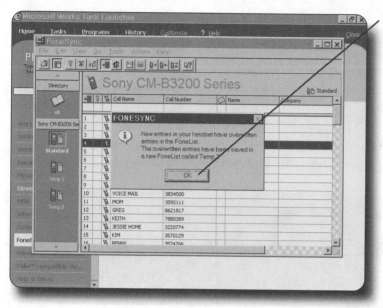

7. Click on **OK**. The message box will close.

Setting FoneSync Options

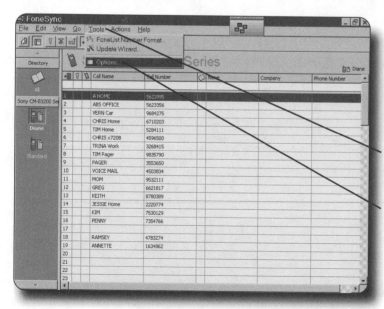

You need to advise FoneSync what priority it should take when, during a full synchronization, a listing has changed in both the FoneList and in the cell phone.

1. Click on **Tools**. The Tools menu will appear.

2. Click on **Options**. The Options dialog box will open.

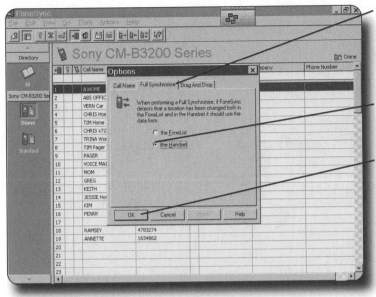

3. Click on the **Full Synchronise tab**. The Full Synchronise tab will come to the front.

4. Click on an **option**. The option will be selected.

5. Click on **OK**. The Options dialog box will close.

Editing FoneList Items

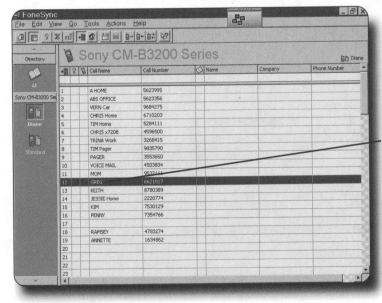

You might find it easier to create and edit phone listings through the FoneSync FoneList rather than by entering them on your cell-phone keypad.

1. Double-click on an **entry** or **a blank row** you want to change. The Edit Phone List Entry will open.

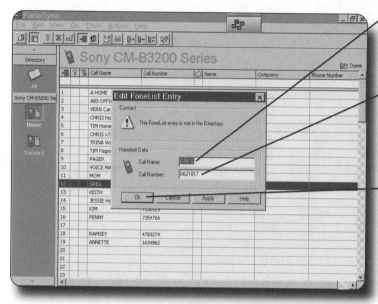

2. Type a **name** for the entry. The name will appear in the Call Name text box.

3. Type a **phone number** for the entry. The phone number will appear in the Call Number text box.

4. Click on **OK**. The entry will appear as modified in the FoneList.

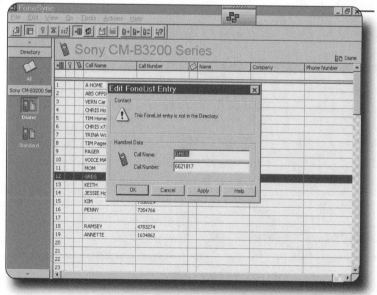

5. Click on the **Close button** to close the FoneSync window.

Glossary

A

Absolute Reference. In a formula, a reference to a cell that doesn't change when you copy the formula. An absolute reference always refers to the same cell or range. It is designated in a formula by the dollar sign ($).

Account Register. The page where you can enter, view, and balance transactions for a specific financial account, such as a checking account or credit-card account.

Active Cell. The selected cell in a worksheet. Designated with a border surrounding the cell.

Address Book. Stores names, addresses, and phone numbers in one handy location.

Alignment. The position of data in a document, cell, range, or text block; for example, centered, right-aligned, or left-aligned. Also called *justification*.

Attributes. Items that determine the appearance of text such as bolding, underlining, italics, or point size.

AutoSum. A function that adds a row or column of figures when the user clicks on the AutoSum button on the toolbar. Same as *SUM*.

AVG. A Works function that calculates the average of a list of values. SYNTAX: =AVG(*list*)

Axes. Lines that form a frame of reference for the chart data. Most charts have an X-axis and a Y-axis.

B

Bar Chart. A type of chart that uses bars to represent values. Normally used to compare items.

Bold. A font attribute that makes text thicker and brighter.

Border. A line surrounding paragraphs, pages, table cells, or objects.

Browser. A software program especially designed for viewing Web pages on the Internet.

Bullet. A small black circle or other character that precedes each item in a list.

C

Category Group. Contains several categories and provides a broader way to identify transactions.

Category. A type of income or expense to which you can apply individual transactions. For example, Food, Salary, and Entertainment are all Financial categories.

Cell. The area where a row and column intersect in a worksheet or table.

Chart. A graphic representation of data. Also called a *graph*.

Choose. To use the mouse or keyboard to pick a menu item or option in a dialog box.

Circular Reference. A cell that has a formula that contains a reference to itself.

Class. A level of classification that applies to multiple categories. Examples of classes could be all financial transactions for a particular individual, pertaining to a home business, or for a rental property to which multiple categories would apply.

Classification. A further layer of identifying and grouping transactions at a higher level across multiple categories.

Click On. To use the mouse or keyboard to pick a menu item or option in a dialog box.

Clip Art. Ready-made drawings that you can insert into a Works application.

Clipboard. An area of computer memory where text or graphics can be temporarily stored.

Close. To shut down or exit a dialog box, window, or application.

Close Button. Used to shut down or exit a dialog box, window, or application.

Column. A set of cells that appear vertically on a worksheet. A single Works worksheet has 256 columns.

Command Button. A button in a dialog box—such as Open, Close, Exit, OK, or Cancel—that carries out a command. The selected command button is indicated by a different appearance, such as a dotted rectangle or another color.

Command. An instruction given to a computer to carry out a particular action.

Compound Formula. A formula, usually in a spreadsheet, that has multiple operators. An example might be A2*C2+F4.

Connectivity Kit. A special serial cable needed to connect your cell phone to your PC.

Copy. To take a selection from the document and duplicate it on the Clipboard.

COUNT. A Works function that counts the nonblank cells in a list of ranges. SYNTAX: =COUNT(*list*)

Cut. To delete a selection from the document and move it to the Clipboard.

D

Data. The information to be entered into a spreadsheet or database.

Database. A file composed of records, each containing fields together with a set of operations for searching or sorting.

Default. A setting or action predetermined by the program unless changed by the user.

Deselect. To remove the check mark (✔) from a check box or menu item, or to remove highlighting from selected text in a document.

Desktop. The screen background and main area of Windows where you can open and manage files and programs.

Dialog Box. A box that appears and lets you select options, or displays warnings and messages.

Document. A letter, memo, proposal, or other file created in a Works component.

Drag-and-Drop. To move text or an object by positioning the mouse pointer on the item you want to move, pressing and holding down the mouse button, moving the mouse, and then releasing the mouse button to place the material into its new location.

E

E-mail. The exchange of text messages or computer files over a local area network or the Internet.

Export. The capability to copy data from one program to another.

F

Field. A piece of information used in a database.

File Format. The arrangement and organization of information in a file. File format is determined by the application that created the file.

File. Information stored on a disk under a single name.

Fill. The changing of interior colors and patterns or the completion of data in a series of spreadsheet cells.

Fill Data. A function that allows Works to automatically complete a series of numbers or words based on an established pattern.

Folder. An organizational tool used to store files.

FoneList. The telephone book provided with FoneSync.

FoneSync. The software, provided with Works Suite 2001, that allows your cell phone and a phone list to synchronize information.

Font. A group of letters, numbers, and symbols with a common typeface.

Footer. Text repeated at the bottom of each page of a document or spreadsheet.

Footnote. Reference information that prints at the bottom of the page.

Form Design View. The view in a Works database that allows the structure of the database to be modified.

Form. A type of database document with spaces reserved for fields to enter data.

Form View. A view in a Works database where one record is displayed at a time.

Format. To change the appearance of text or objects with features such as the font, style, color, borders, and size.

Form Letters. Multiple printed copies of the same document, each with some information that differs slightly, such as name and address.

Formula. A formula is an entry in a worksheet that performs a calculation on numbers, text, or other formulas.

Formula Bar. The location where all data and formulas are entered for a selected cell.

Freezing. The preventing of sections of a worksheet from scrolling offscreen when you move down the page.

Function. A series of predefined formulas used in Works spreadsheets. Functions perform specialized calculations automatically.

G

Go To. A feature that enables you to jump to a specific cell or worksheet location quickly.

Graph. See *Chart*.

Greater Than. A mathematical operator that limits the results of a formula to be higher than a named number or cell.

Gridlines. The lines dividing rows and columns in a table or worksheet.

H

Handles. Small black squares that appear when you select an object, which enable you to resize the object.

Header. Text entered in an area of the document that will be displayed at the top of each page of the document.

Help. A feature that gives you instructions and additional information on using a program.

Help Topic. An explanation of a specific feature, dialog box, or task. Help topics usually contain instructions on how to use a feature, pop-up terms with glossary definitions, and related topics. You can access Help topics by choosing any command from the Help menu.

Hypertext Link. Used to provide a connection from the current document to another document or to a document on the World Wide Web.

I

Icon. A small graphic image that represents an application, command, or tool. An action is performed when an icon is clicked or double-clicked.

Import. The capability to receive data from another program.

Indent. To move a complete paragraph one tab stop to the right.

Internet Explorer. A browser made by Microsoft used to view documents on the World Wide Web.

J

Justification. See *Alignment*.

L

Label. Any cell entry you begin with a letter or label-prefix character.

Landscape. Orientation of a page in which the long edge of the paper runs horizontally.

Legend. A box containing symbols and text, explaining what each data series represents. Each symbol is a color pattern or marker that corresponds to one data series in the chart.

Less Than. A mathematical operator that limits the results of a formula to be lower than a named number or cell.

Line Spacing. The amount of space between lines of text.

List View. A view in a Works database that allows the records to be displayed in a vertical format similar to a spreadsheet.

M

Mail Merge. A feature that combines a data file with a word-processing document to produce personalized letters.

Mailbox. An area of memory or disk assigned to store any e-mail messages sent by other users.

Margin. The width of blank space from the edge of the page to the edge of the text. All four sides of a page have margins.

MAX. A Works function that finds the largest value in a list. SYNTAX: =MAX(*list*)

MIN. A Works function that finds the smallest value in a list. SYNTAX: =MIN(*list*)

Modem. A device used to connect a personal computer with a telephone line so that the computer can be used for accessing online information or communicating with other computers.

Mouse Pointer. A symbol that indicates a position onscreen as you move the mouse around on your desktop.

N

Netiquette. Short for *network etiquette*. Internet rules of courtesy for sending e-mail and participating in newsgroups.

O

Object. A picture, map, or other graphic element that you can place in a Works application.

Online Banking. The ability to download financial transactions, view your accounts, and perform financial activities via an Internet connection.

Open. To start an application, to insert a document into a new document window, or to access a dialog box.

Operator. The element of a formula that suggests an action to be performed, such as addition (+), subtraction (-), division (/), multiplication (*), greater than (>), or less than (<).

Orientation. A setting that designates whether a document will print with text running along the long or short side of a piece of paper.

P

Page Break. A command that tells the application where to begin a new page.

Page Setup. A command that tells the application the paper size, orientation, margins, and other items applicable to the entire document.

Password. A secret code word that restricts access to a file. Without the password, the file cannot be opened.

Paste. The process of retrieving the information stored on the Clipboard and inserting it into a document.

Patterns. Predefined shading and line arrangements used to format cells in a worksheet.

Pie Chart. A round chart type in which each pie wedge represents a value.

Point Size. A unit of measurement used to indicate font size. One point is $1/72$ inch in height.

Point. To move the mouse until the tip of the mouse pointer rests on an **item**.

Portfolio. A feature used to gather and organize images, sounds, and documents.

Portfolio Collection. A unit of storage used by the Portfolio.

Portfolio Item. An individual image, sound, or document stored in a Portfolio collection.

Portrait. The orientation of the page in which the long edge of the page runs vertically.

Print Area. The portion of a worksheet you designate to print.

Print Preview. Shows you how your printed document will look onscreen before you print it.

Properties. The characteristics of text, objects, or devices. Text properties might include font, size, or color.

Q

Queue. A waiting or holding location, usually for printing documents or sending e-mail messages.

R

Range Name. An "English" name that identifies a range and that can be used in commands and formulas instead of the range address.

Range. A collection of cells, ranging from the first named cell to the last.

Record. The collection of field information about one particular element. For example, Joe Smith's record might include field information such as name, address, and phone number.

Redo. To reverse the last Undo action.

Reference. In a formula, a name or range that refers the formula to a cell or set of cells.

Relative Reference. In a formula, a reference to a cell or a range that changes when you copy the formula. A relative reference refers to the location of the data in relation to the formula. A relative reference can be an address or range name.

Right Align. To line up text with the right side of a cell, tab setting, or document margin, as with a row of numbers in a column.

Row. Cells running from left to right across a worksheet.

Ruler. A feature that lets you easily change page format elements such as tabs and margins.

S

Save. To take a document residing in the memory of the computer and create a file for it to be stored on a disk or to save a previously saved document to reflect changes made to that document.

Save As. To save a document with a name you choose or to save a previously saved document with a new name or properties.

Scroll Bars. The bars on the right side and bottom of a window that let you move vertically and horizontally through a document.

Shape. Item such as a circle, rectangle, line, polygon, or polylines in your document.

Shortcut. An icon that represents a quick way to start a program or open a file or folder.

Simple Formula. A formula, usually in a spreadsheet that has only one operator. An example might be B4+B5.

Sizing Handle. The small solid squares that appear on the borders of a graphics box or a graphics line that has been selected. You can drag these handles to size the box and its contents.

Sort. To arrange data in alphabetical or numeric order.

Spell Check. A feature that checks the spelling of words in your document against a dictionary and flags possible errors for correction.

Split Transaction. A transaction that applies to multiple categories.

Spreadsheet. The component in Works that handles calculations and data needing to be placed in a columnar or linear format. Data is stored in small locations called cells.

Stamps. Predefined images that can be added to a Picture It! Publishing image.

Status Bar. The line at the bottom of a window that shows information, such as the current page in a document.

Style. A way to format similar types of text such as headings and lists.

Subcategory. A smaller unit of financial categorization that rolls up to a category. For example, Dining Out and Groceries are subcategories of Food.

Subclass. A smaller unit of financial classification that rolls up to a class.

Submenu. An additional list of menu items opening from a single menu item. Also called a *cascading menu*.

SUM. A Works function that adds a range of cells. See also *AutoSum*. SYNTAX: =SUM(*list*)

Symbols. Characters that are not on your keyboard, such as iconic symbols, phonetic characters, and characters in other alphabets.

Synchronization. The capability to transfer data entered on the Web to a software program on your computer and to enable viewing of data from this program directly on the Web.

Syntax. The exact structure of functions and formulas.

T

Table. A set of rows and columns of cells that you fill in with text, numbers, or graphics.

Tabs. Settings in your document to determine where the insertion point moves when you press the Tab key or use the indent feature.

Task Wizard. An interactive Help feature that prompts the user for key pieces of information and then, using that information, completes a project.

Taskbar. The bar (usually at the bottom of the screen) that lists all open folders and active programs.

Template. A predesigned file with customized formatting, content, and features.

Thesaurus. A feature used to find synonyms (words that are alike) and antonyms (words that are opposite).

Tile. A display format for open windows. Tiled windows are displayed side by side, with no window overlapping any other window.

Title. A descriptive piece of text. Used in charts and spreadsheets.

Toolbar. Appears at the top of the application window and is used to access many commonly used features of the Works applications.

U

Undo. To reverse the last editing action.

Uppercase. A capital letter.

V

Value. An entry that is a number, formula, or function.

Views. Ways of displaying documents to see different perspectives of the information in that document.

W

Word Processing. The ability to type, edit, and save a document.

Word Wrap. To let text in a paragraph automatically flow to the next line when it reaches the right-hand margin.

WordArt. A feature that allows blocks of text to be manipulated into varying shapes and formats.

World Wide Web. A series of specially designed documents—all linked together—to be viewed over the Internet.

Wrapping. A function that causes text to automatically wrap to the next line when it reaches the right-hand edge of a cell or page margin.

X, Y, Z

X-Axis. In a chart, a reference line marked in regular intervals to display the categories with descriptive labels.

Y-Axis. In a chart, a reference line marked in regular intervals to display the values of a chart.

Zoom. To enlarge or reduce the way text is displayed on the screen. It does not affect how the document will print.

Index